SUPERMAN AT FIFTY THE PERSISTENCE OF A LEGEND

SUPERMAN® AT FIFTY!

©1941 DC COMICS Inc.

THE PERSISTENCE OF A LEGEND!

Edited by Dennis Dooley and Gary Engle

OCTAVIA   Cleveland, Ohio

To Jerry Siegel and Joe Shuster

Published by Octavia Press, 3546 Edison Road,
Cleveland, Ohio 44121, 216-381-2853.

Library of Congress Cataloging in Publication Data

Superman at Fifty.

Includes index.
1. Superman (Comic strip) I. Dooley, Dennis. II. Engle,
Gary D., 1947-   . III. Title.
PN6728.S9S87   1987   741.5'0973   87-15221
ISBN 0-940601-00-1

A version of "The Man of Tomorrow and the Boys of
Yesterday" was originally published in the June 1973
issue of *Cleveland Magazine*, vol. 2, no. 6.

"SUPERMAN," the poem, was originally published in
the May 1982 issue of *The Cleveland Beacon*, vol. 2,
no. 4.

TABLE OF CONTENTS

SUPERMAN

Don't believe everything you read in comics.
Superman was born in Cleveland.
Made him plenty tough,
faster than speeding bullets,
stronger than death.
Gave him the blue black hair,
a newspaper beat, desire of flight.

And a healthy fear of kryptonite.

—Timothy Joyce

PREFACE

This book is a tribute to an American legend and to the two kids from Cleveland who created him.

Why, on his 50th birthday, do we honor Superman? No one has said it better than Harlan Ellison in a letter written in response to this project, so, with his permission, we quote him on the subject:

If one of the unarguable criteria for literary greatness is universal recognition, consider this: In all of the history of literature, there are only five fictional creations known to every man, woman and child on the planet. The urchin in Irkutsk may never have heard of Hamlet; the peon in Pernambuco may not know who Raskolnikov is; the widow in Jakarta may stare blankly at the mention of Don Quixote or Micawber or Jay Gatsby. But every man, woman and child on the planet knows Mickey Mouse, Sherlock Holmes, Tarzan, Robin Hood...and Superman.

11

He is more than the fanciful daydream of two Cleveland schoolboys. He is the 20th-century archetype of mankind at its finest. He is courage and humanity, steadfastness and decency, responsibility and ethic. He is our universal longing for perfection, for wisdom and power used in service of the human race.

Of all the literary creations of American fiction, Superman, after all these years, born of a "dispensable, disreputable" genre, is the only one that seems certain to get Posterity's nod. And that is because, simply put, he is our highest aspirations in human form.

This is not to claim for *Superman* the subtleties of Shakespeare or even the hard-boiled poetry of a Raymond Chandler. What *Superman* does have is a kind of elemental power—a simple grandeur of conception—that sticks in the soul and finds its way to the corner of one's smile. Lois and Clark are no Kate and Petrucchio, and Perry White is no Charles Foster Kane. We make no foolish claim for such lyrical flights or such dramatic depths, for these characters were, after all, born in the comic strips, a form of contemporary folk art whose very naivete is a great part of its importance and its appeal.

It is precisely because the characters and stories of *Superman* were created with no more complicated end in view than enter-tainment and the satisfaction of some basic human yearnings that the elements of this modern myth yield such a rich lode of pop cultural lore and say so much about the character and values of America. Like the stories of King Arthur that were so popular in the Middle Ages, the Superman myth has been passed on from one generation to another and retold and reworked by many hands. Boys like Denny O'Neil have thrilled to the stories in their youth and then gone on to become themselves the carriers of the myth, reshaping it to the new sensibilities of a different time, just as Chretien de Troyes and Thomas Malory did with the Arthurian legends of their day.

Such characters and such stories belong, in the end, to the ages and to the nation that produces them. But the two teenagers who *created* them retain a very special position in the history of American culture, and—need one say it?—a very special place in our hearts. It is the purpose of this book, in part, to honor them and to bring them a measure of the recognition they were so long denied. Unhappily, they lost control of their creation all too early on, not through the normal processes of cultural evolution, but through the then standard practices of the comic-book industry. A few years ago, a new generation of executives made its peace with Superman's creators. Their names were restored to their rightful place in the comics and the official histories, and they were guaranteed an annuity for the remainder of their lives.

No one can give back the years. But one can give respect and recognition for a contribution to popular culture that has enriched and brought delight into millions of lives.

It is the practice in scholarly circles to present respected figures on a significant anniversary with something called a Fest-schrift—a festive anthology of essays by their peers on a subject of mutual interest. Here, then, on the 50th anniversary of Superman's publication, is our Festschrift for Jerry Siegel and Joe Shuster. May they enjoy its playful ruminations and more serious reflections.

The first section of the book brings to-gether many little-known facts concerning the circumstances surrounding Superman's real birth in Cleveland, Ohio, in the early '30s and offers some theories about the special alchemy with which two unlikely youngsters transformed the cultural flotsam and adolescent yearnings of their teenage lives into an original creation of enduring character.

The second section, which includes revealing essays by two individuals who have played key roles in shaping the Superman legend, explores the transformations the story underwent over five decades of adaptation for radio, the animated cartoon, film and television. The essays in this section offer many examples of the cross-pollination that strengthened and enriched the myth.

The children who enjoyed those comics or the radio program, or sat transfixed by the TV series or the movie serials have long since turned to the more serious pursuits of the adult world, becoming political scientists, psychologists, priests, physicists, art critics. In the third section, 11 such former fans reexamine the Superman myth in the light of their chosen disciplines in an attempt to answer the book's central question: What accounts for the astounding durability of the Superman legend and its continuing appeal to successive generations of Americans? What is it about this character and story that so endears us in a time when the continually shifting winds of fashion are forever sweeping last month's fad and last year's superstar into the rubbish heap of obsolescence?

The book's final section should provide a sufficient dose of irreverence for any reader who feels we've committed the 20th-century sin of taking popular culture all too seriously. Indeed, as Frederik Smith notes in his essay in the third section, humor has been an integral part of *Superman* from the beginning. The fact that this material lends itself so readily to both the pleasures of affectionate satire and more scholarly pursuits is perhaps the ultimate tribute to the special power of Siegel and Shuster's creation.

On another level, this book is a salute to the city of Cleveland, Ohio, which, like Superman, has a divided character: on the surface mild-mannered and occasionally self-conscious, but when the chips are down a City of Steel, with integrity, with an abiding faith in decency, with a sense of humor, with staying power.

Except for Curt Swan and Denny O'Neil— whom we hereby make honorary Clevelanders—the contributors to this book have all called Cleveland home. Those who have moved on carry with them the knowledge that there's still a place where kids like Jerry and Joe can dream.

This book would not have been possible without the cooperation and encouragement of many individuals, beginning with our spouses, Elizabeth Berrey and Barbara Hawley, whose thoughtful input and continuing support were indispensable. Tim Gorman of Neverending Battle, Inc., has been an invaluable source of information and archival materials, taking time from his own efforts to build a permanent Superman memorial in Cleveland to answer our many calls for help. His impressive command of Kryptonian lore is glimpsed in the piece with which this book ends.

Special thanks must also go to our publisher, Diana Tittle, whose commitment to this project kept it alive and rolling toward its destination, as well as to the eminent Americans from several walks of life who, upon learning of this project, offered their own personal tributes for inclusion. Behind them looms the affection of a nation.

Not all of the people who have helped make this book possible have their names on the contents page. We'd like, therefore, to acknowledge the assistance of Allan Asherman, Paula Bloch, Alicia Ciliberto, Ben Dooley, John Ewing, Mary Fran and Joe Fahey, Louis Giannetti, Mark Gottlieb, John Greppin, Alan Hills, Tom Hinson, Tony Isabella, Susan Jaros, Jeanne Krier, Jerry

Lackamp, Mark Lantz, Louis T. Milic,
Edmund Santavicca, Gail Stuehr, Nina
Sundell, Marjorie Talalay, Dan Thompson
and Sheldon Wigod. Stuart Kollar and Rosa
DelVecchio deserve a special mention for
their help with research and typing. In New
York, Paul Levitz, Chantal D'Aulnis, Joe
Orlando and Pat Mach of DC COMICS
provided welcome assistance in acquiring
permissions and illustrations. Finally,
Thomas Andrae of Berkeley and Gary
Coddington of Pasadena were most helpful
in representing the interests of their friends,
Jerry and Joe.

Dennis Dooley and Gary Engle
Cleveland, Ohio
July 1987

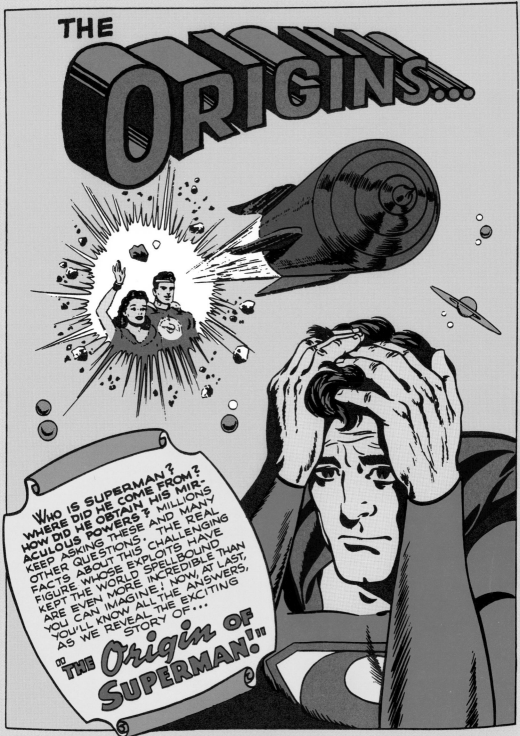

THE MAN OF TOMORROW AND THE BOYS OF YESTERDAY

by DENNIS DOOLEY

They were a couple of Jewish kids from Cleveland. There wasn't much else you would have remarked about the two youthful faces that peer out today from the yellowed page of the Glenville High School yearbook over the unassuming names of Jerry Siegel and Joe Shuster.

Not much here to command the attention of the world, much less seize the imaginations of their contemporaries, nay, of generations still unborn.

In fact, their good parents must have wondered what the two boys would ever do

19

when they graduated. America was on hard times in the early '30s. Hard times for Jews were also in the wind. Hard times for the world, as well, said some of the old-timers, who said civilization was going to hell in a hurry.

Unlike some of their classmates and companions, young Siegel and Shuster had not exactly covered themselves with academic glory, were worth little as athletes and, perhaps hardest of all to bear, entertained no ambitions their families could tell their friends about.

The truth was they thought of themselves as artists—men of original imagination. Maybe Siegel was no Dostoevski, and Joe Shuster, to be sure, was no da Vinci, but when they left high school in 1934, they had already created the most compelling character since Huckleberry Finn—and an authentic, modern-day myth so striking and enduring, it should have made both of them millionaires many times over:

Superman.

The story of how it didn't is a sad one that has been told before. But the story, the full story, of how it all started back in the early '30s in a neighborhood on Cleveland's near East Side has never been written.

Almost everybody knows, at least in its bare outlines, the story of Superman, the starchild placed by his parents into a tiny rocket ship on the eve of the planet Krypton's destruction and hurled, the only survivor of a wonderful race, across millions of miles of interstellar space…to Earth; of how the helpless babe was found in a cornfield by a gentle couple, the Kents, who raised the lad as their own son; and of the miraculous powers young Clark Kent discovered

himself to possess—tremendous strength and X-ray vision, the gift of flight—powers he vowed at his dying foster father's bedside to use only for the good of humankind and the deliverance of the oppressed; to which purposes he hid his true identity behind the bland exterior of timid Kent, the newspaper reporter, emerging from a phone booth or a handy alleyway in his bright red and blue costume with flowing cape and jutting chin whenever evil showed its ugly head or catastrophe endangered the innocent; and, last but not least, of his doomed love, as the ineffectual Kent, for his female colleague on the *Daily Planet*, the raven-haired Lois Lane, whose ignorance of poor Clark's true identity left her continually mooning for yet another glimpse of her manly rescuer, Superman, while Kent, increasingly, ate his heart out at the third desk from the window. Only the occasional stray fragment of the lost world of his infancy, the dreaded kryptonite, could render the Man of Steel helpless as a babe again…until some passing mortal or sudden stroke of grace delivered him once more from the hands of his enemies.

Here was a myth worthy of the Greeks in its intuitive grasp of human aspiration confronted with self knowledge. It reverberated with childhood fears and adolescent dreams revealed on many a Freudian couch. Yet it was a peculiarly American myth. And one that could only have been born in the Depression—indeed, out of the curious configuration of background, persons and events that had shaped the minds of 19-year-old Jerome (born Jacob) Siegel and Joe Shuster.

But how, half a century later, might one reconstruct the womb that gave birth to an idea? The task was made more difficult by the fact that (in 1973 when the first version of this essay was undertaken) no interview with or extended commentary by Siegel or

Shuster was known to exist, nor was their present whereabouts even known. Gone were the Jews of Glenville, married and moved away—to Beachwood, Ohio, or to Florida or the coast. The high school library where they once shared furtive whispers behind history books was now populated by black students from lower middle-class and poor families, the shelves of faded yearbooks and back issues of the school newspaper—like the detritus of a vanished civilization—presided over by a friendly black librarian named A. Grace Lee Mims.

Those far-off summers that followed the Crash, the bustling corridors of old Glenville High, the movies that were playing at the local theaters, the books, the conversations, the extended moment in which all of those friends and particular events came together to ignite a fantastic idea in an 19-year-old boy's brain—were gone, had exploded as surely as the planet Krypton. But, coming almost half a century later to the spot where it had all happened, and persisting doggedly in one's detective work, one began to find tiny splinters of a forgotten summer, a handful of survivors, shards of memories that one could begin to piece together. The picture that emerged was an extraordinary one.

Old Glenville High School, on Parkwood between St. Clair and Superior Avenues, was renamed Franklin Delano Roosevelt Junior High in 1964, but the little room on the first floor where Jerry Siegel and his friends put out the weekly student newspaper, *The Glenville Torch*, from 1931 to 1934, is still there.

If you had opened the door of that room almost any day of the week, back in 1932, you would have come upon one of the most remarkable collections of people ever brought together on the staff of a high school paper anywhere, but that is almost another story in itself. There, banging away at one or another of those old black upright typewriters, you would have seen the youthful forms of Willie Gilbert, who would subsequently carve out a career in New York writing material for such early television shows as *Tom Corbett*, *Space Cadet* and *Howdy Doody* and a little later still a play with the improbable title, *How to Succeed in Business Without Really Trying*; or Jerome Lawrence, who would coauthor *Inherit the Wind*, *Auntie Mame* and other plays; or Seymour Heller, who would wind up out on the West Coast managing a glitzy pianist named Liberace. There was Charlotte Plimmer, who would one day edit *Seventeen* magazine and make a reputation as a foreign correspondent and coauthor, with her writer-husband David, of a number of books; Hal Lebowitz and Wilson Hirschfeld, who would enjoy long and successful careers on Cleveland newspapers; the cartoonist, Bernard Schmittke; and Albert Maslow, who was to win national prominence in the field of psychological testing. And from time to time, there were others. Not least of all, a mysterious bespectacled boy named Jerome Siegel, maybe the zaniest of them all.

The psychic electricity in the air still crackles from the yellowed pages of the *Torch*; the sense of the creative potential, the sheer imaginative energy gathered in that room is palpable.

They all learned how to write on that newspaper and found the beginnings of their individual identities on that weekly feature page. You can thumb through the crumbling back issues and see it taking place, in the regular columns they wrote, and in the constant repartee—the one-liners and good-natured ribs—they indulged in at one another's expense.

Jerry Lawrence was still Jerry Schwartz in those days, writing a literate, often lyrical column called "Spices and Cinnamon"; Willie Gilbert, still Willie Gomberg, and Al

Maslow were responsible for "The Blow Torch," a regularly appearing string of quips and quickies; Charlotte Plimmer was Charlotte Fingerhut then, presiding over a chatty corner called "Thimble Thoughts," a pun on her name, the German word for thimble. ("Reubie Schrank actually thinks that the reason Louis XVIII was a good king — or was he? — was because he was fat and had the gout. Honest, he said so in history class.")

Other popular features with the Glenville student body were Sy Heller and Hy Schulkin's Hollywood-type gossip column, "Subtleville Slander" ("Have you noticed: Martha Yablonsky's dimples?...The alarming number of red heads in this school?...The progress of the Lehman-Shively affair?"); and a relatively short-lived effort, "Burlesquing the News" — "That masterpiece... composed weekly by Jerry (Goober the Mighty) Siegel and Wilson Hirschfeld of Student Council (Phooey!) fame." Buck Segelin was editor, and Al Levine rode herd on sports, while Jerry Mendelsohn knocked out hard-hitting editorials for which he rarely got credit. And the notorious Martha Yablonsky, dimples notwithstanding, seems to have been writing practically half the paper. Was she, at least in part, the original model for Lois Lane, the archtypical ambitious, hard-working female reporter of the *Superman* strips?

"The firm chin in itself indicates the ambition that resulted in her previous offices of editor-in-chief of the *Empire Herald* and *Glenville Torch*," said an anonymous tribute upon her graduation two years later. "The intellectual brow of course corresponds to the 'bookey' strain in our Martha.... What's that you say, Miss Yablonsky? You entertain hopes of being a reporter? Well, more power

to you, my dear."

1932 was the year of the Lindbergh kidnapping and the resignation of New York mayor Jimmy Walker under a cloud of scandal, and the third of the Great Depression. Jack Sharkey took the heavyweight crown away from Max Schmeling in a 15-round decision, FDR won the Presidency from Herbert Hoover, and *The Grand Hotel* with Garbo and Barrymore was named movie of the year. Knute Rockne was dead, and Hitler was making noises in Germany. Back home there were gangsters and Prohibition — and Will Rogers. And the Palace Theatre in Cleveland was packing them in with Olsen and Johnson and crooner Rudy Vallee.

Jerry Mendelsohn bought a used Model "T" Ford for $12 (a bargain even then) and in the balmy evenings he would round up Willie and Jerry Schwartz and Charlotte and a couple of others, and they'd drop by the basement apartment where Al Maslow lived with his old man, who was the custodian of the building, and sit around and talk till all hours over some salami and rye bread and a *glezele-tay* — or maybe they'd sit and kibbitz on Jerry Schwartz's front porch or over at Sid Lobe's. And maybe Sid's dad, who spoke broken English, would wander downstairs looking for a cigarette and then he would pull up a chair and tell them about how it had been in Europe, and they would talk about where the world was going and what it had to do with them. Jerry Mendelsohn would always believe afterward that those long sessions around the kitchen table had had more to do with what they would become than any other thing. Little by little they explored their ties to European culture and tradition, listened to what the old folks had to say and slowly formulated their understandings of who they were.

But one of them was conspicuously absent from these sessions. They saw little of

Jerry Siegel outside of school. He wasn't really part of the crowd. He and Wilson Hirschfeld, the quiet, serious-student type who sometimes sat unnoticed in a corner of the *Torch* room working on a piece for the paper, both lived over on the other side of East 105th. They spent a good deal of time together, but no one was sure what they talked about.

They were both quiet boys, but there it ended. Hirschfeld was a sober sort, neat, industrious. Jerry was something else.

The boy was a paradox. Outwardly shy, thin, unathletic, bumping about behind glasses that slipped down his nose, he lived almost totally within a boyish imagination teeming with spectacular adventures and tales of outrageous daring.

Here was the soul of a D'Artagnan imprisoned in the body of an undernourished delivery boy. He daydreamed his way through school and went through the motions of his after-school job making deliveries for a printing plant, by which labor he earned four dollars a week to help his family make it through the hard times that were on the country, living for those precious hours up in his room during which he did his best to quench that voracious appetite for swashbuckling tales with an all-but-ceaseless intake of dime detective novels and adventure stories by authors like Edgar Rice Burroughs and H.G. Wells and always the latest installment of *Buck Rogers* comics he could get his hands on.

"It was 12 midnight and I was reading the latest edition of *Weird Tales*," begins a mysterious item on the *Torch* feature page for March 10, 1932. "Outside my window the wind moaned dismally…. To my ears had come the sound of claws drawn across glass. And above the whimpering wind had come the wail of a rising chant.

"The magazine dropped from my nerveless fingers. I stared wide-eyed at the win-dow. Glaring in at me were five dreadful faces.

"The shock killed me."

He could not get enough, and when he couldn't buy more he read the same stories over and over again and expanded the plots in his mind. In the dark of his room he merged personalities with "Doc" Savage and Tarzan and the Scarlet Pimpernel.

He would often arrive late for his first class and tiptoe clumsily to his seat while the annoyed history teacher looked on. His shirt would be hanging out, his rumpled striped pajamas visible below the cuffs of his hastily donned pants — foreshadowing Clark Kent's eccentric habit of wearing his Superman costume underneath his clothes in order to save time in emergencies. Siegel was reading history, all right, but in his own choice of authors.

When an unsigned review of The Baroness Orczy's novel, *Child of the Revolution*, appears on the feature page of *The Glenville Torch* for October 20, 1932, there can be little doubt who the reviewer is. "The Reign of Terror — the guillotine descending swiftly on innocent and guilty alike," writes the impassioned critic. "The only hope lies in the aid of the 'Scarlet Pimpernel,' a mysterious Englishman who risks his life to save…the unjustly condemned." Or of Hugh Walpole's gothic thriller, *The Duchess of Wrexe*: "Her sharp, steely eyes reflected all the hate in her heart. The dignified figure, clothed in black, bespoke her power."

"THE UNITY OF THE NATION," Siegel would one day write under different circumstances, "IS THREATENED BY THE MACHINATIONS OF A CUNNING BEING KNOWN AS 'THE LIGHT.' SUPERMAN, DEFENDER OF DEMOCRACY, SWINGS INTO ACTION TO COMBAT A DARK MENACE THAT THREATENS TO ENGULF AND ENSLAVE A CONTINENT!"

The purple prose was appropriate to its

creator's point of view. The youthful Siegel thought naturally in terms of cataclysm and apocalyptic confrontation and the clashing of intergalactic forces bent on good or evil. For if one foot of his creative imagination was planted squarely in the world of the detective story, the other was anchored in the exotic realm of science fiction.

Still another unsigned item, in the October 6, 1932, issue of the *Torch*, announces with a familiar flourish of nouns and adjectives the publication of a new magazine called *Science Fiction: The Advance Guard of Future Civilization*, J. Siegel—owner, editor, secretary, treasurer and office boy, which will feature "action-adventure stories upon this and other worlds."

The work of "several prominent Glenvillites," writing under pseudonyms, we are informed confidentially, appears in its pages. And among its illustrators are *Torch* staff cartoonist Bernard Schmittke and one Joe Shuster.

In a sudden outburst of boyish enthusiasm, the writer of the unsigned news piece confides Siegel's excited expectation that the magazine will soon be featuring the work of "well-known" authors as well, then adds, touchingly, that "until a large enough circulation has been reached to warrant printing, the magazine will remain mimeographed."

"Meanwhile," he rhapsodizes, "a great deal of capital is being used for advertising which is expected to bring staggering results." For it is the youthful editor's hope, through ads placed in *Amazing Stories* and "practically every other pulp paper magazine on the newsstands," to reach somewhere "in the vicinity of five million magazine readers. A few thousand subscriptions are

hoped to be secured from this resort."

In striking contrast to the awkward bespectacled youth known to the halls of Glenville High, the Jerry Siegel of whom one catches glimpses in the feature pages of the *Torch* is a fireball of ambition and energy, a relentless self-publicizer and irrepressible egoist of dimensions that continually take one by surprise. By the spring of his senior year he has clearly set up as something like the Norman Mailer of his class. Under the heading, "IMPOSSIBLE TO SEE:" some one of his classmates has nominated as the first item: "Jerry Siegel and Adolf Hitler indulging in a wild game of pinochle."

With zany flourishes of self-admiring wit, he eats up the adulation with the bottomless hunger of a boy deprived of his true measure of admiration throughout a timid childhood. A letter to the editor (November 17, 1932) congratulates him: "What's happened to your column? Overnight it switched from terrible to splendid. I can't understand the sudden change. Tell me, how did you do it?" Siegel replies, "I ate Grape-nuts."

The remark is characteristic of much of the writing—mostly short, way-out fiction pieces—he did for the *Torch*. What saves Siegel's flamboyant, top-heavy style again and again from bathos is his sense of humor.

In one classic piece, we are treated to a sensationally described murder scene featuring "the extinguished bodies of Phulla Ventzen and Izzy Murphy"—two of Jerry Siegel's favorite characters among his own fictional detectives—upon which enters "Sleuth Jerry Siegel, tripping daintily over rifles, toy cannons, stacks of daggers and such.

"Foul play!" he announces.

When Siegel's trusty assistant arrives, he is shocked to see the detective sitting nonchalantly among the bodies, playing solitaire.

"Say, aren't those guys dead?" he gasps.

"Sure," Inspector Siegel tells him, "from the neck up."

In another classic piece,

MASTER SLEUTH SOLVES
VERY BAFFLING ENIGMA

Jerry Siegel, "master of deduction," is called upon "to solve the mystery of the murder of Doris Blank, 87-year-old maid." After carefully examining the scene of the crime, in the manner of a latter-day Sherlock Holmes, Siegel repairs to the cellar followed by his bewildered assistant. There they find a stash of whiskey, which they proceed to drink.

"How did you find out—hic—that this old lady," inquires the assistant between belts, "had such good stuff here?"

"The old lady ain't murdered," Siegel tells him, "she'sh just drunk."

In the fall of 1932, the paper ran another short-lived series, this time a collaboration between Siegel and Reuben Schrank ("Again Siegel and Schrank crash through with a new column! We call it 'Serialettes'....") which featured the short-short "first chapters" of a succession of flakey mystery sagas that always break off at just the most exasperating point, never of course to be continued. ("If you like this feature, let us know," said Siegel in a note; "if you don't—shut up!")

Siegel's first sustained effort, which was featured on page one of a special *Torch Literary Supplement* (January 14, 1932), was a detective yarn with the lurid title, "Five Men and a Corpse." It also contained his first published attempt at "realistic" dialogue.

If not as high-minded a writer as Jerry Mendelsohn or Jerry Schwartz, Siegel was prolific enough, and the Glenville student body chuckled at the outrageous products of his hyperactive brain. You can still find people who remember reading of the hysterically inept adventures of detectives Phulla Vahncen and "Stiletto" Vance—both una-

bashed takeoffs on the popular patrician sleuth of S. S. Van Dine's books, the indomitable Philo Vance—though nobody can remember any longer what they did; and of the maniacal antics of a whole array of mad scientists and their slobbering assistants. (" 'Are you with me?' the professor asked. Zucker glanced over his shoulder at Miriam's picture. 'In the interest of science,' he replied, and shot another look at the photograph. Silently, the two men clasped hands.")

But his most popular creation by far, during his high school years, was Siegel's muscle bound parody of Tarzan of the Apes, Goober the Mighty ("GOOBER THE MIGHTY DISCOVERS/COUNTLESS FOES IN WILDERNESS"—May 7, 1931). As the story opens, "Goober, Son of the Lion," is flexing his muscles, muttering to himself: "By Jove, one year from now I'll be the strongest man on Earth."

"Cut out admiring yourself and come with me," says Oolala, the lion, Goober's adopted parent. "I smell Looneyack the deer."

" 'I am Goober, Son of the Lion,' he shouted at the top of his voice, as, in a fit of superhuman energy, he snapped a twig between two great hands."

This character retained a certain fascination for Siegel, who appears to have been even more preoccupied with heroes of gigantic strength and powerful physiques than the average boy of his age. Was he answering some painful need to parody what friends say was his own obsession with body-building schemes when he wrote, in "The Return of Goober the Mighty" that autumn:

"Goober, adopted son of Oolala, the lion, lifted his tousled head and drew in a mighty breath. 'If I take breathing exercises one hundred times a day for one hundred years he informed himself, 'I'll have the greatest chest in existence.' He pounded his chest

experimentally with a ham-like fist, then went into a paroxym [sic] of coughing that turned his face purple."

Are we looking here at evidence of the profound self-consciousness that finally issued in the split personality of poor weakling Clark Kent and the Man of Steel? This fascinated self-awareness drove Siegel to observe and write, on the one hand, about the at-times frightening intensity of his involvement with the fantasy life of his brain and the marvel-packed adventures of his numerous alter egos, on the other.

Once, in a lighthearted vein, he described himself at work: "With startling rapidity a thought had unexpectedly smote his brain.... When Jerry was finally galvanized into motion, he certainly was a man to behold!" Siegel describes how he would rip several sheets of theme paper out of his notebook, grab a sharpened pencil, loosen his collar and begin.

"Minutes ticked by and still the boy wrote. Small black marks now covered the page. Tiny beads of perspiration hung on his brow. His look was both haunted and eery. Suddenly, the wild expression dropped from his eyes. His face broke into a jubilant smile. Flourishing the papers before him, Jerry rose up. 'Friends,' he proclaimed to the silent throng of admirers that had gathered about him, There are 1,488,000 seconds till June 10, when summer vacation begins.' "

It was on one warm summer night, he told a reporter from the Saturday Evening Post a few years later, that the story of Superman had come to him in a blinding flash as he lay unable to sleep.

Had time worked the split in him far enough at last that he could see suddenly before him the meek, slope-shouldered figure of Kent, the reporter, banging out at his typewriter the excruciatingly sweet and uninhibited adventures of his other self, who dashed about in a red cape and blue tights leaping buildings, snapping railroad trains like giant whips, knocking gangsters' heads together and rescuing Lois Lane? A hero who could do everything he had ever dreamed, and do it wonderfully, basking in the admiration of women and the envy of his fellow men. The ultimate fantasy, bubbling for years somewhere in the back of his head, too much for him to admit to in a serious way, for fear of humiliation. Until on this night…"all of a sudden it hits me. I conceive a character like Samson, Hercules and all the strong men I ever heard tell of rolled into one. *Only more so*."

That had been the answer. Play the fantasy flat-out, with no hedging. Let it happen. Let this hero be something no other hero had ever been, a person from out-of-this-world altogether, a visitor from the stars who must hide his identity behind the guise of a mortal man and, able to retire from the harsh, demanding light of the everyday, dart forth in times of trouble to amaze and then disappear again from the eyes of humankind. ("BUT WHEN WILL I SEE YOU AGAIN?" Lois Lane would ask her mysterious deliverer. "WHO KNOWS?" the man in the flowing cape would reply gravely, his eyes avoiding hers, "PERHAPS TOMORROW—PERHAPS NEVER!")

The otherworldly origins of Superman stimulated Siegel's imagination with a new intensity: There was no limit to the kinds of exotic powers this hero might possess — invulnerable skin (Superman would be fond of making corny remarks to himself or to the awed reader to the effect that the machine-gun bullets or bazooka shells frustrated foes of law and order persisted in showering upon his body "tickled" or even, on some occasions, felt good), flight (for the first few years, apparently until he got the hang of it, Superman only took what amounted to big jumps), the ability to see long distances, or even—perhaps every adolescent boy's dearest dream—to see *through* things ("IT'S AS IF I HAD X-RAY EYES," blurts young Clark; "HMMM," says Pa Kent).

It was a wonderful morning.

Even before the sun was all the way up, Siegel dashed, shirt hanging out, several blocks to the house of his friend and some-time collaborator, Joe Shuster, to tell him about the newest idea and to get Joe to work up the drawings. It was going to take some refinement, but Jerry Siegel and Joe Shuster knew that at last they had their hands on the idea with which they were going to make it—big.

What they didn't know on that mild morning in 1934 was that it was going to take them four more exasperating years to get a publisher to give the strip a trial run, and that with the first appearance of Superman in a 1938 comic book, one of the very first, they would discover to their dismay that they no longer controlled the rights to their famous character.

Poignantly, the 50th anniversary of their famous character's debut finds the two men still friends, living—far from Glenville, Ohio—in West Los Angeles only a few short blocks from one another.

Some of the missing details of their early collaboration were to come to light many years after that historic summer night in an extraordinary interview conducted with the pair by Thomas Andrae, an instructor of mass communication at the University of California at Berkeley known for his many important contributions to the history of that long-neglected American art form, the comics.

Andrae, whose previous credits include co-editing the *Carl Barks Library*, a 30-volume collection of classic comic book stories by the creator of Scrooge McDuck, first met the reclusive Jerry Siegel in 1976 at a San Diego comic book convention. The historic interview that eventually resulted was published in the August 1983 issue of *NEMO: the classic comics library*, of which Andrae is an editor, under the title, "Of Superman and Kids with Dreams: An Interview with the Creators of Superman, Jerry Siegel and Joe Shuster." A newly expanded version will appear in the 1988 edition of Robert Overstreet's *Comic Book Price Guide*.

In that illuminating conversation, Shuster and the Siegels confirm a number of the hunches advanced by the present author in the 1973 version of this article. They also throw new light on those formative years of the Siegel-Shuster partnership.

Both were 16 when they met. Joe's family had moved to Cleveland from Canada when he was ten, and the talented boy had published his first cartoon illustrations in the Alexander Hamilton Junior High School paper, *The Federalist*.

When Shuster's family moved again, this time to an apartment at the corner of Kimberly Avenue and East 106th Street in the Glenville area, the paper's editor told him to look up his cousin, Jerry Siegel, at Glenville High. Jerry and Joe took to each other like long-lost brothers. Both wore glasses, were shy with girls and were insatiable consumers of science fiction and comic strips, especially of the exotic variety, such as *Flash Gordon* and the surrealistic classic *Little Nemo*.

Shuster, whose family had been hit hard by the times, was forced to do most of his drawing in those days "on brown wrapping paper and on the back of wallpaper." The first drawing of Joe's Jerry ever saw was on the back of a calendar. It was "a beautiful

27

scene of spaceships, rocketships and futuristic skyscrapers in a city of the future.''

Andrae also learned that Siegel had already published, at 14, the world's first science fiction "fanzine," a mimeographed effort entitled *Cosmic Stories* that reportedly featured stories mostly by Siegel himself under such dashing pseudonyms as Hugh Langley. Though his English teacher had pronounced it "trash," Siegel eagerly pressed Shuster into collaborating with him on the even more ambitious *Science Fiction* project. While it did not realize its publisher's earnest goal of "a few thousand subscribers," *SF* was to earn a footnote in the annals of popular culture for a story that appeared in its third issue (January 1933).

"The Reign of the Superman," published by Siegel under the mysterious nom de plume of Herbert S. Fine ("a combination of the names of one of my cousins and my mother's maiden name") and illustrated by Shuster, featured a bald villain in a Mao jacket determined to rule the universe. A couple of months later, Siegel told Andrae, he decided the concept was too good to waste on a villain and got Joe to illustrate a full-blown comic-book story. The cover (its contents were destroyed by Shuster in a fit of disappointment) depicts a strongman in tights and T-shirt: nothing, in short, to write home to Krypton about. (The Superman aficionado will enjoy Tom Andrae's article, "From Menace to Messiah: The Prehistory of the Superman in Science Fiction Literature," in the Summer 1980 issue of *Discourse*, a semi-annual journal of film and literary criticism published by the Center for Twentieth-Century Studies at the University of Wisconsin. "The Reign of the Super-

man," for the curious, is reprinted in facsimile in the August 1983 issue of *NEMO*.)

It was not until a year later, on that famous night in 1934 (not 1932 as the *Saturday Evening Post* interview erroneously asserts), that the vision of Superman as we know him—his flamboyant cape and costume, his otherworldly origins, his dual identity as the mild-mannered reporter, and the unattainable Lois—crashed in on Siegel's brain. Thus was born one of the most famous and touching love triangles in all of American literature. American folklore, anyway.

Did the idea of Clark Kent and Lois Lane spring full-blown into Siegel's imagination or were those two star-crossed characters merely disguised versions—as was so often his habit with the short stories he published in *The Torch*—of real people Siegel knew? (Mildred Gogolick, for example, became mysterious "Gogolick Island," and Goldie Blank became Doris Blank, the 87-year-old corpse-that-wasn't. And so forth.) Again, the past offers tantalizing clues.

A persistent rumor (and one must credit something to any rumor that persists for half a century) has it that there was indeed a girl named Lois, on whom the comic-strip character was based. It seems likely that at least some aspects of the character were based on one or two prominent female reporters connected with *The Torch*, as suggested earlier; but who was *Lois*? For though no one by that name is mentioned on the paper's masthead in those years, the name Lois does have a way of cropping up in the pages of those old newspapers—once in a spoof of Siegel's. Whom was he teasing? Was it Lois Long, who sang in the choral society and graduated in '33; or Lois Ingram, a talented art student who got out a year earlier in '32; or Lois Peoples, class of '31, of whom only a picture remains?

If one searched back a bit further, there was indeed a Lois Donaldson who had been associate editor of *The Torch* back in 1928. (Had Siegel met her through his friend Wilson Hirschfeld's older sister, Mary, who had also worked on *The Torch* about that time?) Oddly enough, in 1928 there had also been a copyreader on the paper with the unlikely name of Maxine *Kent*.

But the most intriguing references involve a girl known as "Lois A." She seems to have come into the Maslow-Mendelsohn crowd — or rather hovered on the edge of it — sometime in the fall of 1931. An item in the "Subtleville Slander" gossip column makes reference to a "Joel G.-Lois A. romance." (A Joel Goldberg was on the business staff of the paper.)

She was Lois Amster, "a very pretty, very nicely-put-together girl…one of the handful of young females that the boys were conscious of." She seems to have dated Al Maslow briefly. She was very bright — and one of those disturbingly self-assured girls who make their male contemporaries uneasy by dating older fellows.

"We wonder if Lois Amster is seeing any more of her red-headed East Hi boy friend?" someone wonders in print in November of 1932. She appears to have been the sort of young woman high school boys lie awake brooding about or trying to get up the courage to ask for a date.

The first time Lois Lane ever appears in the Superman story, an awkward Clark Kent is standing beside her desk in the city room with one hand jammed self-consciously into his pocket, trying to look nonchalant. "W-WHAT DO YOU SAY TO A — ER — DATE TONIGHT, LOIS?" he stammers. "I SUPPOSE I'LL GIVE YOU A BREAK…FOR A CHANGE," says Lois, looking up coolly. ("WHY IS IT YOU ALWAYS AVOID ME AT THE OFFICE?" he asks her later that night while the two of them are dancing. "PLEASE CLARK! I'VE BEEN SCRIBBLING SOB STORIES ALL DAY LONG," she tells

him, trying to be kind. "DON'T ASK ME TO DISH OUT ANOTHER.")

Close enough. But who then was Kent? The probable answer, as in the case of Lois, is maybe a composite of two or three people. The name Clark, for one thing, is not too difficult to trace. Anyway, there's a good bet.

In the "Subtleville Slander" column of February 18, 1932, somebody (the column is unsigned that week) is ribbing student-council president and popular senior-class actor Irv Schnabel (rhymes with *Gable*). "DO YOU KNOW," the anonymous heckler asks, "…CLARK SCHNABEL (OH, GIRLS! YOO! HOO!)" Schnabel's nickname appears to have been something of a standing joke around the *Torch* room. Jerry Schwartz was a close friend, Wilson Hirschfeld served on the student council with him, Willie Gomberg acted on the stage with him and Joe Shuster was often hanging around rehearsals, painting sets.

So Clark Kent's first name, it seems, was very likely intended to call up, for laugh value, the image of Gable in the minds of readers. Clark indeed, with his four left feet and his stammering, bashful ways with women. What could have been more ludicrous? Siegel, in the NEMO interview, confirms the Gable connection, adding that the "Kent" part was borrowed from actor Kent Taylor, and the name of Metropolis from Fritz Lang's 1927 film classic about a city of the future.

As for the rest, there is also a rumor that persists to the effect that Kent was modelled on none other than poor Wilson Hirschfeld — indeed Hirschfeld is said to have once proudly asserted, later denied it. Did Jerry Siegel's soft-spoken friend once confess that he nursed a crush on the class beauty, the Inaccessible One herself, Lois Amster? Did she go out with him once? One former classmate laughed aloud at the suggestion.

"Lois was, well she was a nice girl, but a little stuck up. She was very beautiful, you see. She had guys lined up, waiting to go out with her. Wilson was this little guy sitting at his typewriter in the corner."

(This hunch concerning the identity of the original Lois was later confirmed by a little-known interview with Siegel and Shuster published in the Washington *Star* on October 29, 1975. "Lois Lane was named for Lois Amster, a Cleveland girl," reports the *Star*. But the article also contains a surprise none had previously suspected. It was *Joe* who had "had a crush" on her. "She's a grandmother now in Cleveland," a mature Shuster philosophized, "but I don't think she has any idea that she was the inspiration for Lois Lane.")

As a young reporter on Cleveland's *Plain Dealer* in the years that followed high school, and eventually as managing editor, Hirschfeld was in any case the very image of Siegel's superhero, always stamping out the forces of evil with the selfless dedication and odd single-mindedness of the Man of Steel; breeding enemies every step of the way as casually as he swooped down on the partisans of crime and corruption (he is said to have once remarked that he didn't know anybody with as much integrity as himself); seemingly forever on the phone ferreting out plots, and — curious detail — never allowing himself to be seen wearing his glasses.

In the 1983 *NEMO* interview, Siegel claimed that "Clark Kent grew not only out of my private life, but also out of Joe's. As a high school student, I thought that some day I might become a reporter, and I had crushes on several attractive girls who either didn't know I existed or didn't care I existed.... It

occurred to me: What if I...had something special going for me, like jumping over buildings or throwing cars around or something like that? ...Joe was a carbon copy of me." "I was mild-mannered, wore glasses, was very shy with women," Shuster corroborates. "So in the artwork," says Siegel, "he...wasn't just drawing it, he was feeling it."

And when Lois and other women looked at Superman and sighed, says Siegel, "I enjoyed the fact that he wasn't that affected by all their admiration," reasoning that Superman "would be so advanced that he would be invulnerable in other ways than physical."

But if Joe and Jerry were the models for poor Kent, the model for Superman was... "Douglas Fairbanks, Senior." At least where his physical appearance was concerned. As teenagers Siegel and Shuster had haunted the local movie houses like addicts. The swashbuckling Fairbanks' pictures were among their favorites: "He did *The Mark of Zorro* and *Robin Hood* and a marvelous one called *The Black Pirate* — those are three that I recall we loved," remembered Shuster in 1983. "He had a stance which I often used in drawing Superman. You'll see in many of his roles — including Robin Hood — that he always stood with his hands on his hips and his feet spread apart, laughing — taking nothing seriously." (The physical appearance of Superman's counterpart, too, owed something to the movies, Shuster told Tom Andrae. "Clark Kent, I suppose, had a little bit of Harold Lloyd in him.")

Jerry would try to recreate the excitement of those Saturday-afternoon matinees, too, when they worked together, leaning close in by Joe's shoulder, as he talked him through the story. Though Siegel had never seen a screenplay, he talked instinctively in cinematic terms. "He would describe each scene, and the shot used," Joe recalled years later,

"—long shot, medium, close-up, overhead shot. It was marvelous."

For his part, Joe Shuster squinted through thick glasses at the blurry figures of Clark and Lois taking shape beneath his fingers, his nose only a few inches from the drawing board. He had always suffered from poor eyesight and now, as his creation's powerful X-ray eyes bored through foot-thick walls to expose to the reader the clandestine deeds of dour men, his own vision was deteriorating at an alarming rate. (Touchingly, he—and Siegel—would insist, long after the relentless press of deadlines had required them to hire other artists to do the finished "inking" of Shuster's rough pencil sketches, that Joe ink every face of Superman.)

To make matters worse, the Shusters had no heat in their apartment, and during the cold months Joe was sometimes forced to work with gloves on, often wearing two or three sweaters and a jacket or two. One imagines the two friends hunched over the first story boards of *Superman*, trading bursts of frosty breath excitedly, as they shaped the myth and set of characters that would be their ticket out of the poverty and anonymity of their Glenville boyhoods.

But this was 1934. And the world was not yet ready for Superman. Or at least the adult businessmen who controlled the comics industry. It was too far out, they said. Indeed, when publisher Harry Donenfeld of *Action Comics* was first shown the cover drawing for the first Superman story— four years later—a scene depicting a caped man in tights lifting a car over his head while a stunned gang looks on, Donenfeld is said to have rolled his eyes and pronounced it "ridiculous."

Siegel and Shuster had in the interim submitted Superman to practically every newspaper syndicate around, drawing similar responses. They were able to sell other strips—such as the exotic adventures of Doctor Occult, a "ghost detective" dedicated to combating supernatural evil (which the team produced under the pseudonyms of Leger and Reuths), a humorous strip about a blue-blood nerd named Reggie van Twerp, and the Roaring Twenties-type exploits of a modern day Samson in sports jacket and slacks known as Slam Bradley, who bears more than a passing resemblance to the Man of Steel.

It was not that the sight of grown men dashing about in tights and in some cases even capes was foreign to the comic strips. Siegel and Shuster themselves had grown up on the adventures of Buck Rogers and Flash Gordon. But, as historians of the genre such as Ron Goulart have pointed out, these stories all took place in the far future and/or on distant planets: credible contexts, in the 1930s, for such otherwise improbable antics and wardrobes. Siegel and Shuster's brilliant innovation—which seems ironically to have made their creation just a little *too* exotic for their contemporaries—was to make their hero an honest-to-God extraterrestrial and to set his wonderful adventures on the streets of a contemporary American city.

Other fictional heroes, similarly, had divided their time between duty as a costumed crime-buster and a civilian identity. One thinks of Zorro and the Scarlet Pimpernel. But in each case, the civilian was the real person and the crusader (a la Batman) was the fabrication: a bold fantasy life acted out by the light of the moon. With Superman, it was the wonderful being who was the reality, his civilian identity the fabrication. He was, in 1938, the alien walking in our midst, the benevolent interplanetary visitor decades before *Close Encounters of the Third Kind*, the walking racial memory of another, more perfect Earth. Enter Lois Lane, and the stage was set for a drama whose hook was set deep in the ado-

lescent soul.

A reader poll taken a few months after the first appearance of Superman in *Action Comics* in June 1938 revealed that kids were asking for "that magazine with Superman in it" (Donenfeld having at first decreed that more sensible cover subjects be chosen). And they were going like hotcakes—soon as many as half a million copies a month. American youth could not get enough of Superman. And so, in 1939, he got his own comic book, which was soon selling an incredible one and a quarter million copies bimonthly—in addition to the *Action Comics* in which he still appeared.

So great was the demand for more adventures of Superman that the McClure Syndicate had commissioned Siegel and Shuster that January to do a daily newspaper strip. The following year, 1940, a 15-minute serial which aired three days a week debuted on the Mutual Radio Network, under the sponsorship of—what else?—Kellogg's Pep, forever emblazoning on the American psyche the immortal words, "Up in the sky, look…!" Between 1941 and 1943, 17 lavishly colored animated shorts were turned out for Paramount by Max Fleischer's studios. And in 1942 a full-blown novel by George Lowther was published by Random House.

But if Superman took the various media of the day by storm, he also spawned a whole new genre of comic books as competitors—even *Action Comics* itself—scrambled to get a piece of the new market. By 1942 more than a dozen other superheroes, all more or less patent imitations, had arrived on the scene. In time this doughty band would include such latter-day Olympians as the Flash, the Torch, Hour-Man, Star-Man, Hawkman, Plastic Man, the Ultra-Men, Wonder Woman, Wonder Man, Captain Marvel, Captain America, Dr. Fate, Air-Wave, the Red Knight, Green Mask and Green Lantern.

But there was no catching him. Superman was an authentic American dream; he simply outclassed all rivals and seemed to thrive on having enemies. Indeed—the dark side of the myth—he seemed somehow almost to generate them. The Man of Tomorrow rose unfailingly to the occasion, wrapping girders around bank robbers as easily as Goober the Mighty had once tied a slipknot in an alligator's tail. ("Haven't you fought enough for today?" Goober's wreck of a mother had once asked him. To which the Mighty G. had shaken his head emphatically: "I don't know what I'd do if it weren't for these scrapes of mine.")

Always something of a superpatriot, Superman joined the war effort along with other proud enlistees like Joe Palooka and Terry, while Charlie Chan and Dick Tracy tangled with spies and saboteurs on the home front. (Even Tarzan got into the war, sabotaging German efforts to set up a base in the African interior.) Indeed, the Nazis took such a whale of a beating at the hands of Siegel and Shuster's hero, both on land and in the air, that Nazi Minister of Propaganda Joseph Goebbels himself is said to have bounded to his feet in the middle of a Reichstag meeting waving an American comic book and furiously denouncing Superman as a Jew.

The Fuhrer's furor may have been ignited by a patriotic wartime comic-book episode in which Superman, who has taken part in American war games, gracefully accepts "defeat" with the assertion that "this has been the proudest moment in my life" because he has "seen proof that American soldiers cannot be defeated by Superman or anyone else—not even Mr. Schickelgruber's so-called Master Race!" Standing Patton-like before a huge American flag, the son of Krypton boasts pridefully about "our nation's real secret weapon — the unflagging courage of her men, no matter what the odds, and their indomitable will to win! Against that, Hitler and Hirohito haven't a ghost of a chance!" (Small wonder *Superman* comics were practically standard issue in the duffel bags of American GIs.)

So old crazy Jerry Siegel, in a manner of speaking, had his pinochle game with Hitler after all. He had taken the very name, if not the spirit, of Frederich Nietzsche's Ubermensch — the embodiment of the great German philosopher's doctrine that the "will to power" is the chief motivating force of individual and society — and rubbed their noses in it. Siegel, who himself did a stint in the United States Army during the war, must have savored the moment.

What greeted him on his return to the States was less enjoyable. He and Joe had been irritated by all of the ripoffs of their famous character which had appeared in the early '40s. Now National Periodicals itself, the parent company of *Action Comics*, was publishing the adventures of a new character named Superboy, who purported to be the earlier self of Superman. In 1947, tired of watching others making millions on their character while their own income was declining, Siegel and Shuster went to court to regain the rights to their creation, cancel their contracts with McClure and Donenfeld and recover $5 million in what they claimed was lost income. They were awarded $100,000 in compensation for Superboy, which they divided. But the court denied their claim to ownership of Superman.

Back in 1938, beaten down by years of rejections, the two boys had turned over the first 13 pages of Superman, along with a customary release form relinquishing all rights to the character, in return for a mere

$130, or $10 a page, which they split equally. When their character became an overnight sensation, they had protested what Siegel felt was their exploitation. But they were dismissed, he wrote later, as "inexperienced" young men with swelled heads who were "grossly exaggerating the importance of *Superman*," and told to put their energies instead into "your work with zest and ambition to improve."

Their publisher, Harry Donenfeld, finally agreed to let them do a regular strip, as well, for the McClure Syndicate for a share of the net (reported variously at from 50 to as high as 90 percent) if they would agree to work exclusively for Donenfeld for the next ten years at $35 a page. When Siegel protested, the publisher reminded him that he, Donenfeld, now held all the rights to Superman. The partners had little choice.

Though Siegel and Shuster are estimated to have earned approximately $400,000 from Superman between 1938 and 1947 (worth roughly three or four times that in today's dollars), the Superman industry they had launched took off like a rocket. By 1941 Superman was appearing regularly in 230 newspapers across the country with an estimated circulation of 25 million, as well as multiple overseas translations, and the marketplace was glutted with Superman toys and other spinoff products — altogether bringing in somewhere in the neighborhood of $1.5 million, in 1940-41, to Superman, Inc. While the following year, Siegel and Shuster split maybe $150,000 between themselves and a staff of five artists working out of a one-room office in Cleveland.

The 1947 court victory was short-lived. The following year, their contract with Donenfeld ran out, and they were fired.

This last cruel turn of events was, ironically, perhaps made bearable by another unexpected twist of fate. At a costume party he and Joe attended during the period of

their litigation, Siegel told Andrae, he found himself dancing with a woman named Joanne Carter, whom he had not seen in several years. She was costumed as the popular comic-strip character Dixie Dugan. But her real identity was well known to Siegel. Joanne Carter had once answered an ad for an artist's model placed in the Cleveland *Plain Dealer*, it turned out, by one Joe Shuster. The sketches Joe had subsequently made of her had become the basis for the character of Lois Lane. (Joanne had worked on her own school paper, it came out in the course of several modelling sessions; in fact she had entertained ambitions for a time of becoming a reporter.)

A few months later—it was 1948, the year he and Joe were fired by Donenfeld—Jerome Siegel (a.k.a. Clark Kent) married Joanne Carter (a.k.a. Lois Lane).

And so began the long years of bitterness and frustration marked by further legal attempts, also unsuccessful, to regain ownership of Superman. Though Siegel was retained in the early '60s by DC COMICS (as National Periodical Publications eventually came to be known, after its original line, *Detective Comics*) as an anonymous writer for a reported salary of $20,000 and Shuster, who was then all but legally blind, for $7,500, the millions they saw others making on various Superman deals continued to rankle—as did the fact that their names no longer appeared on the Superman stories.

After another unsuccessful lawsuit and falling-out with DC COMICS in 1963, Siegel went to work as a mailroom clerk at $7,000 a year and Shuster was taken in by his brother Bern. But the two never surrendered

their belief that Superman rightfully belonged to them. In 1975 the news that a $20-million *Superman* movie was in the works drew an anguished cry from Siegel in the form of a nine-page single-spaced press release mailed to a thousand newsrooms around the country. The industry hoopla already surrounding *Superman, the Movie* had been too much for Jerry Siegel to bear, and he asked the public to boycott the film.

Convinced that its rights to the Man of Steel had been reaffirmed by several court rulings over the years, but faced with the prospect of negative publicity damaging to the new movie, Warner Communications, which now owned DC COMICS, at length offered—in exchange for Siegel and Shuster's agreeing to suspend hostilities—to give them each $20,000 a year for life along with medical coverage for themselves and their families and a promise, in the event of their deaths, to take care of Siegel's wife and Shuster's brother. Tired of waging a half-century-long battle, with no hopes of cutting a better deal, the two men, now in their sixties and in poor health, accepted.

Something else may have moved them to let go, at long last, of their demand for legal ownership of Superman.

One final gesture had been thrown into the bargain—one which had cost Warner and DC practically nothing, but which must have been sweet for Siegel and Shuster: Their names were to be restored to their creation.

This month youngsters of another generation will hurry home to curl up with the newest adventure of the caped Champion of the Oppressed. They will swallow excitedly to read the story of his origins, as vivid as the news of a freshly discovered galaxy on the edge of the universe. But the truth is, Krypton has long since exploded. The world that gave Superman birth is long gone. And the pieces of stardust are everywhere.

DRAWING SUPERMAN

by CURT SWAN

I dropped by the Smithsonian when I was in Washington one day this past June to see the new Superman exhibit. Like other Americans who will visit the museum during the exhibit's year-long run, I have a certain fondness for the Man of Steel. He and I go back a long way. For 30 years or so, from around 1955 until a couple of years ago when I more or less retired, I was the principal artist of the *Superman* comic for DC COMICS.

It still surprises me sometimes when I think about it. It was never something I set out to

do. It just kind of happened, the way a lot of good things do. In fact, if anybody had told me when I was a kid growing up in Minneapolis back in the '30s that I would one day be sitting on the set of something called *The Today Show* being interviewed about my work by a young woman named Jane Pauley, or that I would be a guest celebrity at a national comic-book convention, I would have thought he or she was crazy. Television was still only science fiction in those days, and, not only wasn't I much interested in science fiction, I wasn't even particularly into comic books.

My brother Stanley—I was the youngest of five children, and he was the oldest—was an avid reader of the "pulps." But I preferred curling up with magazines like *Collier's* or the *Saturday Evening Post*. I especially liked the adventure stories—I guess because of the illustrations. I was already drawing my head off every chance I got, and I was in awe of those illustrators. I admired their technique, their coloring, their composition, their honesty with the human figure. It was my dream that I would one day be an illustrator, too.

My teachers had recognized my talent early. They were always giving me projects to do, such as calling me up to the blackboard to draw a mural or illustrate some lesson. I remember a school fair we had when I was in sixth grade. Every child in the school was expected to do a project to be sold (I don't remember what they were going to do with the money). I got the idea of doing a comic book. It was a takeoff on the Big Little Books that were very popular in those days, which I had discovered while babysitting for a younger child in the neighborhood. They were fat little paperback books that

contained reprinted comic strips. So I got hold of a desk calendar—the kind with the big numerals on one side and nothing on the other—and I stapled together a whole year's worth of them to make a blank comic book. It was just about the right size. I wrote the story myself. It was about two young boys who ran away from home and the adventures they had. One of the other kids bought it. I was thrilled.

But it still did not occur to me that I might someday make a living drawing comic books. I had more serious ambitions.

My family were serious, hard-working folk of Swedish stock. (Our name was originally Swanson, but some ancestor of mine, my grandmother, I think, decided to shorten it.) My father, John Swan, was born on a farm just across the Canadian border, in Saskatchewan. Later, he and his family moved back to Willmar, Minnesota, a town about 60 miles from Minneapolis where the Swansons had originally settled before moving north. My mother grew up in a nearby town called Litchfield. She was a Hanson. Leotine Hanson. She worked for a while in a local hospital; my father was a railroad man. He repaired trestles.

We were raised Presbyterians, but my father could never quite make up his mind on a religion. I guess he was looking for something—or driven by something: the fear of the unknown, perhaps. He would drag us to a Methodist church one week, a Baptist church, the next. Since I was the youngest, he latched on to me and always took me along with him. I was a very religious person up until the age of 11 or 12, when my brother Lloyd and I began to lie on the grass out under the stars on long summer evenings, just talking for hours about everything, deciding what we thought about things. I sort of lost interest in churches around that time. My brother was quite a philosopher.

This was during the Depression. My family

was lucky. Most of us were able to get work of some kind, and we all chipped in to put food on the table and paid for our own clothes. I got a job with a small letter service doing stencils and deliveries and helping out the printer. I also worked for Sears Roebuck for a short time as a "warehouse man." I remember getting a letter in the mail—I must have been about 17—informing me that I had received a triple-A credit rating. I was proud as a peacock!

It was around this time that I signed up with the National Guard, along with some of my friends. The war in Europe was heating up, and, somewhere around the end of 1940, a bunch of us were inducted into the army—34th Division, 135th Infantry, Service Company—and moved to Camp Clayborn in Louisiana. We went from there to Fort Dix. I was made a sergeant. And the following February, we boarded a ship for Belfast, Northern Ireland. I was stationed at Fintona, near Enniskillen, for about three months. It was there in Northern Ireland, with a war on, that I got my first break as an illustrator.

I met a young GI named Dick Wingert, who was a cartoonist with the army paper, *Stars and Stripes*. (He later created a strip called *Hubert*, which was one of the most successful comic strips to come out of World War II.) We became quite good friends while the two of us were doing murals for the Red Cross club in Belfast, and he suggested that I write to a Colonel Llewellyn about a position on *Stars and Stripes*. I hung back, not thinking of myself as much of a writer.

Then one day as I was dishing out grub to the headquarters staff back at camp— I was officially a mess sergeant in those days—I got this brainstorm. I went to another one of the guys on the staff who was very good with words, he was some kind of writer, and told him what I had in mind and asked him if he would script it for me. He

did, and I sent Colonel Llewellyn an illustrated letter with a silhouette of him—I had no idea what he looked liked—interviewing me and a caricature of myself giving him my resume. The next thing I knew, I was being shipped over to London where they made me a staff artist on *Stars and Stripes*. I did illustrations for the magazine section, war maps showing the progress of the Allies, cartoons, little spot drawings for the sports section—whatever they threw at me.

My unit, back in Belfast, was eventually shipped out to North Africa. After the war, when we got together back in Minneapolis and they talked about their experiences, I was very reticent to join in. They had gone up through Italy, through the worst of it. A lot of our friends were lost.

There was one night in London, however, when my life did flash before my eyes. I was living in a lovely, upper-middle-class neighborhood at the time on the outskirts of London, not too far from Henley Airport, which was probably the reason the Germans had us on their clipboard back across the channel where they were launching the V2s they'd started sending over after the buzz bombs. I had been up most of the night working on a war map and had finally gotten to bed about four or five in the morning, when suddenly I sat bolt upright, listening. I must have heard it deep in my sleep, the way you do with some things. A moment later the V2 came roaring in and hit very close by, rattling everything to hell. That was about the closest I came during the war to meeting my Maker some years ahead of schedule.

For a year or so I roomed with Wingert in London. We were the original Odd Couple. We originated the concept. He was Mr. Filth and I was Mr. Clean. But we had a swell time going to the neighborhood pubs and conversing with the citizenry on all manner of subjects—politics, culture, the Americans

versus the English. I did a mural for an airbase somewhere in the Midlands. It was a wonderful couple of years, except for the bombs.

Wingert and I used to go down to the Red Cross club in London, the Eagle Club I think it was called, to play ping-pong and eat doughnuts. They had comic books spread out on the coffee table, and I remember picking one up one day and thinking, ''Why would anybody want to put that much work into drawing—for a comic book?'' I couldn't imagine anybody wanting to do that for a living.

One day word came through that *Stars and Stripes* needed a staff artist in Paris. Next thing I knew I was living in a little apartment near the Eiffel Tower. I would sit for hours sketching by the Seine. Once I stowed away (with the complicity of the French drivers) aboard a quarter-ton army vehicle filled with copies of *Stars and Stripes* bound for the GIs at the front—to drop in for a surprise visit on my bride-to-be, Helene Brickley, whom I'd learned was stationed just across the Belgian border with the 82nd Airborne, the paratroopers who had moved in ahead of Patton's army. We had met back at Fort Dix, New Jersey. Her family lived in a nearby town and she had come up for one of our dances. She was working for RCA in Camden at the time. Later she had signed up with the Red Cross and turned up, much to my surprise, in London. But when I walked into the dispatcher's office that day in Belgium wearing a raincoat and garrison cap, she nearly fell off her chair. The next time I dropped in, she was living with a French family in a village nearby. We were married in Paris in 1944.

After the war, we agreed that my chances of finding something in the art field were greater in New York than back in Minneapolis. Several other ex-staffers from *Stars and Stripes* were living in New York, and we all used to get together at a little place on Third Avenue called the Campus Restaurant, which is long since gone. This was 1945. One of them was a fellow named France Herron, whom I'd known as a feature writer on the Paris *Stars and Stripes*. Before the war he'd been working in the comic-book business, and now he was back at it, writing for DC COMICS. He suggested I take my samples around to see Whitney Ellsworth and Mort Weisinger at DC. I shrugged and decided I'd give it a try.

They started me out me on a Jack Kirby feature called *Boy Commandos*. ''Well, this will be good for about two years,'' I told my wife. I figured the comic-book business hadn't much longer to run.

I was being paid $18 a page. That didn't sound too bad at first until I discovered how much time it took me to do a single page. I was getting really discouraged until one of the guys in the inking department took me aside and gave me a few tips. In the comic-book business, I had quickly learned, almost everybody specializes. There are pencillers, and there are inkers, who turn the pencils into finished pages, which are then turned over to the letterers and finally the colorists. Not everybody has a style of inking that is appropriate to comic books. Some people are very good at it and very fast. They have to be to make any kind of living at it. In those days the inkers were making even less than the pencillers, about $14 a page. (The writers, I would later discover, were only getting between $8 and $11 a page, depending on the quality of the writing.)

Anyway, this inker's name was Steve Brody. And he told me I was putting too much work into each panel and that he was

40

breaking his arm inking my stuff. He showed me ways to fake things, to suggest things without putting in every last detail. After that I was able to work faster. Soon I was turning out three to four pages a day. At the end of one year I discovered I had earned almost $10,000. That was a lot of money in those days. When a friend of mine who was visiting from Minnesota heard I had made that much, his eyes bulged out and he said, "God! If I was making $10,000, I'd feel wealthy!"

We were living in the Rockaways then, out on Long Island, not far from the old Floyd Bennett Field. We lived only half a block from the beach. There was a board- walk and we would go for long walks on the beach. We were putting away every dime we could spare to buy a little farmhouse in New Jersey.

But I was knocking myself out to make that much money — working up to 14 and 16 hours a day, seven days a week. They had me working on a variety of features: Besides *Boy Commandos*, I was now doing *Tommy Tomorrow* and a thing called *Gangbusters*. I even did some *Superboy* covers — whatever they pulled out of the drawer. I would come by the DC offices with my pencils and pick up a new script. (The offices were on Lexington Avenue then.) At home I had my studio set up in the bedroom or, later, when we got a big enough house, in a separate room. If the story was difficult or I got excited about it, I would work until three or four in the morning. I would usually have music on or sports or maybe a talk show. I liked the Big Bands — Charlie Barnett, Benny Goodman, Glenn Miller — and occasionally I would tune in a symphony concert.

I worked three times up (that is, three times larger than the drawings would even- tually appear). The script usually included a description of what was supposed to be happening in the panel, as well as the

dialogue that went in the balloons. Most of the time I was free to do what I wanted insofar as the scene itself. Only occasionally would a writer suggest a "long shot" or a "closeup." The only other limitations in those days were that you shouldn't show blood or extreme violence and should keep it cool on the sex part.

So I would compose each panel as I saw it, trying to make it interesting and visually balanced. I would sketch in the balloons, too, and the lettering. Most stories in those days ran ten or 12 pages. When I was finished with a story, I would take it back into the city and lay it in front of my editor — usually Mort Weisinger in those days. He would frequently ask me to make changes. He didn't like the way I had some character's face or the way I had carried out the "stage directions" in the script. Weising- er always thought you were just goofing off. It drove me crazy. Occasionally a writer would set a scene, say, on Fifth Avenue and want you to show the crowded street and sidewalks literally, all the cars and the people. Stadium scenes were especially hard to fake convincingly.

At home I was getting more and more tense, throwing things around the room — paper, my art supplies — because I was being asked to draw things I didn't think would work. I was working too hard, anyway. I would get these terrific migraine headaches where I would have to lie down on the bed, and heaven help anybody who dropped a pin. I figured my eyes were going. I got new eyeglasses, but it didn't seem to help. I decided I would have to give up the comic- book business and find something less strenuous.

I took a job with a small advertising studio. (This was sometime around 1951.) It was actually enjoyable. They handled a line of toys and some other things. I worked on displays and occasionally jobs for other

clients. But I was making only $50 a week. My wife panicked when I brought home my first paycheck. I panicked, too. We had just bought a house in Tenafly, New Jersey, and had payments to make. So, after only one month at the agency, I went back to DC. They welcomed me with open arms.

But soon I was lying in bed at home again with a spitting headache. Suddenly it hit me. I had had no headaches during the month I had worked for the studio. It was not my eyes, after all. It was something about working for DC COMICS that was causing my headaches. So I sorted it out and decided it was Mort—or, more likely, a combination of Mort Weisinger and myself, the way I was reacting to his criticisms and demands, swallowing a lot of my anger. I decided the only way to deal with it was to dig in my heels and fight him every inch of the way. It worked. My headaches stopped for good. I also think he respected me more after that, because I fought back. In time, we actually became quite close friends.

It was around this time that I started filling in occasionally for Wayne Boring, the artist who had taken over Superman from Joe Shuster. But it wasn't until around 1955 that I became the primary Superman artist. The first 3-D comics were making their appearance around that time, because of the success of 3-D movies, I guess, and DC wanted to get a 3-D *Superman* book out in a hurry. So Boring and Al Plastino and I were all brought on to the project. We only put out one 3-D *Superman*, but Weisinger was quite happy with my work on it, and soon after that he put me on *Superman* steady. I had done *Superboy* and *Jimmy Olsen* before I did *Superman*, so I was quite

familiar with the characters. I used to study Wayne Boring's work. I liked his style. I thought it suited Superman. Wayne had a real feeling for him, the way he constructed the figure, the flying, et cetera. Joe's Superman had been different. He was not trying to be realistic. His conception of the character was more cartoon-like. And my own style was different from Wayne's, just as Wayne's was from Joe's. I don't think any of this was intentional; each artist just had his own way of drawing.

Mort Weisinger told me early on that he wanted to soften the jaw line that Wayne Boring had put on Superman. I guess it had been Wayne's way of showing strength and power. Mort wanted the drawing to be more illustrative and less cartoony, maybe a little more handsome, with more emphasis on the muscles. I did speak briefly to Wayne Boring about it when I took over drawing the syndicated *Superman* strip in the late '50s or early '60s, a couple of years before they killed it. He knew how difficult Weisinger could be on the subject of Superman's looks. "Just hang in there," Wayne told me, "and don't take any s---."

I didn't have any conscious models for Superman. I suppose I may have been somewhat influenced by Johnny Weissmuller. I had always been kind of fascinated, as a boy, by the *Tarzan* newspaper strip and the Weissmuller movies, and I guess I may have imitated them subconsciously to a degree. Alex Raymond's strip *Rip Kirby* was probably also an influence.

At one point in the '50s, I gave some thought to making Superman look more like George Reeves, the actor who played him on television. I had seen Reeves once on the set, briefly, on one of my trips to the coast. I began to study his features on the TV show, but finally decided that it would be pointless to copy him too literally, though I think I did get his profile a little bit from time

42

to time.

I wanted to show strength, of course, and ruggedness. And *character*. He had to be the kind of person you'd *want* to have on your side.

When I drew Clark Kent, on the other hand, I deliberately softened his features, made them less angular than Superman's. I wanted him to appear more meek. Just sort of a good Joe. I don't know if it worked, but that's what I was trying to do.

Superman's hair was different from Clark's, too, of course. That curl would come down—it was a way of showing action. I guess that had been Shuster's idea: action causing that lock of hair to fall out of place. As for Lois, I just tried to draw her pretty, but I wasn't successful enough for Mort Weisinger. From time to time, he would have Kurt Schaffenberger do Lois.

We also had arguments about showing expression. I felt it was necessary to put lines in the face to show pain or whatever. Mort and I had long discussions about this. He thought they made Superman look too old. I think I finally got through to him by pointing out that even a baby, when it's angry or crying, has lines in its face.

I also used to argue about some of the things the writers came up with. I thought it was rather ridiculous that this character could do anything the writers could dream up, like fly in space or withstand an atomic blast. "If he's that invulnerable, then where's your story?" I used to ask. "You're handcuffing yourselves." But I guess they thought of me as just that stupid artist. Eventually, they had to invent things like all the different-colored kryptonite, which seemed to me a feeble way of getting out of the box they had put themselves in.

Once in the early '50s, I decided to take a course in illustration. I wanted to improve my craft. I had been more or less self-taught.

So I enrolled at Pratt Institute in Brooklyn. Some of the teachers raised their eyebrows when they heard what I did for a living, but my fellow students, who were mostly attending art school on the GI Bill and still trying to break into the business, were a little bit in awe of me. It turned out to be just a review of everything I already knew. It was a long drive in from New Jersey two nights a week at the end of a long day, and I began to find myself nodding off on the way home. So after a few months, I gave it up. So much for my formal art education.

The comics, I decided, were not a bad place for an artist to make a career, after all. Where else could you have the fun of creating an entire city in a bottle? I think Al Plastino had first drawn Kandor, the Kryptonian city that had been miniaturized by the villain Brainiac and thus escaped the destruction of Superman's native planet. But I had a lot of fun inventing all that tiny futuristic architecture, not to mention the view from inside the bottle—with the "giant" figures peering in. I've always regretted that Al Plastino and I never got to play golf together, another passion that we shared.

And it was always a special treat for me when the writers would come up with a story about Mr. Mxyzptlk. Suddenly, there in the midst of a fairly realistic comic book, was this wacky cartoon character. They excused it by explaining that he was from the fifth dimension, of course, and that suited me to a T, because they would go off the edge with some of those plots, and I knew I could have a ball. It was always like vacation time for me to get a script with Mxyzptlk.

But my favorite villain was Brainiac. I could do things with him—his expressions, et cetera—that were tough to do with some of the other villains. Lex Luthor, for example, didn't *look* evil. He was just a bald man. You could put a scowl on his face, and he still wouldn't look evil enough. But Brainiac was

thin, even gaunt, you could see the bone structure of his face. And there's a lot you can do with that to make a person seem more evil. Then, of course, there were those electrodes on his head!

For years my favorite Superman *story* was the one in which Superman and Jimmy Olsen visit another dimension, another world where Jimmy gets a costume, too, and superpowers. (I think his name is Flame Bird or something like that.) I got to create their costumes and those cities. I had fun with that. But I guess the story I'm proudest of is the 1973 version I illustrated of "The Origin of Superman"—showing the last days of Krypton, the baby Kal-El rocketing to earth and being found in a cornfield by Jonathan and Martha Kent, then young Clark discovering his superpowers as a boy and going off to Metropolis to serve the world as Superman. Carmine Infantino did the layout on that story, planning the way it was to unfold, panel by panel. It was so good. We included it in *The Amazing World of Superman*, one of those special large editions we put out for $2 a shot while Infantino was publisher. I am very fond of that one.

Nelson Bridwell did the dialogue, and Murphy Anderson inked my pencils. Murphy's inking was among the best. George Klein's was pretty good, too. But, since this one's for the history books, I'll have to say that my absolute favorite among all the inkers who ever worked on my stuff was Al Williamson, with whom I collaborated just before I officially retired. He was the best. A fine draftsman in his own right, an extremely talented artist, he could render even the little mechanical parts of vehicles. He had a very special flair the others didn't have.

I've worked with some inkers over the years who did not delineate the figure of Superman the way I'd done it in the pencils. They would lose something in the face, the eyes; the features would be just a little off or the muscular structure. It used to get to me. I would have to remind myself, sometimes, that this was only, after all, a comic book and wasn't going to be hung in some gallery. I had inked my own work, of course, back when I was on *Stars and Stripes*, but my style of inking wasn't right for comic books—a little too ornamental. It would take me too much time, and inkers, as I've said, have to work fast to make any money. Fellows like Al Williamson and Murphy Anderson are all the more amazing when you remember that.

The colorists have come a long way, too, since I was starting out in the business. By and large, they always did a nice job. But they were restricted in the old days by what the editors down the hall thought made sense. Those guys believed that a sky had to be blue, so it was blue. It was a long time before the colorists were allowed a little creativity: now, if they want to put a red sky in, they can put a red sky in and even make judgments about the overall treatment of the page. And, as a result, the coloration has improved tremendously.

I guess I was pretty far off base when I predicted, back in 1945, that comic books were only a passing fad and would never survive the '40s. As it turned out, the business was to be pretty good to me.

I've felt fortunate to be associated with *Superman* over so many years. I've met and had the opportunity of working with some wonderful people. I especially remember meeting Jerry Siegel and Joe Shuster, the creators of Superman. I used to see Jerry around the DC offices in the early '60s. This was years after their formal relationship with DC had ended, of course, but he was often there in those days, anonymously scripting stories about Superman and the other characters he and Joe had created. He was soft-spoken, a very likable person. I didn't know him socially, but I ran into him often in the offices.

Joe Shuster was a very shy, introverted person. It always struck me as kind of unusual, since most of the artists I know are extroverts. I believe Joe was living somewhere out on the Jersey shore at the time. His eyes had gotten very bad. I don't know how he supported himself. They were a couple of sweet guys.

I found myself thinking of all of these things, and of these people, after I came back from Washington and the Smithsonian's exhibition. There had been some beautiful displays—blowups of Superman, one of the costumes George Reeves wore in the TV series, a dress of Lois Lane's and lots of other artifacts and comic books—including about a dozen covers I remember having done.

Nice memories.

THE MAN OF STEEL AND ME

by DENNIS O'NEIL

I could probably write you a scene, New Journalism style. Describe walking into Julie's office on a spring or early summer day 17 years ago. Add a couple of telling details—afternoon sun slanting through the blinds? Batman artwork scattered on Julie's desk?—and then describe Julius Schwartz himself. Have Julie glance up from a manuscript, contemplate me through his glasses and say something like, "They gave me a new book to edit. *Superman*. You interested?" If I wrote it well, I might convince you. I might even convince myself. But the truth is, I don't remember how Julie asked me to script *Superman Comics* nor exactly when, nor how I reacted. I am certain that neither of us anticipated my ultimate failure.

Maybe if I'd thought about all the cultural freight Superman carries, I would have been reluctant to accept the assignment. The character is one of the best-known fictional creations in the world, if not *the* best known, and he has the further distinction of having created an industry, something not even Sherlock Holmes managed; before *Detective Comics* publisher Harry Donenfeld featured the benevolent alien introduced to the world by Jerry Siegel and Joe Shuster in the first issue of his new magazine, *Action Comics*, way back in June of 1938, the comic-book business had been extremely marginal, operated by fast talkers with a penchant for getting into whatever the public seemed to be favoring at the moment and getting out when the popular fancy moved on. Cheesy, some might call it. In fact, *Action* was one of the first titles to feature new material; mostly, comics were cobbled together from newspaper strips, altered very slightly, if at all, to accommodate the new format.

McClure Syndicate editor Sheldon Mayer remembers introducing M.C. Gaines, a McClure agent, to Joe and Jerry's brainchild. Shelly, who later worked for Gaines as editor of *All American Comics*, says he convinced Gaines to show the material to Donenfeld, who gave Superman 13 pages of *Action* 1. It is at least possible that Donenfeld thought of the venture as a tryout, a gamble with not much at stake. What the hell, gotta fill the pages with *some*thing, right?

Then, bam. Phenomenon. Within a couple of weeks, newsstands were sold out of *Action* and dealers everywhere were asking for more copies. And that was only the beginning. This guy was *popular*. Not as popular as future pop culture icons would be, not as popular as the Beatles and Presley

in their glory days, but certainly he had a movie-star-size fan following. By 1941, he was appearing in *Action*, *World's Finest*, his own title, *Superman*, and in a daily newspaper strip and starring in his own radio show and in a series of 17 brilliant animated cartoons produced by the Max Fleischer studios and on the backs of Kellogg's Pep boxes and—

Enough. If I'd been thinking of all that when Julie Schwartz called me into his office and asked me to take a shot at scripting *Superman*, I might have begged off. But at the time, it was just another assignment. I was a pro. I accepted the jobs offered me unless there was some personal reason not to. (For example, my opposition to the Vietnam war kept me from doing anything with military heroes for the duration.) I was, and am, a second-generation comic-book writer, which explains my attitude toward Superman. The first generation men—they were virtually all men—were refugees from other fields: illustration, advertising, gag cartoons, the adventure pulps. Although they *created* comic books, I have a sense that they weren't aware of doing anything special, just turning in their stories, collecting their checks, hoping they'd continue to be in demand. In the darkest crannies of their private conversations with mates and buddies, they might have confessed to a craftsman's pride in their work, and in moments of soul-baring *hubris*, they might have mumbled the word *art*, but at least publicly they were humble laborers—literary blue-collar guys. It was a self-deprecation their employers were apparently happy to encourage. Humble laborers don't make demands, don't cause trouble, don't threaten a *status quo* that was giving at least a few of the publishers a sultan's lifestyle. The writers and artists collected no royalties, received no incentives or fringe benefits. Only last year, after I'd been working in comics for

two decades, I learned that I was originally hired by DC in 1968 because a few of the regular scripters had asked—not demanded, *asked*—for health insurance. The reply was instant dismissal. (Today, employment and compensation practices are eminently fair; score one for progress.)

Enter me, then, not worrying about health insurance, benefits nor much of anything else beyond next week's grocery bill. I had been in New York for two years, doing the struggling-writer-with-wife-and-child number, which is charming in movies and sit-coms and an abyss in real life, scrounging occasional journalism assignments and writing comics to pay the rent on two rooms in a lower East Side tenement. Like my forebears, like some of the first-generation people I was soon to replace, I thought of comics as a marketplace, but with this difference: I *liked* them. I respected them. I probably learned to read from them. The doings of the costumed heroes in the funny books were far more interesting to the six-year-old me, a far greater incentive to puzzle out the words, than Dick, Jane, their dumb dog Spot and that miserable ball they were always chasing. I grew up with comics and related media—movie and radio serials and, later, the Superman television program—had enjoyed them, been absorbed and maybe educated by them; their images and the odd combination of picture-and-copy that is the essence of the form were thoroughly internalized by the time I first scraped a razor across my chin. If, as I believe, comics are actually a language with image and word acting as different components of the same unit of information—much as noun and verb are different components of a sentence—it

was a language I learned concurrently with English. I knew it without knowing I knew it.

So, although I shared with the veteran scripters the feeling that comics were mainly a source of income, I respected them as an arena where entertainment had flourished and—here's that word again—*art* was at least a possibility. I remember telling another writer that "you've got to respect comics as an art form but regard them as a job." The last part of that was me being realistic: at $10 or $12 a page, with no hope of future remuneration, a writer had to produce a lot, and producing a lot meant spending a given number of hours every day at a typewriter. None of this waiting-for-inspiration non-sense: If the muse wasn't present, you didn't wait—you just went ahead without her and dragged the words out of yourself with the force of sheer determination. It was nice—hell, it was wonderful—if you could be proud of two or three of the 40 or so scripts you delivered in a year, but if not, tough. What you tried for was a certain level of craft below which you did not sink, ever, a kind and amount of entertainment you could promise because you had *learned how to do it*; you were like a crusty old vaudevillian who got out there and did his tap dance no matter what. Favorite aunt died? Wife ran away with the juggler? Bad news from the dentist? *So*? Do the dance and do it eight times a day and keep your mouth shut. And hey, once in a while, when you're feeling real good or real bad, it is a living *mother* of a tap dance, it is what tap dances ought to be, what they *can* be. No way to predict when that will happen, but when it does, a lot of frustration goes away.

Allowing for a bit of hyperbole, that's how it was with us second-generation comics writers. That's *not* how it is with many of the third-generation folk—colleagues who, bless and preserve them, grew up reading *us*. These guys *care*. For them, comics are an art, the means they will use to reach out and touch their times, the vehicle of their self-expression. That puts them in an awkward position, and the people who employ them in an even more awkward one. If you're a capital-A artist, you nurture your creation until you're ready to send it out to face the harsh world. And it is *yours*, dammit, not to be altered because some Philistine of an editor, some fossil, wants it different. But comics are periodicals. If you're doing a regular title, you have to produce an issue every 25 days featuring characters that belong, not to you, but to a huge, impersonal corporation the minions of which can change your work at will and whim. It is a tormenting conflict for all concerned.

That conflict was not mine when I walked out of Julie's office in 1971. Nor was I concerned that I'd be writing the biggie, the character who had started it all. "Superman literally created this industry," Carmine Infantino had said, truthfully, when he was president of DC comics. "He's the key, the granddaddy of them all." Okay, but granddaddy had been looking a bit wan of late, and Julie was asking me to provide a remedy. That was logical enough. I was, at the time, DC's resident superhero doctor—a still-youthful writer who, always with the guidance of Julie, could transfuse new ideas into old heroes; we had already successfully modernized *Green Lantern* and *Batman*. It sounds like a better trick than it was: Most of the superdoers hadn't been allowed to change much. Conventional wisdom held that once a hero was found acceptable to the readership, said hero would *always* be thus acceptable, and any mucking around with the tried, true (and eventually tired) formulae was equivalent to spitting on the Pope. (This same wisdom may explain why TV shows seldom celebrate a fifth birthday.)

Of course, a few blocks uptown, Stan Lee was demonstrating that the audience had outgrown the formulae. Under Stan's direction since 1961, Marvel Comics had for years been the junk reading of choice on a lot of college campuses and now, in 1971, was clearly claiming the younger comics fans, the group which had always been DC's constituency. Stan's comics were, by DC's lights, heresy—full of self-satire, loose plotting and thoroughly humanized heroes: costumed men and women who whined, complained, argued, self-doubted, self-pitied, laughed, cried, erred—as varied and amusing a bunch as the gods of Olympus. By contrast, DC's superheroes were defined by their powers: The Flash was fast, Hawkman had wings, Green Lantern had a magic ring. Whatever personality they possessed was that of All-Purpose Good Guy, not unlike the priests in Warner Bros. prison movies: a regular fella with the courage of Audie Murphy, the prowess of Ted Williams and the wholesomeness of St. Prisca. Plus the wings or ring or whatever. Inoffensive. Often dull. Sometimes *deadly* dull. If you met a Marvel hero at a party, you'd probably have a pretty lively conversation with him; if you met his DC opposite number, you'd probably remember a dentist appointment after five minutes. Superman was, alas, no exception. "The first thing I said when Carmine asked me to take over Superman was, 'I gotta change him,' " Julie told me recently. Julie acknowledged what Stan Lee was doing right—many of his colleagues preferred to believe that Lee was a whippersnapper upstart who wouldn't last—but instead of imitating Marvel, he preferred to build on DC's traditional strengths.

Briefly and oversimply, DC was classical, Marvel was romantic. DC was well-made plots, clear artwork, a comforting predictability: a Mozart concerto. Marvel was improvised story lines, high energy, surprise: a Charlie Parker saxophone solo. Now, Julie

felt there was nothing *wrong* with the classical approach; on the contrary, much was right. But it needed deepening, broadening, modernizing: add a little Stravinsky to the repertoire and borrow some rhythms from Scott Joplin, maybe. In me, he found a writer: I fancied myself a romantic—actually, an existentialist—but under the long hair, tie-dyed T-shirts and ratty jeans, there was a Jesuit-educated Midwesterner who'd venerate Charlie Parker in public, listen to bebop two days of three...*but*—that third day was Mozart's.

So we turned our attention to Superman. The artwork was no problem. Superman's penciller was Curt Swan, and Curt was the best, a quiet man not much noticed and consequently underrated because he never caused a fuss; he simply delivered anything an editor asked for, met any challenge and did it with the reliability of the tides. I'd never met Curt—we often didn't meet our artists, and sometimes didn't even know who, exactly, would bubble up from the talent pool to add pictures to our words. But, given his reputation, I would have been astonished if Curt's contribution had been anything less than excellent. No, our problems lay in old Supe himself—specifically, in what he had become. Earlier, I mentioned that conventional wisdom mandated no change in lead characters. This does not mean that they *didn't* change, merely that nobody changed them *intentionally*.

They drifted. Evolved. Superman began with rather modest powers and abilities: He could leap over a skyscraper, about an eighth of a mile; he couldn't be hurt by anything less nasty than an exploding shell; he could outrun a locomotive—100 miles

an hour wouldn't seriously tax him; and he was strong enough to bend steel in his bare hands. A formidable fellow, this Superman, but nothing to what he was to become. Within a couple of years of his debut, he was no longer leaping, he was flying. There is disagreement concerning why and where he first took to the air. Some pop historians say he began flying in the Fleischer cartoons; certainly, he *did* fly in them. But Joe Shuster thinks the flying originated with the comic-book version: "He was mostly leaping tall buildings in the beginning," Joe told an interviewer. "There were cases where he would leap off a tall building or swoop down, and at that point he would look like he was flying, I suppose. It was just natural to draw him like that." In other words, he went from *looking* like he was flying to actually *doing* it, with nobody really much noticing. Within a few years, his other powers had also increased, and he acquired new ones from a variety of sources.

His immense popularity was partially to blame. The demand for new Superman material soon exceeded what the Siegel-Shuster team could produce. Shuster hired assistants to help with the art, to put in backgrounds, draw minor characters, ultimately do everything except the layouts and Superman's face. But Siegel couldn't do something similar; a writer either writes a story or he doesn't, and there were too many of them needed for one man to write. When the radio program began, Siegel was consulted on the initial episodes, but after that the radio scripters labored without him. Apparently, he didn't even speak to the writers of the Fleischer cartoons (though Shuster spent a few days in the Fleischer studios sketching model sheets). The result was that Siegel lost control of his creation and Superman began to be shaped by a small army of people, each with slightly different outlooks, emphases, goals. They didn't work in a vacuum, of course; they were probably aware of what their fellow Supermaners were doing and tried to accommodate it—or steal from it. For example, the radio writers introduced Jimmy Olsen, the perennially eager, perennially boyish and not overly bright cub reporter who has been a prominent part of the mythos ever since. (Giving the hero a youthful sidekick, the producers of radio adventure shows discovered, gave the kids in the listening audience somebody in the cast to identify with and thus vicariously participate in the adventure in an even more satisfying fashion.) More importantly, they gave Superman his greatest menace, kryptonite, the glowing, green rock fragments from his home world that can render him helpless and, if he's exposed to them long enough, kill him.

Kryptonite came to be extremely useful because it gave dozens of writers in comics, radio, television and film something that could get their hero in trouble. Exploding shell? The Superman of the Sixties and beyond could sauna in the heart of a sun. Faster than a speeding bullet? Superman regularly beat The Flash, a fellow superhero, and the Flash could travel seven times the speed of light. (Einsteinian physics did not exist in the DC universe.) More powerful than a locomotive? Superman could now wrestle whole planets out of their orbits. Invulnerability, strength and speed that would put a platoon of gods to shame— and these were only the more noticeable of Superman's powers. In April of 1939, he acquired X-ray vision with which he could look at the far end of the cosmos and, in 1959, he "projected [it] across the time barrier" to locate an ape trapped in prehistory; microscopic vision; "supersensory vision," which enabled him to see in total darkness; and "heat vision," which functioned like an extremely powerful laser beam that he used on one occasion to melt a

meteor hundreds of thousands of miles away. Like his vision, Superman's hearing increased in keenness with every passing year. In 1939, he was described as having "sensitive ears" capable of hearing outside the normal human range; by 1960, he was detecting sounds emanating from "a spaceship millions of miles from earth." Enough? Not quite. Even his *breath* became incredible. In 1939, he could "hold his breath for hours underwater"; in 1941, he blew out a raging fire; in 1947, he sucked back an escaping rocket; and in 1959, he extinguished a star with a single mighty puff.

If you read random Superman stories in chronological order, you get a sense of guys around a campfire trying to top each other with tall tales; the yarns build from the extravagant to the preposterous to the silly. There undoubtedly *was* an element of the playful tall-tale tradition in the creation of the Superman saga—comic-book writers *do* enjoy their work sometimes—and an element of desperation, too; after all, at one point, Superman was appearing in no fewer than seven monthly publications in addition to, at various times, television, radio, movies, novels and on cereal boxes. That is a lot of Superman. Editors and writers had to continually devise new stunts, new powers and new uses for the powers Superman already had, competing with what they had done last month, last year, with what their colleagues were doing. It was a maniacally accelerated version of the folk process; like fairy tales and myths, the Superman stories were begun by one creator but embellished and altered by many. Because of the need to *produce*, to fill those pages, meet those deadlines, get the stuff out there, what would have taken generations in the preindustrial era took only a few years. And as with folk tales, and particularly myths, the personality of the hero, as perceived by the public, was a residue left in the collective

51

consciousness after audiences and readers were exposed to several different versions of what was presumed to be the same character.

Like his powers, Superman's personality altered—not as much, perhaps, and certainly not as quickly, but he was unquestionably several different Kryptonians, depending on his age and where he was appearing. At first, Siegel made him brash, a wise-cracking tough guy with a rugged zeal for reform like the macho, blue-collar heroes Spencer Tracy, Pat O'Brien and Clark Gable who were playing on the local screens. (In an early Siegel and Shuster story, for example, Superman gave comeuppance to a chubby capitalist who was exploiting miners.) This is not surprising. ''Joe and I haunted movies, often cashing in milk bottles to finance getting past theater box offices,'' Siegel has said. ''Seated side-by-side in uncomfortable theater seats, we ate popcorn and absorbed 'B movies' galore along with 'A production' films. I was especially impressed by the Warner Bros. movies with their social injustice messages.'' However, proletarian eclat was wholly missing from the Superman novel by George Lowther, published in 1942, as well as from the Superman of radio and animation and by the end of the '40s, it was missing from the comics, too. As Superman had grown more powerful physically, he had become less flamboyant personally, *safer* somehow—a Scoutmaster in cape and boots.

If Superman were a real person, the explanation would be that he had matured. Since, he isn't, speculation is necessary. It may be that Mort Weisinger didn't share Jerry Siegel's liking for those Warner's

flicks. Weisinger, a former pulp editor hired by DC in 1941, had assumed control of the Superman books upon his return from the war and shaped the Superman legend until his retirement in 1970. He was an extremely strong editor with a commanding—some said overbearing—presence; it's not likely that Siegel, or any other writer, ever won a policy argument with him. Soon after the Weisinger regime began, the emphasis in the Superman comics shifted from derring-do to whimsy, humor, blatant fantasy.

As Superman became more and more godlike, he had less and less to do with the problems of ordinary people—not surprisingly, since readers couldn't expect the guy who blew out a star to worry much about greedy mine owners. This newer, lighter, almost droll Superman reflected the mood of the country. More than any other popular art form, commercial comics have mirrored the mood of the audience, possibly because they're produced so quickly that there isn't time for the shaping of personal visions; writers and artists must use what's in the air. Arguably, the public embraced Superman in 1938 because he was an antidote to the gloom of the Depression; that same public wanted its postwar entertainment to be escapist, frothy, devoid of reminders of either the poverty of the '30s or the bloodletting in Europe and Asia. Or so Mort Weisinger must have thought. His writers introduced magic—*real* magic, without the scientific rationale that had inspired Siegel's vision of his creation's powers—and funny aliens and wrote a lot of stories in which Superman's greatest problem was convincing his skeptical girlfriend Lois Lane that he was not Clark Kent. Metropolis became a rather homey place, more like Mark Twain's Hannibal than any genuine big city. Weisinger's people even partially vitiated the Krypton tragedy when they showed readers that

Superman was *not* the only survivor of the doomed planet. It seems that a cousin, Supergirl, also escaped, as did several criminals who had been transported into the "Phantom Zone" before Krypton exploded, and a dog, Krypto, who became Superman's pet, and a whole city, Kandor, which had been miniaturized and put into a bottle. All in all, there was a sizable colony of Kryptonians living on and around Earth.

Details of Superman's infancy and childhood were also revised and expanded. The reason, again, was almost certainly the need to fill pages. Unintentionally parodying scholarship, writers kept "discovering" new data about Superman's early years. In 1945, in *More Fun Comics*, Weisinger and crew debuted *Superboy—The Adventures of Superman as a Boy*. The series, which soon got its own title, related young Clark's exploits in Smallville, before he moved to Metropolis to begin his newspaper career on the *Daily Planet*. His foster parents, Jonathan and Martha Kent, figured prominently in these cheery, rather bucolic adventures, as did a set of supporting characters who rivaled the gang at the *Planet*. These included Lana Lang, Clark's first love, and Pete Ross, his best friend and the only person privy to his secret identity. And if Superman's past could be mined for material, Mort Weisinger must have asked himself, why not his future? In 1958, Superboy journeyed to the Thirtieth Century and joined The Legion of Superheroes, an organization of no fewer than 28 youthful law enforcers whose members range from Superboy clones like Ultra Boy to such unlikely superdoers as Matter Eater Lad.

Weisinger's contribution to the Superman saga was an enormously benign sense of optimism. On the one hand, the Superboy stories paid homage to the values of rural America and the innocence associated with them and, on the other, assured readers that the world would survive to the Thirtieth Century intact and improved, but still recognizable. In our post-atomic age, it is a highly comforting assurance. Super*man* was similarly comforting. After all, he is the most powerful being in the universe—remember that blown-out star—and he's on *our* side. His virtues are our virtues. He believes in the same things we do. As the opening of the television program proclaimed, he fights for "Truth, Justice and the American Way." And he always wins.

There was, however, a price to be paid for all this sanguineness: drama. As the Kryptonian's superness increased, it became increasingly difficult to get him into any kind of trouble, to contrive problems he couldn't logically solve in a second or two, to fabricate worthy foes. Part of Weisinger's answer was to trivialize him in stories that contrasted his might with some minor difficulty or pitted him against a ludicrous enemy. The other part was to rely increasingly on a stable of bad guys who *could* give Superman pause, chiefly Lex Luthor, Brainiac and the mob from the Phantom Zone.

That's the Superman Julie Schwartz and I inherited: a chummy, white-bready sort of fellow toting a complicated biography, a large extended family and godlike powers whose activities had become nearly as predictable as Dagwood Bumstead's. I admit that's possibly an uncharitable description—it's certainly an oversimplified, overly glib one—but I also think it accurately reflects the feelings I had as Julie and I sat down to plot our first Superman story. No need to fabricate a scene here because our plotting sessions were always the same: comfortable, enjoyable rituals. I'd arrive at Julie's office sometime in mid-afternoon, drop the completed script of my previous assignment on his desk and plop onto a chair. He'd grumble something crusty and avuncular, often having to do with my deficiencies as

a speller or my custom of never retiring a typewriter ribbon while it was still in one piece. Then he'd lean back and say, "Well, what've you got?" What I had could be anything from a fully plotted story that needed only to be put on paper to a yawning void. Usually, it was something between those extremes. In any case, we'd spend the next 15 to 90 minutes discussing my ideas. Julie functioned as a benevolent gadfly: He'd criticize my logic, demand clarification, offer suggestions and, rarely, insist on the incorporation of a point he considered essential. If my cupboard was utterly bare, if I lacked even a starting point, he'd supply something. We might disagree, we might argue in a restrained, friendly way, but the mutual respect we'd developed always enabled us to reach a satisfactory compromise. He never insisted I write something I felt was unequivocally wrong, and I never allowed my ego to challenge his experience and authority. I'd leave his office with a clear notion of what I was going to write and, after a day or two of letting it ferment in the imagination, I'd begin the three-to-four day process of actually realizing a script. I used (and still mostly use) a modified film-script format. Here's a sample:

1 - EXT. DC OFFICES. DAY. O'NEIL LEAVES BUILDING. HE'S ENTHUSIASTIC.
O'NEIL: (thought) Gee whillikers, I can hardly wait till I get home and start slapping down some SUPERMAN PROSE!

2 - INT. O'NEIL'S STUDY. HE IS CLUTCHING HIS HEAD, STARING DESPAIRINGLY AT A BLANK SHEET OF PAPER IN A PORTABLE TYPEWRITER.

CAPTION: Later —

O'NEIL: (thought) Oh my gosh....

How enthusiastic was I, really? Don't know. Can't say. Not very, probably. Across town, at Marvel, the writers and artists were evolving a caste system based on the titles they were working on: the guys doing Spider-Man and the Fantastic Four were that free-lance community's satraps, while those contributing less popular titles were humble citizens. (Money didn't enter into it: The amount a free-lancer earned was almost entirely determined by how productive he was.) But I wasn't aware of that happening at DC. So the fact that I was writing *Superman*, the original superhero, the most popular of them all, wasn't important. Getting the job done was, and the job, Julie and I agreed, had to begin with a return to our hero's roots. A depowerization. Look, we said, faster than a speeding bullet, more powerful than a locomotive and able to leap tall buildings with a single bound should damn well be *enough* for any middle-aged superdoer.

We weren't *cruel* revampers: We'd let him keep the X-ray and telescopic vision and much of the invulnerability — he needn't sweat the exploding shells that would have done him in back in the '30s — and we were willing to concede the flying, but the godlike stuff had to go. Stars were theretofore to be considered safe from Superman's breath. And, while we were at it, we'd give his personality a good decloying, deep-six the white bread. Oh, one more thing we wanted to lose: kryptonite, the all-purpose menace, the *deus ex-machina* in reverse used and used and used until it had become a green-glowing bore. We were reserving judgment on Supergirl, Kandor, Krypto, the Phantom Zone villains and the rest of the continuity detritus. Maybe we'd use it, maybe not.

From this revisionism, we hoped to gain opportunities for conflict and drama and to make Superman attractive to the new comics readers, an audience no longer satisfied with the old shorthand character-izations. These sophisticates sometimes made me feel like a junior clerk suddenly summoned to the executive suite who realizes he's wearing white socks: Comics had always been comfortable—a real home for writers anyd artists with inferiority com-plexes—because by universal acclamation they were *trash*, and nobody has any expec-tations of the trash man. But now the trash man was being asked to display company manners. While we had been busy meeting our deadlines, an artistic Gresham's law had been operating unnoticed; comics were no longer the lowest-common-denominator en-tertainment; that dubious honor had de-volved to television. Comics were *written* and had to be *read*, and in a post-McLuhan age, readers, woe was us, wanted a hint of depth, of complexity. From *Superman*? Yes, we suspected, from Superman. Well, okay, can do. No big problem, actually. The possi-bility for interesting characterization already existed—was, in fact, in the very fabric of his conception. If Superman existed, he would be doubly alienated, being both extraterres-trial and much, much stronger than anyone else, and this alienation would *have* to tor-ment him. By simply using what we already had, we could bring psychological realism to the Superman mythos.

First, though, the depowerization. In our first story, titled "Superman Breaks Loose" and published late in 1970, a planet-wide chain reaction renders all the kryptonite on Earth inert, no more harmful to Superman than ordinary lead. Our hero learns this and, naturally, welcomes it. What he doesn't know is that the same reaction created a duplicate Superman from the sand of the desert in which the event took place. Over the next several issues, this gritty doppel-ganger gradually drained Superman's pow-ers until they were at what was, for us, a comfortable level.

A few days ago, just before beginning this reminiscence, I happened on a summary of the ancient Mesopotamian epic of *Gilga-mesh* and realized, bemused, that this is my Superman story. Yet, to the best of my recollection, I'd never read *Gilgamesh* be-fore, had never studied mythology in either high school or college. Not that I would have hesitated to borrow from a Mesopotamian poet: The rule is, if you steal from your con-temporaries it's plagiarism, but if you steal from antiquity it's research, and research, far from being a sin, always adds a note of class to a comic book. So I *would* have, but I didn't. If I had to guess at an explanation, I'd cite Jung's theory of archetypes, the no-tion that some stories and myths are recre-ated every generation by the very mecha-nism of the human consciousness. (Shirley MacLaine would probably say that I'd lived an earlier, Mesopotamian, life, I have my doubts.) In *Gilgamesh*, the hero and his double become united. In Superman, the doppelganger leaves the Earth and....

The rest of the saga belongs to Whittier's sad words of tongue or pen. You remember: "The saddest are these: It might have been." After writing 13 issues, I begged off the assignment, an act damaging to both my sense of professionalism and, potentially, to my bank account. Now, 16 years later, I couldn't say why I abandoned Superman, and I probably couldn't have done any better then. I only knew that I was spending up to

three weeks on Superman scripts and not enjoying the work. By contrast, Batman scripts took three days and were often fun. The difficulty I was experiencing was, obviously, a symptom. I don't think there was any one disease, though; there were probably several. It's true that I was playing the dreary role of the whiskey-swilling Irishman, that my marriage was coming apart like wet tissue paper, that a brief fling as a proto-celebrity had created terrible self-doubt.... All that is significant, perhaps, but not conclusive. None of it explains why Batman wasn't as difficult to tug from a typewriter as Superman. Instead, let me offer, tentatively and shyly, an hypothesis: A writer must find a way to make a character symbolically real for himself. You've got to *connect* somehow, and the route to the connection is through your own deepest dreams and fantasies.

Now, my fantasies are quite modest, generally concerned with human perfectability. I might imagine myself training and training until some glorious autumn morning I run the New York Marathon in 1:59:59 and receive a gold medal and admiring glances from three or four not-really-unattractive women. It won't happen but it *could*, to somebody, some day; it is, remotely, possible. I have never fantasized about having inhuman power conferred on me by an outside agency, nor shared what psychologists say is a common wish-fantasy, that of having been born to high station and misrouted in infancy; not for a second have I believed I was ever a baby prince spirited away by a wicked serving girl. Tremendous, unearned power and exalted lineage are a lot of what Superman is about, and those are

not my dreams. Writing Superman stories, I was operating on craft, professionalism and technique, and in the end they weren't enough. Not for Superman. I couldn't find a connection with even a vastly scaled-down version of this demigod; I couldn't locate his symbolic reality.

Others, before and after me, could. A few issues after my last, the cover of *Superman* showed old Supe muscling around a planet. The message was clear: The wimped-out Superman had been a temporary aberration and the Weisinger-spawned cosmos-hopper—the Superman I'm sure many readers considered the genuine article—was back. The reason, Julie says, is that our changes didn't help sales.

But a few of our innovations did survive. For example, Julie felt that the television generation might not be able to relate to a newspaper reporter and had me write a slight alteration in Clark Kent's professional status; he became a TV newsman in addition to continuing as the *Daily Planet*'s ace reporter. We developed a few gimmicks to go with the new job, such as a van that enabled Clark to be on-camera while Superman was simultaneously chasing villains, and we updated his off-the-rack blue suit and nerdy hornrims and haircut to a conservatively elegant look befitting a media star. (*Gentlemen's Quarterly*, the fashion magazine, did a piece on Clark's new wardrobe which I helped write— a heady experience for a man who didn't own a necktie at the time.) I'm told most of these additions were integrated into the burgeoning mythos and became as familiar to Superman readers as the *Planet*'s city room. I can't testify to that because I stopped reading Superman. No sour grapes here, no

56

malice. It's just that when someone else does a series I've written, the characters, particularly the hero, seem hopelessly, hideously, unequivocally *wrong*. I'm not alone in this: Other writers, friends of mine, have confessed that when I've taken over a series *they'd* done I have — no offense — totally botched it, and I've had to reply that, on the contrary, I was serving their vision slavishly, thank you very much. In matters of aesthetics, objectivity is in the eye of the beholder.

For me, the adventures of Superman ended on December 21, 1971. For Julie Schwartz, they continued until the summer of 1986, when DC's publisher and president, Jenette Kahn, decided a cosmic housecleaning was necessary. The mythos had become unwieldy. Superman's success, almost a half-century earlier, had spawned hundreds of imitations by both DC and its competitors. (At one point, in the '40s, there were more than 30 comic-book publishers in New York City, most of them doing superheroes.) Almost from the beginning, editors learned that having the superdoers meet and interact was a good way to stir reader interest and boost sales. "Crossovers" became common. As a result, a fabricated "universe" — the universe inhabited by superheroes — came into existence. Because so many editors, writers and artists were constantly adding to that funhouse mirror image of the real world, it was not consistent. Until the late '60s, consistency in comic books was seen as no particular virtue. Writers were making it up as they went along for what they assumed was a highly transient audience. Most of the people in the field considered their work eminently disposable, something to be enjoyed for a short while and then used to paper the birdcage. But, gradually, that changed: Readers were writing in complaining that elements in current stories contradicted what had been established earlier and, sometimes, offering tongue-in-cheek "explanations" of the glitches. Consistency, editors realized, was important to the new breed of readers and continuity could be used as a story device. The nature of the audience had changed: Comics didn't have as *many* readers as they'd had 15 years earlier, but those fewer readers were *involved*; comics were important to them. They insisted the creators pay attention to chronology and detail. But there was *too* much chronology and detail.

Julie and writer Gardner Fox devised a neat strategem: They posited multiple Earths, each with its own set of superheroes. This not only generated story possibilities, it provided alibis. The Flash did something his fans knew was impossible for him? Hey, no problem — that was the Flash of Earth *Two*. By 1986, there were at least seven separate universes in the DC cosmos and the concept had become self-defeating; only one or two people on the DC staff knew which hero belonged on what Earth, and why, and when, and story lines were getting mired in detail that was at best dramatically unimportant, at worst tedious. Yet it was detail that could not be ignored, not without risk of alienating the loyalest readers. Superman was the biggest problem: Of the dozens of heroes DC had copyrighted, he had the longest history, had appeared the most places, had the largest supporting cast. In the summer of 1986, the editorial staff devised a plot that would destroy all but one of the multiple Earths, killing dozens of characters in the process, leaving only a single version of each. As part of the massive revamping, DC decided to recreate Superman. Writers John Byrne and Marv Wolfman updated his origin so that the spacecraft bearing him landed near Smallville only 30 years ago. His powers were substantially decreased — not as drastically as I'd decreased them, but enough to make him merely awesome. Clark Kent was no longer

a fumbling loser; he became a Pulitzer Prize winner who moonlighted as a successful novelist (with a closetful of designer clothing). His friends and foes were given attitudes and personalities that marked them unmistakably as creatures of the '80s. Fifty years' worth of adventures were invalidated, and that was regrettable, particularly to oldsters whose childhoods were colored by those adventures—we feel somehow betrayed—but the invalidation enables Superman's current biographers simply to tell their tales, to be storytellers instead of pseudo-historians. To be what Jerry Siegel and Joe Shuster were.

So the rebirth was desirable, but I have a feeling it wasn't really necessary. Superman is, finally, an idea, an ideal, a hope and a dream, the happy fantasy of millions, and anybody compounded of those things can't be killed by exploding shells, nuclear bombs nor even by that greatest of foes, the passing of time.

THE MAN WHO CHANGED THE COMICS

by THE EDITORS

They are now classic moments in the iconography of Growing Up in America: the youngster discovered reading a comic book behind a school book; the child finishing a comic book in bed after lights out with the aid of a flashlight; the surly parent telling the pimply-faced teenager who's brought home a bad report card, "Maybe it's time you graduated from comic books to more mature reading matter." The fact is, the comics were not always regarded as "kid's stuff."

But, largely as the result of the phenomenal success of *Superman* comics in the late

'30s and early '40s—and that of the horde of imitators he inspired—the young comic-book industry focused quickly on the youth market and was soon cranking out industrial-strength "kid's stuff" with a zeal and efficiency that would have impressed Henry Ford. It would be decades before it even occurred to anybody again that a comic book could be for anybody but kids.

For, in addition to almost single-handedly launching the whole comic-book business and establishing, virtually overnight, the validity of the whole idea of comic books as mini-anthologies of original stories and not merely reprints from newspaper strips, Superman also changed the course, as it were, of a mighty pop cultural river.

The 1920s and '30s had seen the flourishing, alongside the comic strips clearly aimed at youngsters, of an impressive number of illustrated story strips that just as clearly were aiming—in their sophistication of character, theme or graphics—at adult readers. Indeed, it was not considered beneath anyone's maturity to follow and enjoy such wry (occasionally even poignant) features as *Moon Mullins* or *Bringing Up Father*, Frank King's *Gasoline Alley* or Gene Ahern's *Our Boarding House* (which gave the world Major Hoople). Ring Lardner's classic story "You Know Me Al," praised by literary critics for its stunning grasp of authentic American speech and its trenchant depiction of the small-town character, was done as a comic strip. And the gifted J.R. Williams, a machinist from Alliance, Ohio, created the popular *Out Our Way* and *Bull of the Woods* (whose title character was the tough foreman of a machine shop).

The appearance of the comic book, ex-plains contemporary comic-book writer Harvey Pekar, might have offered exciting new possibilities to the creators of such "adult" strips—with its opportunity for extended stories contained in a single book instead of having either to be strung out over many issues of a newspaper or developed and quickly resolved in a handful of panels. But it wasn't long, says Pekar, before no self-respecting adult would be caught dead with a comic book.

Superman himself would go on—in other media—to win the affection of the entire family and eventually even to enjoy a certain cachet among adults of another generation. But, much as the coming of the Beatles in effect destroyed the careers of many a pop singer of the early '60s by creating an insatiable market for an entirely new kind of music, Superman had changed what might have been the course of the American comic book. With a few notable exceptions, comic books for adults would not surface until the so-called "underground comics" of the Vietnam era.

Once again, Cleveland was to step to the fore with the publication in 1976 of Harvey Pekar's *American Splendor*, an annual comic book featuring slice-of-life stories in which Harvey himself and the city of Cleveland play the leading roles. Written exclusively by Pekar and drawn by a variety of Cleveland artists including Gary Dumm, and frequently featuring work by underground comix legend R. (*Zap, Mr. Natural*) Crumb (who began his career as an illustrator with the Cleveland-based American Greetings Corporation), *American Splendor* offers its readers a steady dose of social realism and deadpan irony modelled on the literary humor of

George Ade and Lardner, which Pekar uses to explore the working class and ethnic mores of his Cleveland roots. The result, particularly when paired with Crumb's distinctive graphics, is comic-book art of a high order: deliberately uncinematic, gritty, philosophical, opinionated and funny, with the kind of tone one might expect from oral history. In short, it is difficult to imagine a comic book further from the commercial mainstream standards of *Superman*.

Though this latterday Cleveland original has found recognition in the form of two hardcover collections of his work published in 1986 and '87 by Doubleday and recent guest appearances on *Late Night With David Letterman*, Pekar's dour comic-book-story alter ego, who is a kind of Clark Kent without a secret identity to redeem his dismal workaday existence, is forever complaining about the lack of fame and fortune accorded serious comic books.

A forthcoming comic-book story done by Pekar and Dumm with a cameo contribution by Crumb for a commemorative comic book that will be sold to raise money for a Siegel and Shuster memorial in their own home town features a tongue-in-cheek diatribe against the Man of Steel for "ruining" the business for "serious" artists. A panel from that story is previewed here.

Privately, Pekar admits he too grew up on the daring adventures of Superman and his gaily costumed colleagues ("the weirder their powers, the more I liked 'em; there was one guy who was even supposed to be *dead*.") And as for Superman's ruining the industry: "I guess you can't blame Siegel and Shuster for that; they were just a couple of guys like me, trying to do something they believed in. As a matter of fact, I probably ought to be grateful they made such an impact on the business. It left this whole area wide open for me to move into."

FROM PANEL TO PANAVISION

by PHILIP SKERRY
with CHRIS LAMBERT

Like many of my generation—the post-World War II baby boomers—I first encountered Superman in the "funny books," as we called them in my home town of Chelsea, Massachusetts. I remember heading down to Margolis' drug store every week to get the latest *Superman* funny book and gazing at the brightly colored pages with men in strange green suits sporting orange hair. And of course, I eagerly anticipated the arrival of Superman with his cobalt blue, scarlet red and canary yellow costume. His heavily muscled figure usually dominated the frame, plunging diagonally down in flight, lifting skyscrapers off their foundations, punching villains right out of the panel. After scanning the pictures, I would read the dialogue in the funny balloons that seemed to grow out of each character's head. Given this visual feast of color, action and dynamic movement, was it any wonder that my dull black-and-white school books lay unopened on the kitchen table?

What I didn't realize at the time, as I gobbled up funny book after funny book, was that "reading" those brightly colored panels was like watching a film frame by frame. Each panel was a camera shot — long, medium, close-up; each point of view was a camera angle — high, low, eye-level, bird's eye; each series of panels taking place in one location or at one time period was a cinematic shot or sequence. In my ignorant bliss of adolescent fantasy, I was not aware that comic books were educating a generation of youngsters — including me — in the visual language of film and later television.

In a sense, the spread of the legend of Superman paralleled the growth of consciousness of a new group of visually literate individuals — perhaps the first real film generation — who came to know the Man of Steel (or the Man of Tomorrow, as he was first called) through his various visual incarnations — in the ubiquitous comic books, in animated cartoons, in Saturday serials, in B-films, in TV and finally again in films, only this time big-budget (BIG-BUDGET!) epics from the "new" Hollywood. Each one of these contributed in some way to the growth of Superman's identity and helped to make the Superman legend a mainstay of American popular culture.

The legend of Superman is encoded into the consciousness of this film generation in heroic-sounding phrases, repeated over and over in almost every visualization, in a kind of incantation, a Homeric recitation:

...it's Superman, strange visitor from another planet, who came to Earth with powers far beyond those of mortal men. Superman, who can change the course of mighty rivers, bend steel in his bare hands, and who, disguised as Clark Kent, mild-mannered reporter for a great metropolitan newspaper, fights a never-ending battle for Truth, Justice and the American Way.

My friends and I knew these lines by heart, just as we knew the Pledge of Allegiance, America, Miss Robbins' verb table and the Lord's Prayer.

Hidden away in these phrases are three identities: Superman, or the Man of Steel; Kal-El, or the strange visitor from another planet; and Clark Kent, the mild-mannered reporter. As a youngster, I naturally responded to the Man of Steel; with a long knotted towel around my neck and in my underwear, I would leap from chair to couch in imitation of the exploits of Superman. The other identities of Superman really didn't interest me at the time, but now I realize that one reason for the persistence of the legend in comics, television and film is the multifaceted nature of the character.

It was inevitable that Superman would make his way from the comics to the movies because the very essence of the character — strength and flight — could best be captured in the art of movement — in cinema — and because comics are themselves a kind of primitive cinema. The first "moving pictures" were actually animated strips placed in persistence-of-vision mechanisms like the phenakistiscope or the zootrope. Superman, though, started not as an actual image but rather as an idea in the science fiction-obsessed mind of young Clevelander, Jerry Siegel. It was Siegel's friend, Joe Shuster, who gave visual life to Siegel's conception of a superhuman creature with a secret identity. When Superman finally appeared

in Harry Donenfeld's *Action Comics # 1*, a most important chapter in popular culture was about to be written. For the next 50 years, Superman and his doppelgangers would appear in each of the key media of popular culture—comics, radio, cartoons, television and film. In the process, these various forms would cross-pollinate each other, creating a richness and diversity of stories and characters that continue today.

When I first encountered Superman in the late '40s and early '50s, much of the legend had already been established. The "faster than a speeding bullet" prologue had been created for the radio show, which the Mutual Network began broadcasting in a 15-minute format in 1940, featuring the voices of Bud Collyer and Joan Alexander and produced by Robert and Jessica Maxwell. The radio show also introduced kryptonite, Superman's Achilles heel. Meanwhile, the comics had given Superman an earthly past, with foster parents—the Kents—and a boyhood in Smallville; and a series of supervillains—the Toyman, the Prankster and, of course, Superman's archenemy, Lex Luthor.

Superman flew out of the pages of comic books and into the frames of films in 1941 in a series of animated cartoons produced by Fleischer Studios and Famous Studios. Brothers Max and Dave Fleischer began their animation career in 1920 with their "Out of the Inkwell" series starring Koko the clown. Produced by Max and directed by Dave, this series introduced the technique of Rotoscoping, creating an animated character out of a human character in motion by tracing the live-action character in ink, frame by frame. In the '30s the Fleischer Studios were the main rivals of the Disney Studios in anima-

tion, particularly with the release in 1939 of the animated feature film *Gulliver's Travels*. The brothers parted company in 1941, but Dave continued with the studio and produced *The Adventures of Superman* using the Rotoscoping technique.

These Fleischer cartoons were influenced both by the comic books and the Mutual Network radio show. In fact, Fleischer hired the actors from the radio show—Bud Collyer and Joan Alexander—to provide the voices for his cartoon versions of Superman, Clark and Lois. Collyer, for the radio show, had developed two voices for the Man of Steel. For the somewhat wimpy Clark, Collyer used a Caspar Milquetoast tenor, but for the brawny Superman he dropped a few octaves into the baritone range. This same distinction was retained in the Fleischer cartoons. The comic books, too, contributed to the Fleischer series, particularly in the artwork and story structure. Each cartoon was ten minutes long, much like the eight-page "get-to-the-point" stories that were being produced, four per book, during the late '30s and early '40s. The animated figure of Superman in Fleischer's cartoons was based on model sheets provided by Joe Shuster.

Turnabout is fair play in the fertile field of popular culture, for the Fleischer series actually influenced Superman comics. In *Superman # 19*, published at the time of the Fleischer series, a humorous tale involves Clark's frantic efforts to keep Lois from seeing segments from one of the Fleischer cartoons because she would then know his real identity. One panel shows the Paramount logo (the studio that distributed the cartoons) and the 1942 copyright date. During the cartoon, Clark feigns a choking incident in the theater and later kicks Lois' purse. Both of these distractions prevent her from seeing Clark switch identities to Superman. Poor dumb Lois never figures out what is going on, but she does stand up and cheer when Superman saves her screen counterpart from a certain death under the foot of a gigantic robot.

Fleischer's version of the hero plays an important role in the history of animation, for it represents the first prolonged departure from Hollywood's preoccupation with animal characters in cartoons. Disney had adopted Rotoscoping in his *Snow White* of 1937, but since the Fleischers developed the technique and used it for *The Adventures of Superman* series, the credit for integrating the human body with cartoon adventures really belongs to them. An interesting footnote to the Fleischer influence involves the *Mighty Mouse* cartoon series. Paul Terry's character was actually an attempt to synthesize two of the most important figures in American popular cartoon mythology: Superman and Mickey Mouse.

Back in Chelsea, when I took a break from reading comics, I trekked to the Strand, a theater in the rundown neighborhood where I lived. The Strand featured the best (or worst, if you will) of Hollywood's B-film assembly lines, including movies from Monogram and Republic and from the more prestigious minor studios like Columbia and RKO. It was at the Strand that I saw reruns of Fleischer's *Superman* cartoons during the all-day Saturday cartoon and serial shows that cost a whopping 15 cents for admission. I remember how thrilling it was to sit in the almost total darkness of the Strand, to eat Jujubees and Necco Wafers and to watch Superman actually fly.

Seeing these cartoons today, through my more experienced and admittedly jaded eyes, I see things that I couldn't possibly have seen in the Strand. In the "Mad Scientist" (1941), for example, the first of the Fleischer series, the style is undeniably expressionistic, as if the Fleischer artists had all seen *Citizen Kane* (also released in 1941) before they began drawing their animated cells. The oblique camera angles, the extended shadows, the chiaroscuro lighting, the diagonal lines, even the freeze frame of the scientist turning into the front-page picture in the *Daily Planet*—all seem right out of Welles' masterpiece. The technicolor hues are also gorgeous, retaining even today the vividness of the original dyes while other less stable coloring processes, like Eastman color or Deluxe, are fading away on the original negatives.

The characters in the Fleischer cartoons were familiar ones to *Superman* readers and listeners. The mad scientist, for example, is very much in the comic-book Luthor tradition, which portrays the scientist as an overreacher who transgresses the laws of God and man in order to attain knowledge or power; in this case, he invents an Electrothanasia Ray, which threatens to destroy Metropolis. Lois Lane, of course, appears in her expected role as an ambitious reporter, eager to scoop her unambitious colleague, the meek Clark Kent. Perry White, known as "Chief," also makes a brief appearance. Jimmy Olsen is not yet on the scene. Lois is captured by the mad scientist and then rescued by Superman, who destroys the deadly ray, jails the mad scientist and thus saves Metropolis.

Altogether, 17 *Adventures of Superman* cartoons were produced from 1941 to 1943. The first nine were made by Fleischer Studios, and almost all were directed by Dave Fleischer. The last eight were made by Famous Studios, the first being the jingoistic "Japoteurs" (1942) about Japanese saboteurs and their attempt to skyjack an American bomber to Tokyo. The plots of all 17 cartoons are predictable and rather dull.

What stands out is the wonderfully imaginative, highly stylized look of the animation.

The Strand also provided a steady stream of serials, those multi-episode films that were the mainstay of the B-studios. Like cartoons, serials began in the silent period, with Selig's *The Adventures of Kathlyn* (1914), each installment culminating in the cliff-hanger. This was followed by the always-imitated *Perils of Pauline*. In the sound period, serials borrowed freely from comic strips and comic books—*Dick Tracy*, *The Green Hornet*, *Red Ryder*, *Captain Marvel*, *Batman* and, of course, the first and most famous superhero, *Superman*. Why it took a full decade for Superman to appear in a live-action format is puzzling, since other comic-book characters had made the leap much earlier. The serial *Batman*, for example, came out in 1943 and *Captain Marvel* in 1941. Republic Studios, which produced numerous serials, inquired about filming *Superman* in 1940, but negotiations stalled with National Comics, owner of the rights to Superman. In fact, Republic announced twice that it would produce a Superman serial, but it would not accept National Comics' demand that National have complete control over script and production. Finally, in 1947, Columbia Studios acquired the serial rights to Superman.

Columbia was a notch above Republic in prestige and quality. True, it was not one of the major studios—MGM, 20th-Century Fox, Paramount, Warner Brothers—but it did have in its directorial stable the great Frank Capra. Columbia's serial division had produced *Mandrake the Magician* (1940) and *Batman* (1943), among others, so a Superman serial was a natural.

Sam Katzman was the producer, and he had a reputation for penny-pinching despotism and for never ending up in the red on any production. Assigned to direct was the serials veteran Spencer Gordon Bennet, who began his career in the '20s with such titles as *The Green Archer* (1925), *Hawk of the Hills* (1927) and *The Tiger's Shadow* (1928). His most famous serials, in addition to the Superman series, were *Batman and Robin* (1949), *Captain Video* (1951) and *Blackhawk* (1952). For the Superman serial, the cast included Kirk Alyn (Superman), Noel Neill (Lois), Tommy Bond (Jimmy Olsen) and Pierre Watkin (Perry White).

In the film industry, serial production was different from film production. The best contemporary phrase to describe what happened back then is ''quick and dirty.'' Serial production is legendary for its speed. The units would shoot 60 to 70 sets a day, as opposed to eight to ten for a feature-length film. One crew would rehearse while another was shooting. Moreover, the shooting ratio (feet shot to feet used) was 3:1, while feature production was closer to 10:1 or 12:1. On the average, a good unit would get in the can ten to 15 episodes a month. Given this pace, the quality of the serials was not very high, although Superman is something of an exception. In Gary Grossman's *Superman: Serial to Cereal*, published in 1976 by Popular Library, director Tommy Carr describes the methods Katzman used:

On Superman and his other more important serials, we cracked down, paid more attention to details, made better scenes and took more time with the first three episodes than the others. Sam would run the first three for a prospective distributor in hopes of selling the entire package. If they liked them, they'd take whatever else we delivered....From then on it was downhill. While this was normal for other studios as well, Sam didn't hesitate telling us to make the first three good, especially on Superman.

Columbia produced two Superman serials, each with 15 installments: *Superman* (1948) and *Atom Man vs. Superman* (1950). These were the first live-action versions of the Superman legend, for legend it had become. Ten years' output of comic strips, comic books, radio shows and cartoons had given Superman the proportions of a myth. The hooplah surrounding the production of the serials created anticipation in the audience, which the studio wisely took advantage of. In his entertaining memoir, *A Job for Superman* (1971), Kirk Alyn, the first flesh-and-blood Superman, recalls the clauses in his contract. The Superman set was closed; he couldn't wear his costume (Columbia called it a "uniform") on the lot; Alyn would be billed only as Clark Kent in the credits; finally, all his personal appearances had to be approved by the studio in advance. Of course, the viewing public, as well as the rest of the entertainment industry, were curious about all these secret goings-on. *Variety*, in its October 18, 1948, issue, carried this piece:

HAIL TO THE FORGOTTEN MAN!

This is a salute to Hollywood's unknown actor. Most thesps are embittered over one thing or another, but the one with the most reason to hate the world is the star of Columbia's "Superman." Col. doesn't want to insult the cliff-hanger's moppet audience with the advice that anyone but the great man himself could play the role.

A toast, then, gentlemen, to that Superman among men, the mere man who plays Superman: Kirk Alyn.

What manner of man was this mere mortal who was playing Superman? He was a former ballet dancer who had entered show business accidentally, the result of auditioning for a part as a joke. After a career on stage and on tour with Olsen and Johnson's *Hellzapoppin*, Alyn ended up in Hollywood in 1942, where he did B-films and serials for Republic and Columbia. According to Alyn, he landed the role of Superman in a 15-minute interview during which he was ordered to take off his shirt and pants for producer Sam Katzman, who was sufficiently impressed to offer him the position. Katzman was no fool. He realized that an actor *had* to be impressive in his underwear if was going to play Superman, for as any kid who has romped around his house in underwear and towel can tell you, Superman does all his great deeds in his underwear.

Being the first anything is no easy task, and Alyn both takes pride in and laments assuming the role of the Man of Steel. The lament is a common one for the actors who play Superman: typecasting, plain and simple, and the effect of typecasting on a film career. The pride comes into play when Alyn discusses the technical problems that plagued the serials. The two characteristics of Superman that worked so well in animation—strength and flight—were the two most difficult technical problems for the Columbia crew. Special effects were not well advanced in the late 1940s, particularly in the penurious serials division of Columbia and most certainly not with the stingy Sam Katzman. At first, the special-effects crew persuaded Katzman to allow them to use wires and a steel breastplate for the flying sequences. Alyn was hoisted up, the wires were opaqued against the back lighting and several scenes were shot. Unfortunately, Alyn's legs had no support, so he had to rely on his stomach muscles to keep his legs up during the endless hours of shooting. He lost 17 pounds, he claimed, none of it fat.

67

More unfortunate, though, was the fact that the wires showed in the rushes, so Katzman fired the special-effects crew and decided to forego live-action flying, relying instead on animation. In the finished serials, Alyn jumps out of the frame and an animated character takes over for the flying scenes. For landings, the animated character alights behind an obstacle of some sort—a boulder or building—and then the "real" Superman walks or runs into the scene. Admittedly, it was a compromise, but the kids in the audience—including me—loved it. Less effective were the few live-action flying scenes. For these Bennet and crew settled on a camera trick to suggest flying: The camera was positioned horizontally while Alyn stood vertically with a fan blowing in his face and painted scenery positioned behind him. When the film was projected—*voila*! Superman seemed to be flying.

Strength tricks were somewhat easier to pull off, but again these involved editing techniques to suggest Superman's superpowers. For example, an out-of-control car comes careening down a crowded street: shot of Superman jumping into the street; shot of car heading straight for the camera; shot of Superman stopping the car with his arms on the hood. The kids in the audience never saw Superman stop the speeding car. What they *saw* was a speeded-up shot of a car coming to a halt.

Despite the limitations of budget and special effects, *Atom Man vs. Superman* (the second Columbia serial) was a huge success and still holds up today. Each chapter opens dramatically with Superman bursting through a screen-size reproduction of a *Superman* comic book cover. (We see the

same kind of intertextual tribute in the 1978 *Superman, the Movie*.) Next is documentary footage of a huge atomic blast, followed by the series title. The plot of the serial is a familiar one. Atom Man (actually Luthor in disguise) tries to use his evil genius to destroy Superman. The scheme is foiled, of course, but not before dozens of fights, last-minute rescues and cliff-hanger endings. Alyn plays Superman in the traditional way. "When I was Clark Kent," Alyn writes, "I played him for light comedy. When I got to be Superman, I puffed out my chest, pushed my voice down and became authoritative." Alyn plays up the meek side of Kent, who wears wire-rimmed glasses and delivers his nasally sounding lines so unassertively that he appears a somnambulist. Noel Neill's Lois is her expected plucky self, while Jimmy Olsen, played by Tommy Bond, has an angry edge. Pierre Watkins' Perry White is just irascible enough to be irritating. Lyle Talbot plays a convincing Lex Luthor, who, with his bald pate, beady eyes and mellifluous voice, seems the very essence of the evil scientist.

Columbia's serials drew more heavily from the comic-book legend than did the earlier Fleischer series mainly because more than a decade had passed since the invention of Superman by Siegel and Shuster; thus, the writers had more material to draw on. There was even a brief scene depicting the last days of Krypton, with Jor-El and Lara sending their son to Earth. Yet the first serial, *Superman*, is not altogether satisfying. Like the cartoon series, it was right on the money as far as representing the official comic-book version of the Man of Steel. But Kirk Alyn, while facially adequate, was somewhat thin and seemed short compared with artist Wayne Boring's comic-book rendition of a Herculean man from Krypton. The serial limited itself to mundane displays of strength while the comic-book Superman was traveling through time and visiting other worlds, exploits the serial could never aspire to. In fact, the character was so late in making the jump from monthly publication to silver screen that by the time the four-color hero transferred to cinema, cinema had already visited the pages of his *Superman* magazine twice: first, in the episode alluding to the Fleischer cartoon (described above) and second, when Orson Welles himself appears in a story with a twist on his Martian invasion hoax (*Superman* # 62). Although Kirk Alyn did a splendid job as Clark/Superman and Lyle Talbot outshone a later campy Gene Hackman as Luthor, the two serials were made far too late to remain current with what was happening in the pages of Superman's own magazine.

Much of the science and technology in *Atom Man vs. Superman* seems silly and primitive today, but there is one aspect that is truly prophetic. Luthor has created his "greatest invention," which he uses in destructive ways. It is none other than television. To the film world of the early '50s — and especially to the serials — television was indeed a destructive force, for its development created economic havoc in Hollywood. The advent of television meant the demise of the B-film as well as the serials. The audiences for these entertainments were now home watching their eight-inch Crosleys and adjusting their rabbit ears for the best reception, rather than sitting in theaters like the Strand or sending their children to Saturday matinees.

My family joined Luthor's TV conspiracy in 1951, a year important in the Superman saga as the date of the first Superman film.

That's right — 1951. The film was entitled *Superman and the Mole Men*, directed by Lee Sholem; it was sort of a pilot for the TV series that was to begin that year. The second cinema Superman was named George Reeves (actually George Bessolo), a former boxer turned actor turned Man of Steel. Of the 200 actors who auditioned for the part, Reeves had the right look for producer Robert Maxwell, who had produced the Superman radio series in the '40s, and for director Tommy Carr, who had co-directed the first Kirk Alyn serial. In the crucial Lois Lane role, Maxwell cast Phyllis Coates, later replaced by Noel Neill of the serials.

Superman and the Mole Men was an undistinguished film effort, but it was auspicious as a Superman vehicle: It launched the career of George Reeves and led to one of the most durable series in television history. In the film, Clark and Lois cover the story of the deepest oil well ever dug. Unfortunately, the drilling accidentally invades the underground world of the Mole Men, who stumble into the light through an unused drilling hole. These weak creatures are discovered by xenophobic townspeople, who try to kill them. Superman, of course, comes to the aid of the Mole Men and teaches the townspeople something about tolerance and acceptance. The production values of the film are of marginal quality, with undistinguished special effects. The flying is accomplished through animation and through some live-action sequences using a harness and wire rig that worked adequately but not convincingly. Yet this modest film (it was only 67 minutes long) marked the beginning of a long series of Superman stories that reached people not in theaters but in their own living rooms. In the process, the Superman legend reached a new audience — the American family — comprising not only readers of comic books and Saturday matinee-goers, but also mothers, fathers, aunts, uncles and grandparents, all of whom watched the series together.

The Adventures of Superman ran from 1951 to 1957; in all, 104 episodes were broadcast, the last half of which were shot in color but originally broadcast in black and white. The production crew for the first half of the series included executive producer Robert Maxwell, co-producers Barry Sarecky and Bernard Luber and directors Tommy Carr and Lee Sholem. The overall feel of these shows had more to do with 1930s and '40s gangster films than with the comic-book characters and stories. In fact, many of the shows had a distinct *film noir* look, especially in terms of the dark, expressionistic lighting and the alienated, trapped characters. The episodes depicted people full of fear and tension: blackmailers, killers, smugglers. The sets were empty warehouses and back alleys (many of which Clark would run into to change).

Although the look and feel of these early episodes might have been borrowed from another medium, the interpretation of Superman's character reveals something new. The comics, the cartoons, the radio show, the serials — all had presented dramatizations of Superman's triple identity — the mild-mannered reporter, the Man of Steel, the visitor from another planet. Because they appeared more frequently, the comics had elaborated on the three identities with the most imagination. Superman was given a boyhood in Smallville as Superboy; Lana Lang appeared and Ma and Pa Kent were given identities. Kal-El, the being from another planet, also developed an identity separate from that of Superman. There were stories about what Kal-El's life on Krypton might have been like with parents Jor-El and Lara, his dog Krypto and his cousin, later to become Supergirl. In the comics, Superman himself grows and changes. He encounters

new enemies, like the Toyman, and takes on new powers, like traveling through time. But Clark Kent, his double, stays about the same — meek and mild-mannered.

Suddenly onto the stage comes George Reeves, with his pugnacious jaw and battered nose (it had been broken six times). This was no Caspar Milquetoast; this was an investigative reporter with the *chutzpah* of Hildy Johnson in the Ben Hecht and Charles MacArthur play *The Front Page*, or the tenacity of the fighting DA in Warner Brothers pictures, frequently played by a young Humphrey Bogart, or the grittiness of "Steve Malone — District Attorney," a series National Comics had in its own anthology comic book, *Detective Comics* (where, by the way, the present DC COMICS gets its name in homage to its own flagship publication).

All the other Superman versions tried to distinguish between Superman and Clark Kent through either a change in voice or a change in posture — or both. But Reeves and his early director Tommy Carr brought Superman and Clark very close together, so close in fact that Superman seems to be a natural extension of Clark's courage, not a Walter Mitty-type fantasy projection. Carr, in fact, has stated, "There was little difference between our Superman and our Clark Kent." Once, after wrapping up an early episode, Carr exclaimed, "This episode's got everything: drama, mood, action, adventure. Hey, wait a minute. We forgot to put in Superman!"

Carr's oversight not only expresses the series' attitude toward its major character(s) but also reveals much about the structure of the half-hour shows. This short format did not allow much time for exposition, rising action, crisis, climax and falling action — the classic plot structure. So Clark gets much more involved in the action and saves Superman for the problems that he—Kent— can't solve. For example, in one episode, "The Golden Vulture," Clark snoops around a suspected smuggler's ship, gets caught, then takes on the whole crew in a smashing fistfight. At one point, he stops fighting for a moment when Lois appears, comically answering her pleas to do something by replying, "I would if you'd only get out of here!" Earlier, in the heat of the battle with the smugglers, Clark had asked, "Superman, where are you?" Because he can't reveal his true identity to Lois, both are captured and then Clark, to Lois' horror, is made to walk the plank. Underwater, Kent changes to the Man of Steel for the superhero's perfunctory appearance. Such was the formula for many of the episodes.

The intimacy of the new medium of television had much to do with this new interpretation of the Clark Kent/Superman connection. Some critics have sfaulted the characterization because of the lack of a clear distinction between the two. Even Kirk Alyn believed that Reeves' Clark was always getting in Superman's way. What these observers fail to recognize is the way the medium influences the message. In the comics, for example, writers and artists concentrated on motion, hence the focus on Superman's deeds. The animated features were an extension of the comics with the added dimension of movement, so it was natural to give emphasis to the strength and flight of the Man of Steel. The serials were divided into 15 segments, each providing a kind of advertisement for the next. Action was necessary to keep the kiddies coming back each Saturday. Also, the darkness of the theater and the gigantic size of the images tended to give the movie experience

a dreamlike quality of fantasy. But television is altogether different. Its small screen is the obverse of the movie screen; its images are small and tightly framed and physically near enough to invade the viewer's personal space. A kind of intimacy with the viewer is established, which is underscored by the position of the TV as a piece of furniture. You go to the movies, but you live with TV.

When we got our TV set in the early '50s, the characters who came into our home were part of our lives: Milton Berle, Sid Caesar, Captain Video, Kukla, Fran and Ollie. And of course Clark Kent. This human part of the three-sided character—the one most like us—works best on television simply because of the nature of the medium. Perhaps it was because the Man of Steel seemed so tiny on our eight-inch Crosley. He didn't even have the vivid colors of the comic books to give him life. Or perhaps it was simply easier to "live" with Clark Kent because he seemed so believable. But the real reason, I think, is that Reeves' Clark was a more interesting character than the other Clarks, more fully developed, less klutzy—a hero in his own right.

The first 26 episodes, in particular, highlighted this combative, pugnacious Clark Kent. The producer, Robert Maxwell, tended to go for scripts with lots of action, and writers Eugene Solow, Dick Hamilton, Dennis Cooper and Ben Freeman gave him plenty of it. Whatever the script, Clark was always in on the action. In "The Mind Machine" (#8), for example, a gangster named Lou Cranek, under indictment for racketeering, forces the scientist Dr. Stanton to use his new invention to brainwash a potential witness. Clark, the tenacious investigative reporter, asks an aviator friend to fly him over the gangster's suspected lair. Suddenly realizing that Lois, one of the witnesses against Cranek, is in danger, Clark slugs his friend, the pilot, so that he can change into

Superman. It is the quick-thinking Clark who saves the day. Typically, Superman is brought in to give the show a denouement.

For the production years 1953-57, the *Superman* staff underwent some key changes. Unhappy with the violence of the first 26 episodes, National Comics brought in one of its own, Whitney Ellsworth, to produce the series. Ellsworth, who had been with National when the Fleischer series was made, visualized Superman as family entertainment. Beginning with the 1954 shows, *The Adventures of Superman* seemed tamer, showing crooks as bumblers rather than as villains. The gradual shift away from violence is also a reflection of the mood in the early '50s. Dr. Frederic Wertham's attack on sex and violence in the comics had spread to other media, particularly the infant medium of television. Still trying to find the medium's own identity and trying to establish the family as its audience, the TV networks bowed to the pressure.

The budget limitations facing Ellsworth forced him into reusing sets (the hideout in "The Mind Machine," for example, is the same as in "The Phantom Ring") and designing utilitarian costumes that the major characters could wear in all the episodes (Clark's double-breasted suit, Jimmy's bow tie, Lois dark tailored suit). Except for the one early change from Phyllis Coates to Noel Neill, the cast remained the same throughout the series: Jack Larson played Jimmy, John Hamilton played Perry White, Robert Shayne played Inspector Henderson and, of course, George Reeves played Superman.

During the last year of production, 1957, the show seemed to grind to a creative halt. Reeves, paunchy and visibly aged, seemed bored with his role. The series had gone through numerous writers and directors. The quality of the series had deteriorated, with flubbed lines remaining in the broadcast version and with hackneyed scripts and characters becoming commonplace. The series had, unfortunately, become a kiddie show. In the director's chair for the penultimate episode, Reeves tried a last-gasp effort to revive the show's initial excitement. Episode 103 was entitled "The Perils of Superman" and contained situations right out of the serials: Lois Lane is tied to railroad tracks, Perry White is strapped to a buzzsaw, Jimmy Olsen is in a car hanging over a cliff. Needless to say, Superman comes to their rescue, but he couldn't rescue the series.

It is the reality of television that all shows must come to an end, and so it was for *The Adventures of Superman*. A pilot for a 1960 *Superboy* show was a dismal failure, as was a pilot for *Superpup* (1958) with, believe it or not, Bark Bent and Perry Bite. Both society and television had changed during the 1950s. The seeds had been planted for a revisionism in the 1960s that would use superheroes as the prime targets for campy satire, such as *Batman* on television and DC COMICS' *Justice League of America*.

For the next two decades, the Man of Steel was absent from live-action television and movies. He did make an appearance, though, in 1966-67 in an animated TV series called *The New Adventures of Superman*, with the durable Bud Collyer and Joan Alexander providing the voices. Produced by Filmways, these cartoons were highly reflective of the three eight-page stories that were then in each issue of the comic book. Like the comics, too, the stories featured innumerable secret identity coverups, the evil machinations of Superman's rogues gallery (Luthor, Brainiac, Mr. Mxyzptlk) and the pristine style of the Curt Swan-George Klein artwork, both of whom had taken over the art chores from Wayne Boring at DC. Superman did make a live appearance during the decade. That was on the legitimate stage in *It's a Bird...It's a Plane...It's Superman*, written by David Newman and Robert Benton, who would later collaborate on the scripts for the Christopher Reeve *Superman* movies.

The two-decade hiatus of Superman perhaps can best be understood as a reflection of a cultural trend. The generation that had grown up on Superman in the comics, in the serials and on TV had become wary of heroes or establishment representatives of the official "Truth, Justice and the American Way" line. I remember when *Batman* made its debut on television. I was in my last year of college, and memories of *Superman* seemed hopelessly lost in my youth. Now, on TV, was a new kind of tongue-in-cheek hero, with a phony stentorian bass voice, on a show featuring cartoon-like balloons saying "wham" and "sock" and with a Pop Art look that owed much to the influence of Lichtenstein and Warhol. Adam West's Batman was the "hero" of my generation because he wasn't a hero at all; he was a caricature of a hero, a self-conscious poser who meshed perfectly with the disillusionment of the young. Superman could find no place in such a world.

It took a combination of factors to bring Superman back on the scene. First was the renaissance of science fiction films and television shows in the 1970s. Films like *Silent Running*, *Star Wars*, *Close Encounters* and *Star Trek*, in combination with TV shows like *Buck Rogers*, *Battlestar Gallactica* and reruns of *Star Trek* and *Lost in Space*, signaled a renewal of interest in the science fiction genre (just as the success of *The Adventures of Superman* reflected the popularity of science fiction in the '50s). Second was the revitalization of the Hollywood film industry. The studio system had been dismantled during the '50s in a series of economic blows. The first was an antitrust action against Paramount which broke up the monopoly the studios had on production, distribution and exhibition. The second was the loss of much of film's audience to the new kid on the block, TV. Hollywood had been in a financial funk for most of the '50s and '60s, searching for a new audience, which it eventually found in the 16- to 24-year-old range. At the same time, the growth of independent production, coupled with the development of international financing and international filming (films shot outside the U.S. are usually less expensive to produce), meant more and bigger productions could be mounted. Finally, and perhaps most importantly, a major revolution in special effects helped give the production of science fiction films an authenticity they heretofore had lacked. Stanley Kubrick's *2001: A Space Odyssey* prefigured the special-effects revolution, which found full flower in Lucas' *Star Wars* series, in Spielberg's *Close Encounters* and in the *Star Trek* movies, among others. Miniaturization, innovative makeup techniques and computerization—all added up to a new and exciting look for films.

It is, in part, because of these trends, then, that *Superman, the Movie* was born. Financed by the international trio of Alexander and Ilya Salkind and Pierre Spengler, the movie was shot in Canada, England and the U.S. and made use of the most advanced special effects to date. A huge production, it cost over $40 million and took more than 350 days of shooting (part of this footage was used for *Superman II*). The producers obviously hoped to capitalize on science fiction's renewed popularity and to appeal to the new generation that had become the marketing target of most Hollywood films.

For the first time in a generation, comics readers and science fiction fans got to see a version of Superman that was very close to the contours of the myth. The producers and director Richard Donner worked from an original story by Mario Puzo. Scriptwriters David and Leslie Newman and Robert Benton added a few original touches. They gave us a very different sort of Krypton from that presented a generation earlier. Here was a delicate, crystalline world with the fragility of glass sculpture, perhaps effete, but with the traditional wisdom and superior knowledge. In addition, the "S" on Superman's costume is shown on Krypton as some type of family crest, since it appears on Jor-El's costume, too. What's refreshing about these innovations is that they're presented to us seriously, not satirically. The same is true for Clark's boyhood in Smallville and his nurturing by Jonathan and Martha Kent.

But then the film divides against itself by presenting a wisecracking, toupee-changing Luthor and his two cronies, the empty-headed Miss Teschmacher and the inept, oafish Otis. It is hard to believe that Luthor, whom we know from previous treatment as one of the most brilliant scientific minds of the 20th century, would surround himself with such moronic losers, until you realize that the filmmakers have changed gears and slipped into the ironic-satiric mode of TV's *Batman*. The film suffers for it. Yet *Superman, the Movie* succeeds despite this weakness. Technology had certainly come a long way since George Reeves jumped on a springboard for takeoffs, or leaped from a ladder for landings and then lay on a matted-out table for flying scenes in front of a rear projection of the city. With new photographic processes and with improved flying rigs, in combination with a giant Chapman crane, *Superman, the Movie* made viewers believe a man could actually fly.

Three years later, in *Superman II*, viewers saw more people fly as three escaped prisoners from the Phantom Zone (they had been spirited there at the beginning of *Superman, the Movie*) headed to Earth with the same powers as Superman. Led by Zod (Terence Stamp), they forced the leaders of the United States to bow to their superior strength. With Superman temporarily losing his powers because of his love for the earthling Lois Lane, the ensuing super-battle is a comic book lover's dream. Even Luthor is toned down considerably since, despite his high IQ, he is mightily outmatched by Zod and his followers.

The characters in the first two Superman movies are close to the early comic-book versions. Jimmy Olsen (Mark McClure) is relegated to minor status, and Perry White is played by a youngish Jackie Cooper, who seems as if he would be more at home in the *All the President's Men* newsroom than at the *Daily Planet*. (Joe Shuster confided to *NEMO* magazine in a 1983 interview that he had been hoping they would cast "the fellow who played Lou Grant: Ed Asner.") Margot Kidder's Lois has the feistiness of Phyllis Coates' earlier performance in the role. Her raspy voice and tomboyish looks give us a less glamorous heroine but, perhaps, a more liberated one than in earlier versions. Reeve's Superman harkens back to the more traditional, dichotomous character, with perhaps more fumbling, bumbling and slapstick than have been associated with Clark Kent in previous characterizations. In Reeve we see the comic-book character come full circle. In fact, Reeve was chosen, among other reasons, because he somewhat resembled Superman as drawn by Curt Swan.

John Byrne, the writer/artist behind the current DC revamp of the comic book, has modeled *his* Superman after Reeve.

I've saved *Superman III* for last because it is the worst of the Superman visualizations and unworthy of extended consideration. When the decision to adapt the comic-book hero for the third time came up, the scriptwriters (again, David and Leslie Newman and Robert Benton) must have said to themselves, "Oh, comics, as in stand-up comics, as in funny." The first 20 minutes of *Superman III* hit an all-time low for heroic action. The slapstick is so absurd it even features one of English comedian Benny Hill's regular sidekicks, Bob Todd. The casting of Richard Pryor as the computer expert, Gus, further accentuates the film's schizophrenia: We actually have two movies, one with the ever-mugging, boorishly hip Pryor, the other with an ineffectual, self-conscious Superman and an equally unattractive, simpering Clark Kent. The only good scene occurs when Superman's imperfect double, Bizarro, almost destroys the Man of Steel in a situation right out of the comics.

That Superman is alive and well after 50 years of mixed treatment in the media is a testament to the vitality and durability of the Jerry Siegel/Joe Shuster creation. I have a faith, born in the dark back at the Strand and nurtured in front of the eight-inch Crosley, that the Superman legend will live on (despite whatever horrors may be visited on us by *Superman IV*), for—God knows—the world needs him now more than ever. In a recent *Action Comics* (#554), writer Marv Wolfman and artist Gil Kane concoct a story about a future Earth where the heroic ideal has been extinguished by alien invaders. Two young boys, defying their elders, imagine and then draw a picture of a great hero to fight the invaders. The hero is, of course, Superman. The two young boys are named—you guessed it—Jerry and Joe. Voltaire once said that if God did not exist, it would be necessary to invent him. The same is true for Superman.

THE **PERSISTENCE** OF A LEGEND

INVULNERABILITY... STRENGTH, SPEED... ALL THESE THINGS, AND MANY MORE... COMBINE TO MAKE *SUPERMAN* THE MOST POWERFUL BEING ON EARTH! BUT THERE IS ANOTHER SIDE TO THE *MAN OF STEEL*... A DARK SIDE HIDDEN FROM BOTH THE CROWDS OF ADMIRERS AND THE EVIL MEN WHO HATE AND FEAR HIM!

STORY BY:
DENNY O'NEIL

ART BY:
CURT SWAN
&
MURPHY ANDERSON

S-560

SUPERMAN BREAKS LOOSE

WHAT MAKES SUPERMAN SO DARNED AMERICAN?

by GARY ENGLE

When I was young I spent a lot of time arguing with myself about who would win in a fight between John Wayne and Superman. On days when I wore my cowboy hat and cap guns, I knew the Duke would win because of his pronounced superiority in the all-important matter of swagger. There were days, though, when a frayed army blanket tied cape-fashion around my neck signalled a young man's need to believe there could be no end to the potency of his being. Then the Man of Steel was the odds-on favorite to knock the Duke for a cosmic loop. My

greatest childhood problem was that the question could never be resolved because no such battle could ever take place. I mean, how would a fight start between the only two Americans who never started anything, who always fought only to defend their rights and the American way?

Now that I'm older and able to look with reason on the mysteries of childhood, I've finally resolved the dilemma. John Wayne was the best older brother any kid could ever hope to have, but he was no Superman.

Superman is *the* great American hero. We are a nation rich with legendary figures. But among the Davy Crocketts and Paul Bunyans and Mike Finks and Pecos Bills and all the rest who speak for various regional identities in the pantheon of American folklore, only Superman achieves truly mythic stature, interweaving a pattern of beliefs, literary conventions and cultural traditions of the American people more powerfully and more accessibly than any other cultural symbol of the 20th century, perhaps of any period in our history.

The core of the American myth in *Superman* consists of a few basic facts that remain unchanged throughout the infinitely varied ways in which the myth is told—facts with which everyone is familiar, however marginal their knowledge of the story. Superman is an orphan rocketed to Earth when his native planet Krypton explodes; he lands near Smallville and is adopted by Jonathan and Martha Kent, who inculcate in him their American middle-class ethic; as an adult he migrates to Metropolis where he defends America—no, the world! no, the Universe!— from all evil and harm while playing a romantic game in which, as Clark Kent, he hopelessly pursues Lois Lane, who hopelessly pursues Superman, who remains aloof until such time as Lois proves worthy of him by falling in love with his feigned identity as a weakling. That's it. Every narrative thread

in the mythology, each one of the thousands of plots in the 50-year stream of comics and films and TV shows, all the tales involving the demigods of the Superman pantheon— Superboy, Supergirl, even Krypto the super-dog—every single one reinforces by never contradicting this basic set of facts. That's the myth, and that's where one looks to understand America.

It is impossible to imagine Superman being as popular as he is and speaking as deeply to the American character were he not an immigrant and an orphan. Immigration, of course, is the overwhelming fact in American history. Except for the Indians, all Americans have an immediate sense of their origins elsewhere. No nation on Earth has so deeply embedded in its social consciousness the imagery of passage from one social identity to another: the Mayflower of the New England separatists, the slave ships from Africa and the subsequent underground railroads toward freedom in the North, the sailing ships and steamers running shuttles across two oceans in the 19th century, the freedom airlifts in the 20th. Somehow the picture just isn't complete without Superman's rocketship.

Like the peoples of the nation whose values he defends, Superman is an alien, but not just any alien. He's the consummate and totally uncompromised alien, an immigrant whose visible difference from the norm is underscored by his decision to wear a costume of bold primary colors so tight as to be his very skin. Moreover, Superman the alien is real. He stands out among the host of comic book characters (Batman is a good example) for whom the superhero role is like a mask assumed when needed, a costume worn over their real identities as normal Americans. Superman's powers—strength, mobility, X-ray vision and the like—are the comic-book equivalents of ethnic characteristics, and they protect and preserve the vitality of the foster community in which he lives in the same way that immigrant ethnicity has sustained American culture linguistically, artistically, economically, politically and spiritually. The myth of *Superman* asserts with total confidence and a childlike innocence the value of the immigrant in American culture.

From this nation's beginnings Americans have looked for ways of coming to terms with the immigrant experience. This is why, for example, so much of American literature and popular culture deals with the theme of dislocation, generally focused in characters devoted or doomed to constant physical movement. Daniel Boone became an American legend in part as a result of apocryphal stories that he moved every time his neighbors got close enough for him to see the smoke of their cabin fires. James Fenimore Cooper's Natty Bumppo spent the five long novels of the Leatherstocking saga drifting ever westward, like the pioneers who were his spiritual offspring, from the Mohawk valley of upstate New York to the Great Plains where he died. Huck Finn sailed through the moral heart of America on a raft. Melville's Ishmael, Wister's Virginian, Shane, Gatsby, the entire Lost Generation, Steinbeck's Okies, Little Orphan Annie, a thousand fiddlefooted cowboy heroes of dime novels and films and television—all in motion, searching for the American dream or stubbornly refusing to give up their innocence by growing old, all symptomatic of a national sense of rootlessness stemming from an identity founded on the experience of immigration.

Individual mobility is an integral part of America's dreamwork. Is it any wonder, then, that our greatest hero can take to the air at will? Superman's ability to fly does more than place him in a tradition of mythic figures going back to the Greek messenger god Hermes or Zetes the flying Argonaut. It makes him an exemplar in the American dream. Take away a young man's wheels and you take away his manhood. Jack Kerouac and Charles Kurault go on the road; William Least Heat Moon looks for himself in a van exploring the veins of America in its system of blue highways; legions of greyhaired retirees turn Air Stream trailers and Winnebagos into proof positive that you can, in the end, take it with you. On a human scale, the American need to keep moving suggests a neurotic aimlessness under the surface of adventure. But take the human restraints off, let Superman fly unencumbered when and wherever he will, and the meaning of mobility in the American consciousness begins to reveal itself. Superman's incredible speed allows him to be as close to everywhere at once as it is physically possible to be. Displacement is, therefore, impossible. His sense of self is not dispersed by his life's migration but rather enhanced by all the universe that he is able to occupy. What American, whether an immigrant in spirit or in fact, could resist the appeal of one with such an ironclad immunity to the anxiety of dislocation?

In America, physical dislocation serves as a symbol of social and psychological movement. When our immigrant ancestors arrived on America's shores they hit the ground running, some to homestead on the Great Plains, others to claw their way up the socio-economic ladder in coastal ghettos. Upward mobility, westward migration, Sunbelt relocation—the wisdom in America is that people don't, can't, mustn't end up where they begin. This belief has the moral force of religious doctrine. Thus the American identity is ordered around the psychological experience of forsaking or losing the past for the opportunity of reinventing one-self in the future. This makes the orphan a potent symbol of the American character. Orphans aren't merely free to reinvent themselves. They are obliged to do so.

When Superman reinvents himself, he becomes the bumbling Clark Kent, a figure as immobile as Superman is mobile, as weak as his alter ego is strong. Over the years commentators have been fond of stressing how Clark Kent provides an illusory image of wimpiness onto which children can project their insecurities about their own potential (and, hopefully, equally illusory) weaknesses. But I think the role of Clark Kent is far more complex than that.

During my childhood, Kent contributed nothing to my love for the Man of Steel. If left to contemplate him for too long, I found myself changing from cape back into cowboy hat and guns. John Wayne, at least, was no sissy that I could ever see. Of course, in all the Westerns that the Duke came to stand for in my mind, there were elements that left me as confused as the paradox between Kent and Superman. For example, I could never seem to figure out why cowboys so often fell in love when there were obviously better options: horses to ride, guns to shoot, outlaws to chase and savages to kill. Even on the days when I became John Wayne, I could fall victim to a never-articulated anxiety about the potential for poor judgment in my cowboy heroes. Then, I generally drifted back into a worship of Superman. With him, at least, the mysterious communion of opposites was honest and on the surface of things.

What disturbed me as a child is what I now think makes the myth of *Superman* so appealing to an immigrant sensibility. The shape-shifting between Clark Kent and Superman is the means by which this mid-20th-century, urban story—like the pastoral,

19th-century Western before it—addresses in dramatic terms the theme of cultural assimilation.

At its most basic level, the Western was an imaginative record of the American experience of westward migration and settlement. By bringing the forces of civilization and savagery together on a mythical frontier, the Western addressed the problem of conflict between apparently mutually exclusive identities and explored options for negotiating between them. In terms that a boy could comprehend, the myth explored the dilemma of assimilation—marry the school marm and start wearing Eastern clothes or saddle up and drift further westward with the boys.

The Western was never a myth of stark moral simplicity. Pioneers fled civilization by migrating west, but their purpose in the wilderness was to rebuild civilization. So civilization was both good and bad, what Americans fled from and journeyed toward. A similar moral ambiguity rested at the heart of the wilderness. It was an Eden in which innocence could be achieved through spiritual rebirth, but it was also the anarchic force that most directly threatened the civilized values America wanted to impose on the frontier. So the dilemma arose: In negotiating between civilization and the wilderness, between the old order and the new, between the identity the pioneers carried with them from wherever they came and the identity they sought to invent, Americans faced an impossible choice. Either they pushed into the New World wilderness and forsook the ideals that motivated them or they clung to their origins and polluted Eden.

The myth of the Western responded to

this dilemma by inventing the idea of the frontier in which civilized ideals embodied in the institutions of family, church, law and education are revitalized by the virtues of savagery: independence, self-reliance, personal honor, sympathy with nature and ethical uses of violence. In effect, the mythical frontier represented an attempt to embody the perfect degree of assimilation in which both the old and new identities came together, if not in a single self-image, then at least in idealized relationships, like the symbolic marriage of reformed cowboy and displaced school marm that ended Owen Wister's prototypical *The Virginian*, or the mystical masculine bonding between representatives of an ascendant and a vanishing America — Natty Bumppo and Chingachgook, the Lone Ranger and Tonto. On the Western frontier, both the old and new identities equally mattered.

As powerful a myth as the Western was, however, there were certain limits to its ability to speak directly to an increasingly common 20th-century immigrant sensibility. First, it was pastoral. Its imagery of dusty frontier towns and breathtaking mountainous desolation spoke most affectingly to those who conceived of the American dream in terms of the 19th-century immigrant experience of rural settlement. As the 20th century wore on, more immigrants were, like Superman, moving from rural or small-town backgrounds to metropolitan environments. Moreover, the Western was historical, often elegiacally so. Underlying the air of celebration in even the most epic and romantic of Westerns — the films of John Ford, say, in which John Wayne stood tall for all that any good American boy could ever want to be — was an awareness that the frontier was less a place than a state of mind represented in historic terms by a fleeting moment glimpsed imperfectly in the rapid wave of westward migration and settlement. Impli-

citly, then, whatever balance of past and future identities the frontier could offer was itself tenuous or illusory.

Twentieth-century immigrants, particularly the Eastern European Jews who came to America after 1880 and who settled in the industrial and mercantile centers of the Northeast — cities like Cleveland where Jerry Siegel and Joe Shuster grew up and created Superman — could be entertained by the Western, but they developed a separate literary tradition that addressed the theme of assimilation in terms closer to their personal experience. In this tradition issues were clear cut: Clinging to an Old World identity meant isolation in ghettos, confrontation with a prejudiced mainstream culture, second-class social status and impoverishment. On the other hand, forsaking the past in favor of total absorption into the mainstream, while it could result in socioeconomic progress, meant a loss of the religious, linguistic, even culinary traditions that provided a foundation for psychological well-being. Such loss was particularly tragic for the Jews because of the fundamental role played by history in Jewish culture.

Writers who worked in this tradition — Abraham Cahan, Daniel Fuchs, Henry Roth and Delmore Schwarz, among others — generally found little reason to view the experience of assimilation with joy or optimism. Typical of the tradition was Cahan's early novel *Yekl*, on which Joan Micklin Silver's film *Hester Street* was based. A young married couple, Jake and Gitl, clash over his need to be absorbed as quickly as possible into the American mainstream and her obsessive preservation of their Russian-Jewish heritage. In symbolic terms, their confrontation is as simple as their choice of headgear — a derby for him, a babushka for her. That the story ends with their divorce, even in the context of their gradual movement toward mutual understanding of one

**Superman, I've always thought, is an angel.
I base this assumption on the fact that all the
fathers of the church up until Aquinas thought
that angels had bodies, if only "spiritual or
ethereal bodies" (Platonic philosophy permitted
only God to be Pure Spirit). It has always seemed
reasonable to me that on other planets the
evolutionary process is further along and has
therefore come much closer to developing
angels than we have. Probably the angel stories
found in all of the world's religions are traces of
the work in our world of Superman and his
relatives. Who is to say I'm wrong?**

Andrew M. Greeley, best-selling author and social commentator

another's point of view, suggests the divisive nature of the pressures at work in the immigrant communities.

Where the pressures were perhaps most keenly felt was in the schools. Educational theory of the period stressed the benefits of rapid assimilation. In the first decades of this century, for example, New York schools flatly rejected bilingual education—a common response to the plight of non-English-speaking immigrants even today—and there were conscientious efforts to indoctrinate the children of immigrants with American values, often at the expense of traditions within the ethnic community. What resulted was a generational rift in which children were openly embarrassed by and even contemptuous of their parents' values, setting a pattern in American life in which second-generation immigrants migrate psychologically if not physically from their parents, leaving it up to the third generation and beyond to rediscover their ethnic roots.

Under such circumstances, finding a believable and inspiring balance between the old identity and the new, like that implicit in the myth of the frontier, was next to impossible. The images and characters that did emerge from the immigrant communities were often comic. Seen over and over in the fiction and popular theater of the day was the figure of the *yiddische Yankee*, a jingoistic optimist who spoke heavily accented American slang, talked baseball like an addict without understanding the game and dressed like a Broadway dandy on a budget—in short, one who didn't understand America well enough to distinguish between image and substance and who paid for the mistake by becoming the butt of a style of comedy bordering on pathos. So engrained was this stereotype in popular culture that it echoes today in TV situation comedy.

What was true for Jews was true for other ethnic groups as well. Irish, German, Italian, Slav—each had the image in popular culture of a half-assimilated American. Some were comic, others not. But none confirmed wholeheartedly the American dream. A case in point is George McManus' long-running comic strip *Bringing Up Father*, about an Irish-American bricklayer who wins the Irish sweepstakes. His sudden and fabulous wealth is the realization of the American dream. The energy of the strip, however, arises out of his failure to wear his new identity well. While his wife makes a fool of herself slavishly following fashion and aping the forms of high culture, he longs for the freedom to put aside his ascot and morning coat, go unshaven, put his feet up on the furniture, smoke cigars or sneak out to the old neighborhood for cards with the boys or bar meals of corned beef and cabbage. The clear moral of the strip has been from the beginning that the reward of pursuing the American dream is a longing for what one loses in the process.

Throughout American popular culture between 1880 and the second world war the story was the same. Oxlike Swedish farmers, German brewers, Jewish merchants, corrupt Irish ward healers, Italian gangsters—there was a parade of images that reflected in terms often comic, sometimes tragic, the humiliation, pain and cultural insecurity of people in a state of transition. Even in the comics, a medium intimately connected with immigrant culture, there simply was no image that presented a blending of identities in the assimilation process in a way that stressed pride, self-confidence, integrity and psychological well-being. None, that is, until Superman.

The brilliant stroke in the conception of Superman—the *sina qua non* that makes the whole myth work—is the fact that he has two identities. The myth simply wouldn't

work without Clark Kent, mild-mannered newspaper reporter and later, as the myth evolved, bland TV newsman. Adopting the white-bread image of a wimp is first and foremost a moral act for the Man of Steel. He does it to protect his parents from nefarious sorts who might use them to gain an edge over the powerful alien. Moreover, Kent adds to Superman's powers the moral guidance of a Smallville upbringing. It is Jonathan Kent, fans remember, who instructs the alien that his powers must always be used for good. Thus does the myth add a mainstream white Anglo-Saxon Protestant ingredient to the American stew. Clark Kent is the clearest stereotype of a self-effacing, hesitant, doubting, middle-class weakling ever invented. He is the epitome of visible invisibility, someone whose extraordinary ordinariness makes him disappear in a crowd. In a phrase, he is the consummate figure of total cultural assimilation, and significantly, he is not real. Implicit in this is the notion that mainstream cultural norms, however useful, are illusions.

Though a disguise, Kent is necessary for the myth to work. This uniquely American hero has two identities, one based on where he comes from in life's journey, one on where hes going. One is real, one an illusion, and both are necessary for the myth of balance in the assimilation process to be complete. Superman's powers make the hero capable of saving humanity; Kent's total immersion in the American heartland makes him want to do it. The result is an improvement on the Western: an optimistic myth of assimilation but with an urban, technocratic setting.

One must never underestimate the importance to a myth of the most minute elements which do not change over time and by which we recognize the story. Take Superman's cape, for example. When Joe Shuster inked the first Superman stories, in the early '30s

when he was still a student at Cleveland's Glenville High School, Superman was strictly beefcake in tights, looking more like a circus acrobat than the ultimate Man of Steel. By June of 1938 when *Action Comics* no. 1 was issued, the image had been altered to include a cape, ostensibly to make flight easier to render in the pictures. But it wasn't the cape of Victorian melodrama and adventure fiction, the kind worn with a clasp around the neck. In fact, one is hard-pressed to find any precedent in popular culture for the kind of cape Superman wears. His emerges in a seamless line from either side of the front yoke of his tunic. It is a veritable growth from behind his pectorals and hangs, when he stands at ease, in a line that doesn't so much drape his shoulders as stand apart from them and echo their curve, like an angel's wings.

In light of this graphic detail, it seems hardly coincidental that Superman's real, Kryptonic name is Kal-El, an apparent neologism by George Lowther, the author who novelized the comic strip in 1942. In Hebrew, *el* can be both root and affix. As a root, it is the masculine singular word for God. Angels in Hebrew mythology are called *benei Elohim* (literally, sons of the Gods), or *Elyonim* (higher beings). As an affix, *el* is most often translated as "of God," as in the plenitude of Old Testament given names: Ishma-el, Dani-el, Ezeki-el, Samu-el, etc. It is also a common form for named angels in most Semitic mythologies: Israf-el, Aza-el, Uri-el, Yo-el, Rapha-el, Gabri-el and — the one perhaps most like Superman — Micha-el, the warrior angel and Satan's principal adversary.

The morpheme *Kal* bears a linguistic relation to two Hebrew roots. The first, *kal*, means "with lightness" or "swiftness" (faster than a speeding bullet in Hebrew?). It also bears a connection to the root *hal*, where *h* is the guttural *ch* of *chutzpah*. *Hal*

translates roughly as "everything" or "all." *Kal-el*, then, can be read as "all that is God," or perhaps more in the spirit of the myth of *Superman*, "all that God is." And while we're at it, *Kent* is a form of the Hebrew *kana*. In its *k-n-t* form, the word appears in the Bible, meaning "I have found a son."

I'm suggesting that *Superman* raises the American immigrant experience to the level of religious myth. And why not? He's not just some immigrant from across the waters like all our ancestors, but a real alien, an extraterrestrial, a visitor from heaven if you will, which fact lends an element of the supernatural to the myth. America has no national religious icons nor any pilgrimage shrines. The idea of a patron saint is ludicrous in a nation whose Founding Fathers wrote into the founding documents the fundamental if not eternal separation of church and state. America, though, is pretty much as religious as other industrialized countries. It's just that our tradition of religious diversity precludes the nation's religious character from being embodied in objects or persons recognizably religious, for such are immediately identified by their attachment to specific sectarian traditions and thus contradict the eclecticism of the American religious spirit.

In America, cultural icons that manage to tap the national religious spirit are of necessity secular on the surface and sufficiently generalized to incorporate the diversity of American religious traditions. Superman doesn't have to be seen as an angel to be appreciated, but in the absence of a tradition of national religious iconography, he can serve as a safe, nonsectarian focus for essentially religious sentiments, particularly among the young.

In the last analysis, Superman is like nothing so much as an American boy's fantasy of a messiah. He is the male, heroic match for the Statue of Liberty, come like an immigrant from heaven to deliver humankind by sacrificing himself in the service of others. He protects the weak and defends truth and justice and all the other moral virtues inherent in the Judeo-Christian tradition, remaining ever vigilant and ever chaste. What purer or stronger vision could there possibly be for a child? Now that I put my mind to it, I see that John Wayne never had a chance.

A FLAG WITH A HUMAN FACE

by PATRICK L. EAGAN

Defender of Truth, Justice and the American Way! What candidate for American political office wouldn't immediately adopt this campaign slogan, were it not already so closely associated with another champion of the people. The very phrase calls up a vivid image of a muscular man in blue tights and crimson cape, bold "S" rampant on a golden shield, his clear eyes and jutting chin proclaiming a nobility of spirit and compassion for the underdog. In his concentrated gaze, the strong silence of Gary Cooper is fused with the pure heart

of Jimmy Stewart—in one stroke Robert Jordan in the last scene of *For Whom the Bell Tolls* preparing to meet the enemy onslaught alone and Lindbergh in *The Spirit of St. Louis* staring out across the blue Atlantic—and all the while Old Glory, the same flag that flew over Fort McHenry, yes, and Iwo Jima, rippling confidently at his back.

On second thought, what contemporary politician would risk measurement by such a standard? For, in the popular imagination, Superman is just that: an ideal figure, an emblem of our patriotism, a flag with a human face. He is a man who puts principles ahead of personal advantage, seeks nothing for himself, only to be of service and to do the job that no one else can—or will—do. For half a century this popular hero and his story have reflected some important truths about America's political psyche and political ideals, including some of the complexity and the disturbing contradictions that mark the national soul.

Take that memorable slogan, for starters. Let fools and philosophers worry about defining "Truth" and "Justice"; any candidate knows his or her constituency will sit up and salivate like Pavlov's dog at the mere mention of both terms, whatever they mean. And as for "the *American Way*," every aspirant to political office in the land knows that this magical phrase transcends abstraction; it is a theological term whose function is to stir the civic faith, and it lies at the very heart of our political creed.

Actually, the American Way is less a single concept than a set of ideas or basic principles having to do with the role of government and the accepted rules of the political game. It is, in short, our civic dogma, and every schoolchild knows that God is its author and Superman its guardian.

And what is this American Way Superman is sworn to defend while he is out there slugging it out for Truth and Justice? Our textbooks say it is government by consent of the governed. It is human rights protected by government. It is the right to rebel when our rights are chronically violated. It is the freedom of the individual to pursue his/her own destiny.

This is our political catechism. And because we are committed to these principles, we value an open society as opposed to a rigid class structure. We support the rule of law over human whim, and we insist on defined limits to governmental authority. This political religion is instilled in every citizen by family, schooling and the political process as monitored by CBS election headquarters. Its canons have guided the national conscience for 200 years, save for those occasional wartime interludes when we let our fear of certain ethnic groups such as the Cherokees or, a little later, the Nisei get the better of our democratic impulses. Economic crises, corruption in government, foreign wars, the disintegration of political parties, technological change and ideological drifts to the conservative right or liberal left have not shaken the national commitment to the American Way of political life. The republic has survived it all, civil liberty has been expanded and mistrust of government is as alive and well today as (some would say even more so than) it was in 1776. In fact, the resilience of the American Way is so remarkable that, while Superman's dedication to its defense is certainly appreciated, it almost seems superfluous.

To be accurate, the explicit identification of the Man of Tomorrow with the defense of "Truth, Justice and the American Way" seems to date, as nearly as can be determined, from the popular Superman TV series (1951-57). Actually, the famous lead-in to the show refers to Superman fighting "the never-ending battle for Truth, Justice and the American Way"—a sentiment and phrasing that no doubt resonated differently for TV audiences of the McCarthy period than for audiences of post-Vietnam America.

In any case, loyalty to these same principles has been unremitting in the Superman comic books before and since. Superman's victories over criminals, foreign tyrants or extraterrestrial invaders are always testimony that the American Way is the true way, the just way. "When the mighty Man of Tomorrow discovers threats endangering the well-being of our great nation," begins one *Superman* tale from the 1940s, "he launches a battle against the saboteurs that will long be remembered."

America's champion never sleeps. Under his street clothes, and presumably his pajamas, this doughty knight is always dressed for combat. When Lois exclaims in the November-December 1943 issue of *Superman* comics that it "would be something to see Clark Kent in uniform!", the timid reporter shares a furtive aside with the reader: "You've seen me in uniform before, Lois...one with a red cape!" "Millions of *Superman* readers will recall," whispers an editor's note, "that Clark Kent tried to enlist, but was rejected for faulty vision (IMAGINE!) when his X-ray vision penetrated the eye-chart and read a different chart in the next room. Since then, he has learned that Superman could be of more value on the home front operating as a free agent." Indeed, a more dedicated superpatriot never leaped a tall building.

Yet the adventures of Superman also present a paradox rooted in the same collision of opposing values that perplexed the authors of the American Way, the framers of our Constitution. When Clark Kent de-clares, "This is a job for Superman!", we have learned to expect one of two possible challenges for the immigrant from Krypton: Either Superman is being called upon to reinforce the powers of a legitimate government that is too weak or ineffectual to maintain law and order on its own. (This usually takes the form of coming to the aid of the police or, in some instances, the armed forces or agents of the federal government.) Or his mission is to prevent the *abuses of power*—whether by a government or by an individual, often some evil genius or supervillain, who has usurped the powers properly accorded a legitimate government. Lex Luthor and Brainiac claim the right, without benefit of the political process or the rule of law, to curb the liberties of America's citizens and to dispose of the country's assets as they please. They are, in effect, self-appointed political dictators who must be deposed.

Thus Superman's life's work parallels a problem—one might even say the fundamental dilemma—that confronted the Constitution's framers: how to establish a government that is sufficiently strong to control evil (Hamilton's concern), but not so strong that it becomes a greater evil that controls us (Jefferson's worry). The framers responded to that challenge by adopting a federal system of government (in which the powers of the individual states are countered by the authority of a central power) and then setting up an arrangement of "checks and balances" between the executive, legislative and judicial functions of that government.

This initial formula for limited government has worked fairly well across the decades, but not without occasional strain. Maintaining a governmental system that is neither too weak to sustain law and order nor so strong as to inhibit liberty remains the constant challenge of American politics, just as it does in the adventures of Superman. "The

90

I don't think that anyone who has chosen a life in public service hasn't wished they could call in Superman to help in a time of national emergency. President Kennedy certainly would have enjoyed having him handy during the Cuban missile crisis.

Edward M. Kennedy, U.S. senator

Wizard with the Golden Eye" (March 1974), described as "a tale of power and how it is used…and abused," has the Man of Steel struggling to subdue a retired scientist whose misguided attempts to solve all of civilization's problems, such as overpopulated cities, by the use of the magical powers he has harnessed, lead to one disaster after another.

Indeed, Superman himself must guard against the inadvertent misuse of his own extraordinary powers. "When I think how close Superman came to becoming a destructive force," Lois reflects at the conclusion of one hair-raising adventure. "It's a lucky thing he's on the side of law and order."

Of course, this entire preoccupation with good government is based on a presumption that pervades the American political tradition, a presumption from which the *Superman* series seldom if ever strays. This is the notion that the primary, if not exclusive, purpose of government is to maintain law and order, to police, to regulate behavior, to "keep us off the grass." In short, the essential function of government is seen as a remedial one—rooted in the necessity to control human behavior that is selfish or ignorant. The Prankster's dangerous stunts

are an example of the former, Bizarro's clumsy destructiveness, of the latter. But they in themselves are never the occasion for the dash to the nearest phone booth. Superman's extraordinary powers are called upon because, and only when, government is failing to deliver on its primary mission.

This view of government—as the keeper of law and order—has been challenged as impoverished and even untenable in the modern world. It makes no allowance for any *positive* or creative governmental activity such as supportive involvement in the arts, education, science (other than for military purposes) and health. Nonetheless, the prevailing view of government in the American political tradition is this remedial one. And the chroniclers of Superman's adventures, on the comic page or on the screen, tenaciously follow the conventional view of government as existing primarily to save us from ourselves. This is the very role, of course, that Superman aspires to. And fans of the Man of Steel will find few, if any, examples of their hero exercising his powers to bring about the real and lasting improvement of the human condition; rather, they will find (as Umberto Eco notes in his essay, "The Myth of Superman") an obsession with preserving the status quo.

91

In Superman, Eco argues, "we have a perfect example of civic consciousness, completely split from political consciousness" (*The Role of the Reader*, Indiana University Press, 1979). Rather than use his powers to change the conditions that breed urban crime or poverty, Superman devotes his energies to rounding up criminals and delivering gigantic Christmas baskets to the poor. "As evil assumes only the form of an offense to private property," says Eco, *"good is represented only as charity."*

Superman may be "the champion of the weak and the oppressed," but, in a profounder sense, he is also the champion of law and order.

Superman thus embodies a distinctly conservative strain running through the American political psyche. This Hobbesian view of human nature as tending toward corruption is even seen in the otherwise "advanced" civilization of the planet Krypton, which, far from having achieved a utopia, is plagued by supercriminals. It seems that on that ill-fated star, as on Earth, the citizenry is forever trapped between wanting the freedom from fear that protective power offers and dreading the loss of personal freedom at the hands of unprincipled persons with that power: the control of fear vs. the fear of control.

Alongside this paradoxical approach to power within our political creed is an even more disturbing pattern: the notable discontinuity between what we *say* is the American Way and what is practiced in its name in the day-to-day life of the nation. Here, too, the adventures of Superman offer instructive examples.

Americans have consistently maintained a high level of official reverence toward the Constitution and commitment to the rule of law. We generally eschew "taking the law into our own hands." We are "a government of laws," we say, "not of individuals." Our public morality condemns violence and acquiesces in the use of force only as a last resort to preserve the peace. Heroes such as Gary Cooper in *High Noon* or, more recently, the gentle figure of David Carradine as Cane in the *Kung Fu* TV series are peace-loving men who unholster their weapon or fly into a slow-motion ballet of destruction only when the bad folks just refuse to let them alone. Presumably, Superman would like nothing better than to spend his life as docile Clark Kent, leaving law enforcement to the paid professionals and justice in the hands of the authorities.

Yet, our experience would suggest that this commitment to the official order on the part of many Americans is another one of those principles more honored in the breach than in the observance. Violence is a familiar phenomenon in the United States. The advocates of the right of the individual to "bear arms" consistently defeat the proponents of gun-control legislation. And the story of the solitary individual who, back to the wall, shoots it out with the "forces of evil" is a recurrent one in our history, our literature, our movies, our television shows and the front pages of our newspapers. The Lone Ranger and Rambo may be fictional, but Wyatt Earp and Eliot Ness—and Bernhard Goetz—were/are very real people.

"Nine of the most dangerous fiends who ever walked the Earth—stalking me like a pack of wolves," says a worried Superman *sotto voce*, as the assembled nemeses of his career encircle him menacingly (May 1976); "I'm in for the fight of my life." Talk about old Wyatt facing the Clantons at the O.K. Corral! At least he had Doc Holliday with him. In "The Kid Who Knocked Out Superman" (December 1972), the Man of Steel must go it alone against a gunslinging desperado in Wild West garb who arrives on a winged horse to threaten Metropolis.

The popularity of such *High Noon*-type

stories, in any case, is worth pausing over.

Though Americans are often found loudly espousing the rule of law, while their actions and popular heroes celebrate the "law" at the end of a gun barrel, Superman is no Rambo. (The Batman of 1987 is something else again.) He does not take a life or maim his enemies, no matter how treacherous their behavior. He is a respecter of the law, of due process and the right to a fair trial. Yet there is a sense in which his adventures grow out of — and satisfy — a need in us to see an individual from time to time stand tall against the "outlaw pack" who menace society and, to put it in the more graphic words of one of our vice presidents, kick some ass.

There are times, Americans seem to believe, when freedom of the press, freedom from self-incrimination and legal police procedure (such as getting a warrant to search a suspect's premises) get in the way of protecting the public interest. Damn it, we know they're in there (if there were only some way we could see through the walls we wouldn't *need* a warrant) and they've got the loot, so hang the protocol and let's just bust in through the roof and take them by surprise! In short: This is a job for Superman.

How easily we Americans suspend our scruples when Clark Kent slips into a phone booth, not to call the police or get a lawyer, but to become Superman — a being who, not being of this Earth, is exempt from the normal restraints that weigh upon the rest of us — who will emerge to "fight the never-ending battle for Truth, Justice and the American Way." Even if one or two fundamental civil rights have to be temporarily set aside in the process.

He even has a uniform, complete with an impressive badge across his chest, which proclaims his qualifications as a champion of the beleaguered taxpayer. If some of us are loathe to admit the quiet satisfaction we derive from reading about the response of subway vigilante Bernhard Goetz to an anticipated mugging, even as we may wince at its cold brutality, we can revel unabashedly in Superman's victories over gangsters, bullies, corrupt politicians, evil geniuses or extraterrestrial would-be dictators like Zod or Brain Storm (December 1975). The comparison may be disturbing, but it holds more than a grain of truth. The big difference, of course, is that Superman doesn't maim or kill people.

He does, however, reflect America's deeply rooted obsession with crime and with the maintenance of law and order. (What other country dines so insatiably on stories of crime and criminals — beginning with the nightly news and running right through the prime-time cop shows?) At the same time, Clark Kent's role as a reporter reflects another quintessentially American idea: that the press is the necessary check on the exercise of power in a free society. How ironic that Clark Kent must forsake his reportorial role — and his perspective as a journalist! — to take up his role as social avenger. Luckily, Lois Lane is still around to stick up for the interests of the Fourth Estate and the people's right to know.

Nor does Superman's defense of the American Way stop at the territorial frontiers of the United States. His mission is global, even galactic. With the same zeal that carried us into such episodes of national muscle-flexing or patriotic fervor (depending on your point of view) as the Mexican War, the Spanish-American War, the Battle of Wounded Knee or, more recently, the invasion of Grenada and the "lessons" delivered by U.S. jet fighter-bombers to Libya's Colonel Khadafy, Superman takes his defense of the American Way to any shore or neighboring solar system perceived to threaten those ideals.

To be sure, the objects of his intervention are always a devilish crew with no respect for God or human life. "On a remote isle, where men are forced to toil for an evil master, one mighty being strikes back!" begins "The Revolt of the Super-Slave" (November 1969). An exiled South American general named Satanta, we learn, is using slave labor to raise the contraband "zykk" flowers used to make a form of nerve gas banned by the United Nations. Superman helps an unlikely hero named Pancho lead a coup against the island's evil ruler.

In the *Superman* comics of the '70s, reflecting America's growing uneasiness with terrorism at home and abroad, an almost continuous sense of menace seems to hang over the modern American city. Stories with titles like "The Man Who Murdered Metropolis" (January 1974) or "The Parasite's Power Play" (April 1975) feature wackos with bombs or other horrific doomsday machines holding Metropolis and America hostage until the Man of Steel intervenes.

The Monroe Doctrine began as a U.S. policy intended to deter European powers from Latin American expansion (though it has been argued that this policy served well America's own imperialist ambitions in the same region). In *Superman*, this doctrine seems to have been extended. The world view with which the reader is presented tends to be bifurcated: On the one hand, we have the United States and the American Way, and, on the other, foreign powers with their non-American or *un*American ways. How could it be otherwise when Truth and Justice are allied with the former? Any other ways, it follows, must be false and unjust.

On to the Bay of Pigs!

This is not to impugn Superman's actions or motives in a given story, which, given the villainous behavior of the evil foreigners, are usually quite understandable, even laudable; our purpose here is merely to understand the appeal of such "intervention" sagas to Americans and the zest with which we tend to embrace them.

It should not be surprising that the *Superman* comics of the 1940s reflect such a world view, as other media of the day reveal that this perspective then enjoyed a wide popularity among Americans, as it had, indeed, for decades. This "us against them" approach to international politics was reinforced for many Americans following World War II by the emergence of the Soviet Union as a world power. Darned if we didn't find ourselves up against a supervillain, flexing its missiles and peering into our laboratories with its sinister X-ray vision.

In *Superman*, the anxieties and obsessions of the cold war era, as we have seen, most often take the form of a cosmic duel between Superman and the supervillain of the month, some scary figure from another star or parallel dimension who threatens to subjugate, or even destroy, the world with his awesome powers. Though the two foes seem evenly matched at best, and victory by either side impossible, we know that the fate of humanity/democracy rides on the broad shoulders of the Man of Steel. The swapping of violent, titanic feats is frightening, as whole forests are uprooted and molten comets hurled in both directions. But in the end, it is usually Superman's ingenuity, that good old Yankee can-do attitude, that wins the day. Whew! Another close one, we sigh. But the world is safe for another day.

What lies behind such stories and their appeal is the old American fear of power-gone-mad. There must be a way to protect

us, these tales seem to be saying, against the unbridled self-interest of a Brainiac or a Galactic Golem (who feeds on energy!). Since Hiroshima, we can imagine nothing more terrifying than an evil intelligence that has harnessed the forces of nature and is prepared to use them ruthlessly to advance its sinister ends. How touching that Superman, the symbol of those powers harnessed in the service of the good, is haunted by the fear of kryptonite and its deadly radiation. Like us, he knows that the very source of his wonderful powers may also have produced the seeds of his destruction.

Over and over, in fantasies, Superman revisits the scene of his native planet's demise and watches the Great Council fail to heed the warnings of his father, the brilliant scientist Jor-El, that Krypton is about to be blown to atoms in a spectacular nuclear chain reaction originating deep in the planet's core. In some stories Superman blames himself for his parents' death; in others, for the "deaths" of various loved ones ("Oh, no! I've killed Lois!" wails the stricken Man of Tomorrow on more than one

cover). It is, finally, his own power he fears, as much as the power of his enemy of the moment, with whom he is typically locked in what often seems an endless, maddening dance of distrust and deception. One slip, one super-thrust when he should have parried — the message is continually brought home to him — and he himself might bring about the destruction of Metropolis.

For all his colossal powers, a melancholy realization seems to haunt Superman: He is the only survivor of a once-great civilization. Since the advent of our own nuclear age, a similar nightmare haunts many an American. Like a sudden chilly breeze on a balmy evening, the uncomfortable truth has overtaken us. Krypton is here, and Jor-El is pleading in the halls of Washington and Moscow. Will humankind heed him this time?

Superman is also a constant reminder, as we have seen, of the delicate balance between control and freedom a democratic nation must work to maintain and of some of the strengths and dangers inherent in the American character.

In short, Superman, like all popular culture, reflects some things about ourselves we need to know and think about from time to time. He is an image we should keep before us.

READING SUPERMAN

by FREDERIK N. SMITH

n Mordecai Richler's comical, poignant story entitled "The Summer My Grandmother Was Supposed to Die," a group of young boys discuss the mythology of America's heroes:

" 'Why is it,' Arty wanted to know, 'that Tarzan never shits?'

" 'Dick Tracy too.'

" 'Or Wonder Woman.'

" 'She's a dame.'

" 'So?'

" 'Jees, wouldn't it be something if Superman crapped in the sky? He could just be

flying over Waverly Street when, whammo, Mr. Rabinovitch catches it right in the kisser.'

"Mr. Rabinovitch was our Hebrew teacher.

" 'But there's Tarzan,' Arty insisted, 'in the jungle, week in and week out, and never once does he need to go to the toilet. It's not real, that's all.' "

I don't mean to overload this little passage, but it does suggest the paradoxical relationship we have with Superman and his super-brothers and -sisters, a relationship which admits their otherworldliness and yet willingly suspends any disbelief we may have. How is it that we can embrace such myths and at the same time recognize their inconsistencies? Part of the answer is undoubtedly the same resistance to reality that keeps our children for so long (thank God!) thinking we're some sort of paragons. Or kept us when we were children so firmly clutching our belief in Santa Claus: The fact is, I no more want to surrender my enjoyment of Superman than I wanted to back off my belief in the paunchy, high-flyer from the North Pole, and while I may have wondered why he didn't get stuck in the chimney, around my parents I kept my mouth shut for a long time. (Come to think of it, after all that milk and cookies, how come *he* never had to use the toilet?)

But another part of the answer to the question of why such inconsistencies don't seem to prevent our enjoyment of Superman and his like, I would suggest, is that we enjoy Superman not merely as *myth*, but also as *literature*. That is to say, there are storytelling features of the continuing saga — and of its telling — that appeal to the reader in much the same way that certain features of *literary* storytelling do.

To see what I'm talking about, you'll have to begin by taking two steps backward from an all-too-common assumption: namely, that comic books are an essentially visual medium that makes only the most perfunctory or simplistic use of language.

When in our highly visual age we think of the superhero comics, we think first of the visual depiction of action. Bang! Pow! Splat! It is ironic, however, that much of what is unique in these comics is not visual at all. Although we talk of *reading* (not looking at) the comics, we tend to forget that comic-book sequences are stories told in words as well as pictures. Indeed, comic books have a place in the long history of narrative form in literature. A comic like *Superman* can be appreciated, without distortion, from a literary perspective, and whether or not we are conscious of its power, *language* is the major source of our fascination with Superman. It is the language in *Superman* that makes our response qualitatively different from our response to Mutt and Jeff, or Archie or Joe Palooka.

True enough, some aspects of the narrative in *Superman* derive from popular culture. No wonder that this comic has been around for so long, for it speaks to our desire to have things action-packed but uncomplicated, ultimately reassuring us that everything will turn out all right. ("Any kid could tell you," Jimmy Olsen says at the end of one strip, "that crime doesn't pay.") For example, some of the most characteristic features of *Superman* are reminiscent of stage melodrama: The stories are based on action, circumstance and omniscient manipulation of events rather than the tracing of motives or the development of character; the characters are types, arranged always on either side of a line separating good and evil; poetic justice is superficially secured through the simple rewarding or punishing of characters according to their deeds; and always there is an appeal not so much to the morality of the audience (which is assumed) but to the audience's adrenalin. That is why the strip is replete with action scenes, why jet streams trail behind Superman and why 90 percent of the dialogue is punctuated by exclamation marks. And, of course, things must be made to *seem*, again superficially, to have fallen under the control of the villain — only to be recovered at the 11th hour by the superior strength or cunning of the hero.

In America this kind of drama has long held a grip on the popular imagination, as in the Gold Rush melodramas of Colorado, Nevada and California, where, oddly enough, the villain wore a cape; in the Saturday matinees, where we watched, week after week, dismayed yet delighted, as a squirming heroine was tied to the tracks and a locomotive approached in the distance; in the old radio dramas, such as *The Lone Ranger*, where the hero's identity, like Robin Hood's and Clark Kent's, was kept a secret in order to preserve the possibility of future good deeds; and, in a more sophisticated way, in a novel (and later a film) like *Shane*, where characterization, although subtler, is still diagrammatic, the emphasis on action (or pending action) and Shane's identity shrouded in mystery. This is the stuff that we as a nation grew up on.

But there are also literary roots to the two-dimensional Superman. One might see in him a faint echo of the 18th-century's klutzy Gulliver or boyish Tom Jones, who were already at that time comic diminishments of Homer's Odysseus. I can likewise see in the comic book a 20th-century world not altogether different from that of Joyce's *Ulysses*, where classical heroics are alluded to but understood to be well beyond our (all-too-human) reach. The basic premise of *Superman* is patently absurd: an ordinary newspaper reporter transformed into The Man of Tomorrow, racing across the sky, determined to stamp out evil and defend the American Way. Yet behind the absurdity is a naive, comic-book acceptance of the righteousness of Superman's cause, as well as a delight in the sheer imaginativeness of it all. What if...? As in a pastoral poem, the world projected in the pages of *Superman* is not an imitation of reality but an image of what reality cannot possibly offer. Paradise is lost, but Superman pretends as if it were not. The world of the superheroes permits us to look back at the Golden Age by peering into the World of Tomorrow. God and Nietzsche may be dead. Superman persists.

The verbal and visual complexity of a typical *Superman* comic strip is, I believe, far greater than we usually imagine; its representation has generally kept pace with the developing complexity of narrative in film and television. While thought balloons, asides to the reader (apparently, as in the theater, not overheard by the other characters) and narrative bridges delivered by an omniscient narrator have existed from the beginning, the *Superman* comics have over the years developed these techniques into an art. If one compares a typical sequence from the '30s with a sequence from the '60s, '70s or '80s, the difference perceived is not so much in the illustration as in the handling of narration; the character of Superman himself remains that of the prototypical virtuous hero who has come to slay some modern-day dragon. Whatever changes we might track in Superman's character, I would suggest those changes are slight in comparison with the changes in narration. The reader of *Superman* can even expect the strip to toy with the nature of narrative itself; as past and present (and, in at least one sequence, future) are brought together, the

As a kid growing up in Harlem, I read _Superman_. But I soon found him too mild. I preferred the much more magical transformation of Captain Marvel. Clark Kent just took off his tie and glasses; Billy Batson said SHAZAM! and he was changed into this wonderful being. Besides, a reporter was something pretty remote from my existence. By the time I was 12, I had moved on to comics with titles such as _The Vault of Horror_ and _The Crypt of Terror_ and eventually to Erskine Caldwell.

Claude Brown, author, *Manchild in the Promised Land*

narrator's words and Superman's thought are made almost indistinguishable, and it often becomes difficult to identify the intended audience for Superman's words—Superman himself? Lois? another character? perhaps the reader?

Furthermore, like much literature, *Superman* has since the early '40s exhibited a marvelous self-consciousness of form. For example, on one occasion Lois begins to suspect that Clark is Superman and begins to search through her scrapbook, reviewing the many escapades they have shared; on another occasion the couple goes to the movies together to watch an animated Superman film which Clark fears will reveal the identity (everyone else seems to know) of her mild-mannered colleague at the *Daily Planet*. And throughout *Superman*'s 50 years runs an interesting tension between the newspaper's need to report fact and its responsibility for covering the incredible adventures of the most famous citizen of Metropolis. "This is a newspaper," Perry

White reminds Clark, "not a science-fiction magazine!"

In fact, a stylistic self-reflexivity is one of the most characteristic traits of *Superman*. Over the years, the comic book has demonstrated a more-or-less consistent awareness of its own artificiality, which is quite in keeping with its borrowings from melodrama, where the villain overtly twists his mustache before engaging in his villainy, and where the hero may pause before performing an heroic deed long enough to flex his muscles. In an early episode Superman says, while hurriedly pulling on his street clothes, "Enter Clark Kent!" In another he even jokes about his ability to fly: "Good thing I'm not subject to vertigo!" A similarly ironic self-consciousness is apparent when Superman, costumed in his usual blue tights and red cape, bursts into a suspect's office and accuses him of "amateur theatricals." Elsewhere, as Lois is snatched from danger by Superman, she calls out his name and he answers: "Right! And still playing the role

99

of gallant rescuer!" In another sequence, as the villains are lifted seemingly out of reach in a construction scoop, they sing, "Up, up, and away!" In the next frame Superboy says, while knocking them out: "That's MY theme!"

Of course such self-consciousness is not restricted to the pages of comics and the stages of melodramas. Shakespeare builds a play-within-a-play in *Hamlet*, and in *Six Characters in Search of an Author* Pirandello develops a whole drama around the idea of a play struggling to be born. There are numerous, well-known examples of novels about novel writing, poems about poetry. One might go so far as to say that self-reflexivity is the quintessential gesture of literature, or at least of modern literature. But the complexity of *Superman*'s self-consciousness is worth noting. In this respect, it is very modern and at one with Joyce, Beckett, Borges, Robbe-Grillet and Nabokov.

An example. In the "Case of the Funny Paper Crimes," the 1942 sequence in which Clark and Lois come to realize their shared fascination with the comics, we initially find ourselves watching a struggling pair atop a speeding railroad car, then hear Lois ask for the comics page out of the *Daily Planet* Clark is reading, then look over her shoulder as she reads the same strip he was reading about the struggle atop the train. As Lois hands back the newspaper, Clark says:

"Odd how those impossible characters get a grip on you. Take Torgo, for instance— the menacing giant in *Prince Peril*. You and I know that it's impossible for such creatures to exist—yet we enjoy reading about them."

And then ("even as Clark speaks") we are launched into a "real-life" situation as Torgo threatens downtown Metropolis. In this episode, arising from the machinations, we learn in the penultimate frame, of an unemployed cartoonist who has devised a ma-chine to bring comic-strip characters to life, Superman must defeat a conglomeration of villains out of the comics, aided at last by a team of comic-strip heroes. The sequence even contains a poignant allusion to the world outside the comics, for the villainous cartoonist is, as drawn in that next-to-last frame, the spitting image of Joe Shuster, who confesses, "Nobody knows me! I wanted to be a celebrity—the creator of a famous comic strip. But no one would buy my strips."

The rapid shifting back and forth between the "real" world of Metropolis, Clark Kent and the *Daily Planet* and the "fanciful" world of the comics is in this sequence marvelously inventive. (The villain's machine can even reduce a "real" Lois into a two-dimensional cartoon image.) As fact and fiction are intentionally scrambled in the comic book we hold in our hands, we are never quite sure which realm we are in at any given moment. This underscores the ambivalence of Superman/Clark Kent, who himself inhabits both worlds. The final frame shows Clark and Lois back in the office, where she admits, "Every time I look at a comic page I still can't believe my incredible adventures with the strip villains ever happened!" Clark's response? "It's funny—but it's true!"

Paradoxically, unlike the imaginary *Prince Peril*, the sort of strip that would unblinkingly insist on its own reality, the blurring of "fiction" and "reality" in *Superman* helps sustain the reality of our hero. The same might be said of the humor in the comic book (something our serious age tends to forget), which enables us to get a good chuckle and yet keep up at least the *idea* of the existence of these characters. Not so the humor in Swift, Fielding and Joyce, however, which tends to put Gulliver, Tom Jones and Leopold Bloom in a disadvantageous light; in *Superman* the paper-thin hero survives in spite of the comic elements, or

perhaps because of them. Indeed, he plays top banana.

Told he can come back to see the governor in the morning, Superman breaks down the door of the mansion, saying, "I'll see him NOW!" In the midst of some heroism or other, he wryly comments, "Nice workout, I must say!" Appearing before the troops during the war years, he departs rapidly, saying over his shoulder to no one in particular, "I hate to go A.W.O.L. — But this is no time for explanations!" Tossing a powerful land mine out into the atmosphere, Superman muses, "Hmm! That one will change the moon's geography a little!" Such cocksure asides as these span the full 50 years of *Superman* comics, and, typically, the jokes fail to diminish Superman's powers. Indeed, they serve to underscore them.

A few other verbal tricks (from several different writers) help establish the recognizable comic style of *Superman*. There are frequent games with cliches, for example, which are decidely out of sync — and thus refreshingly humorous — in this high-powered strip. Blasting through a wall into a den of thieves, Superman apologizes, "I do hope I'm not butting in!" Banging two villains' heads together, Superman humorously moralizes, "Mustn't steal! It's not nice!" Similarly, interrupting a pair of underwater crooks, Superboy quips, "The party's over! Now you're going bye-bye!"

Perhaps not surprisingly, the pun, considered one of the cheapest but nonetheless most enjoyable brands of verbal humor, appears throughout the series. For example, blasting a wrecking ball to smithereens a split second before it reaches Lois, Superboy crows, "The ball is over!" In the same

episode, when a villain brings the arm of a construction scoop down on him, he smiles in the direction of the reader, hands on hips, and jokes, "This is ONE scoop that doesn't bother me!" At the end of this same story, making good on his promise to buy Lois an ice cream sundae if she gets a byline in the school paper, Clark watches her order two scoops and glumly declares, "Scooped again!" Groaners, sure, and counter to the high drama of the desperate situations in the stories proper; but, like the quippy cliches, the adolescent puns in *Superman* are enjoyable in themselves and serve as useful reminders that these are, after all, the *funnies*!

Close to the comic techniques in *Superman* are those in the Anglo-Saxon *Beowulf*, where the hero, locked in mortal combat with the monster Grendel, yanks off the arm of the beast: "There altogether was Grendel's grasp," says the narrator. Quite a handshake, he seems to be saying, flatly. The understatement here, like the similar understatement in *Superman*, reduces not the hero but the villain. Nor do such jokes steal anything from the heroism just then on display; functioning as asides to the reader, either from the character or some omniscient narrator, these jokes are in effect winks in the audience's direction, a momentary bond between us and the hero. The villain has been excluded.

There are in the *Superman* comics a few comments behind the hero's back, as when an exuberant young Lois tells Clark how wonderful Superboy is and the omniscient narrator editorializes: "Better get used to that, Clark! It will be just the same when you become Superman!" But as we have seen, most of the jokes originate with Superman himself and function as asides to the reader, pointing to an understanding between us, a realization that things are under control and will work out for the best, and suggesting that we may enjoy the excitement without fear that things could ever be otherwise. *We as readers* see past villainy, past imminent disaster, and into a double identity that Lois only suspects. As Clark leaves the theater with Lois at the end of the Superman film, we witness the exchange of winks between Clark and the celluloid hero. It's not simply that we are let in on the jokes; we are repeatedly put in the delightful position of knowing more than the villains, knowing more than Lois, and given the opportunity of being Superman's confidant. (This same effect is created in one of Christopher Reeve's *Superman* films when Clark, in a moment of crisis, glances around in search of a place to change, spots one of those contemporary half-length phone booths, then turns in the direction of the audience and sighs.)

Such disarming intimacies, plus occasional addresses to us in the comic-book stories from the editor ("You guessed it, Dear Reader, this plump fellow is none other than the Toyman!"), are irresistible. In a few issues the reader is even invited to send in a postcard, voting on the outcome of a particular sequence or saying whether or not more appearances of a certain villain are desired. The reader is either Superman's pal or the editor's darling, and I admit it, I'm happy with either role. Any attempt to explain the longevity of *Superman* would have to consider the stories, yes, but also the appeal to generations of READERLY EGOS like mine!

SUPERSTAR, SUPERMOM, SUPER GLUE, SUPERDOOPER, SUPERMAN

by DAVID B. GURALNIK

When Superman first zoomed onto the American scene in 1938, cape streaming, leotards nicely filled, the impact he made upon a Depression-weary, hero-hungry public was so great that many people just take it for granted that his name inspired the many words beginning with *super-* now dotting our linguistic landscape. Well, was this the case? Let's look at some of the facts.

The word *super* is found in ancient Latin as both a preposition and an adverb, meaning variously "over, above, on top (of), beyond." What frequently happens to such

103

particles in many languages is that they also become prefixes—compare, for example, *out*, *over* and *up* in English—and that's what happened to *super*. Classical Latin is rich with such compounds as *supercilium*, meaning "an eyebrow," literally that which is "above the *cilium*, or eyelid." That word entered English as the adjective *supercilious*, describing a facial expression with one raised eyebrow, which reveals a haughty or disdainful attitude. Some other such English borrowings directly from Latin include *superstition* from *superstitio*, meaning "excessive fear of the gods," but literally "a standing still over, as in awe or amazement," *superfluous* from *superfluus*, "overflowing," and *superlative*, a word that in itself describes many of those formed with *super-* and that derives from Latin *superlatus*, the past participle of a verb meaning "to carry beyond." During the Middle English period, a number of other such terms entered our language either right from Latin or, very often, by way of Middle French, a language derived from Latin.

By the middle of the 15th century, *super-* appears as an active prefix used directly in English to fashion neologisms, or coinages. It was used by a number of Elizabethan writers and even more widely after the 17th century. Shakespeare, the great neologizer (more than 1,700 of the 17,677 different words used in his writings were his own creations), coined the verb *supervise*, using it in *Love's Labour's Lost*, in a sense now obsolete, to mean "to look over, or inspect," and some other compounds, including the adjectives *superserviceable* and *supersubtle*, in which *super-* had by now acquired a newer denotation, "much more or greater than is usual; extremely; exceedingly." In the late 19th century, *super-* was adopted by chemists and other scientists as a convenient combining form, often as a correlative to *sub-* (e.g., *supersalt*, a salt with an excess

of acid, as against *subsalt*, a no-longer-used term for a basic salt).

In 1885, the German philosopher Friedrich Nietzsche published his poetical work *Also Sprach Zarathustra* (*Thus Spake Zarathustra*), in which he postulated an idealized, superior, dominating individual, regarded as the goal of the evolutionary struggle for survival. He designated this hypothetical being an *Ubermensch*, translated at that time in English as an *overman*, or occasionally *beyond-man*, and in French as a *sur-homme* or occasionally *superhomme* (French *sur*-derives from Latin *super-* and is the usual prefix, but both are employed in Modern French). Then in 1903, George Bernard Shaw published his *Man and Superman*, a comedy based on the Don Juan legend and expanding upon Shaw's conception of social evolution; that is the earliest citation we have for the English compound *superman*. Shaw's use of the term is clearly in allusion to Nietzsche's conception, and immediately thereafter *superman* became the translation of choice for *Ubermensch*, gradually, however, acquiring the looser, more generalized denotation of "any man with extraordinary powers or abilities."

In an interview with Jerry Siegel and Joe Shuster in the August 1983 number of *NEMO: the classic comics library*, they tell of an early collaboration in a fanzine entitled *Science Fiction*, subtitled "The Advanced Guard of Civilization," they began circa 1933. This, a story by Siegel with illustrations by Shuster, they titled "The Reign of the Superman." In this story "the Superman" (note the use of the article) was a bald-headed villain who looked "a lot like Telly Savalas." A few months later, it occurred to Siegel that "a Superman as a hero rather than a villain might make a great comic strip character." The first effort at such a strip in 1933 was rejected by the publisher to whom it had been submitted, and Shuster tore up

Superman represented an innocent and happy thought about power. It was right for Cleveland and the world then; would that it were right now!

Herbert Gold, novelist

and threw away most of the material. A pencil sketch of the cover survives and was published in the NEMO interview. On it the hero is still referred to as "The Superman" and described as "A GENIUS IN INTEL-LECT—A HERCULES IN STRENGTH—A NEMESIS TO WRONG-DOERS." The first appearance of *Superman* (sans article) in print was in the now landmark *Action Comics* #1 in June 1938, and thereafter the word acquired the secondary meaning of "a man with superhuman powers." One cannot help speculating whether the shift from villain to hero might not have been influenced in part, even if only half-consciously, by Hitler's perverted use of Nietzsche's *Ubermensch* as a basis for the well-publicized Nazi pseudo-racial theories. Two Jewish boys at Glenville High School in Cleveland in the 1930s could not have been entirely unaware of that propaganda.

And that brings us back to the question of whether it may not have been the great popularity of Superman that played the major role in stimulating neologisms formed with *super-* and having the sense of "being one that surpasses all or most others in that class." The evidence for such a supposition is not overwhelming. For one thing, the free use of that prefix in English coinages was already, as we have seen, well-established by 1938. Even the slangy adjective *super* as

a counterword for "exceptionally fine; excellent; outstanding" was a common American usage in the 1920s (isolated instances of such a use go back as far as Dickens' *Pickwick Papers* of 1837). The emphatic reduplication *super-duper*, also written *super-dooper*, however, first appeared in print in 1940. Such American superlatives as *superhighway* (first citation, 1925), *supermarket* (first appearance in print, 1933, but apparently common in oral usage in California in the 1920s; in French it is a *supermarche*, in Spanish, a *supermercado*), *supercolossal* (1934), *supercity* (1925), *superstar* (in the Hollywood sense, 1925), *superstate* (1929) and many others suggest that *Superman*, rather than leading the way up the stream, was actually swimming in a current teeming with such compounds. If anything, Nietzsche's, which is to say Shaw's, neologism may have been the stimulant. Immediately following the appearance of *Man and Superman*, we find *superdramatist* and *supercritic* (both coined in 1903), *superwoman* (as an analogue to *superman* in 1906, but with a new, specialized meaning in recent years: "a woman who successfully combines roles as a career-woman, wife and mother," first cited in 1976), *supertramp* (1908), *Super-Dreadnought* (a ship with armament exceeding that of a Dreadnought, 1909), *super-goddess* (1911), *supernation* (1914), *super-*

patriot (1917) and hundreds of others, mostly nonce formations — that is, coinages having only a one-time use.

It is quite possible, of course, that the appearance of *Superman* reinforced the popularity of *super-*, for the coining continued unabated, with such terms as *superbomb* (an early designation for the fission bomb in 1940, then later applied to the even more devastating fusion, or hydrogen, bomb), *superpower* (as describing the U.S. and the U.S.S.R., 1944), *superjet* (1958), *superrich* (1969), *Super Glue* (a trademark, 1977), just to offer a few examples. The first championship playoff game between the two major football conferences was held on January 15, 1967, following the 1966 season. The moguls of professional football were casting about for a suitable name befitting such a great media event. Although unauthenticated, the accepted story is that Lamar Hunt, founder of the American Football League, overheard his daughter refer to a small rubber ball with an unusual capacity for rebounding as her 'super ball' and that immediately suggested to him *Super Bowl*, the name that with its imposing Roman numerals continues to designate that annual happening. The Yale Bowl had by 1914 made *bowl* a synonym for a football field, and the Pasadena Rose Bowl Game of 1917 had made *bowl game* the popular term for such a postseason encounter.

A super example of a word formed with *super-* is the fanciful coinage popularized in a song of the 1964 film *Mary Poppins* and used chiefly by children to suggest the ultimate in approval, *supercalifragilisticexpialidocious*. A lawsuit was brought against the producers of the movie by two songwriters of unpublished songs composed in 1949 and 1951, having titles similar to, but not identical with, that of the *Mary Poppins* song. The court, however, ruled against the plaintiffs, partly because the songs themselves were dissimilar and partly because of sworn testimony of even earlier oral uses of the term.

Superman, inspiring as he did a number of imitators in the comic strip and animated cartoon industries, is clearly responsible for at least one usage patterned after his own sobriquet. In the 1960s, a series of comic books about a whole stable of characters with *superhuman* (first citation, 1633) qualities used in combatting crime, injustice and evil was brought out with the overall title of *Superheroes*. In the more general sense, however, of some public figure greatly admired for certain accomplishments or talents, *superhero* goes back to at least 1917, with *superheroine* following shortly thereafter.

As a productive prefix, *super-* has by no means lost any of its appeal or utility, and the citation files in dictionary offices are bulging with relatively recent coinages employing that prefix, hundreds of them nonce formations that will probably never find their way onto the pages of dictionaries. Scientists continue to recognize the prefix as a particularly serviceable one, and among the neologisms of the past decade or so are such formations as *superalloy* (one that can withstand temperatures of up to 1,800 degrees), *superdense* (as descriptive of the core material of a quasar), *superovulation* (the production of more than the normal number of ova at one time — an objective of the bioengineers working with farm animals), *superbug* (another bioengineering construction, a bacterium produced by gene-splitting, that consumes and digests petroleum quickly, as after an oil spill, but also applied to a strain of insect that has developed resistance to insecticides), and *superrat*, one that has developed an immunity to the usual rat poisons and can pass that immunity on to its offspring.

Among the more general terms of recent

coinage are *supercentenarian*, a person who, despite *superbugs* and *superrats*, has managed to reach an age of well over 100 years; *superdean*, a college official who exercises hegemony over other, presumably lesser, deans; *supermom*, an idealized mother, often a *superwoman* (see above) who is particularly adept at her parenting role; and *superterrorists*, those who, it is projected, will carry out their antisocial activities with atomic weapons and against whom perhaps even Superman would be unavailing.

FEMALE MEETS SUPERMALE

by JOANNA CONNORS

Before we talk about Lois Lane and Superman, I think it might be a good idea for you to go back and reread Freud's *Interpretation of Dreams*. Could you do that, please? Turn to the part where Freud discusses typical dreams; dreams almost everyone has dreamed in the same manner. He talks about dreaming of being naked in public, dreams of the death of a relative and dreams of — flying.

I went back to the *Interpretation* after reading through years and years of Superman comics. I was new to Superman; when

I was a girl, Superman and other heroes were for boys. Archie and romance comics were for girls. I remembered the television shows with George Reeves and Noel Neill, but only vaguely. Because my father worked for a newspaper, I usually spent the half-hour looking for holes in the *Daily Planet* setup: I thought the paper and reporters had been created with little attention to accuracy. I had marginal interest in the Clark Kent/Lois Lane/Superman triangle.

Of course, that's what caught my attention this time around. As the world changed, they remained the same. For someone interested in men and women, these two (or three) were like an unopened tomb to an archaeologist.

But we're getting away from Freud (if that's ever possible). So: As I read these comic books, I kept wondering why Lois Lane loved Superman.

I see that the guy has a wonderful ability to save Lois Lane from terrible predicaments—which Lois has a wonderful ability to create, by the way. I see that he is an astonishing physical specimen. I see that he possesses the qualities a girl might enter on a computer dating form for her ideal mate: he's kind, generous, thoughtful, self-confident, trustworthy, able to leap tall buildings in a single bound. You get the idea.

Still, Superman seemed to take the quality of respect a little far. Beyond her many dreams (in one Lois Lane comic book from the '70s, Lois dreams that she becomes "Mrs. Superman," and says, "Only you, Superman, could take me to the moon") and beyond scenes that Superman always erases from her memory, the only physical contact they share is when he's flying her to safety.

Really, now. Fifty years of loving devotion for that?

Then I saw *Superman, the Movie*, released in 1978. If you saw it, you probably haven't forgotten the sequence in which Superman takes Lois Lane for a spin in the air. I don't know if Mario Puzo, who wrote the original story on which the screenplay was based, had looked up what Freud had to say about flying, but that flight was so—well, it was erotic and amusing and utterly charming at the same time—that I recalled the "take me to the moon" dream and went immediately to my old college textbooks to look up dreams and flying.

What Freud actually said about flying may surprise you. It did me. Like most people who took "Intro to Psych" in college, I pretty much remembered the flying-as-sex explanation and forgot his primary interpretation.

Freud first links dreams of flying to childhood games, when adults swing children through the air or make them "fly" by running across the room with them on outstretched arms. Children feel remarkably joyful and free during these games, he writes, and when they grow up their relive those feelings in dreams. The only problem is, the adult mind takes what Freud calls "voluptuous" feelings of excitement and turns them into feelings of anxiety.

Later on in the book—when he's discussing a patient who had recurring dreams of his teeth being pulled—Freud returns to the theme of flying. Here he does discuss the erotic nature of these dreams: He writes that some dreamers seem to be saying, "If only I were a little bird!" Which, the translator of my edition explains, is a reference to the German words "vogel," meaning bird, and the slang word "vogeln," meaning to copulate. Freud then gives a nod to colleagues who invariably attach an erotic interpretation to dreams of flying.

OK? Found the passages? It's easy to become distracted in *Interpretation of Dreams*. I had no idea dreams of tooth extraction were common, for instance.

Maybe this flying connection was obvious to everyone else, even from the comic books—"Yeah, Superman and Lois *fly*, nudge, nudge, wink, wink." It at least explains those 50 years of love and puts the "super" back in Superman.

What interests me more, however, is Freud's primary interpretation. And to understand that, we have to look at Lois Lane and Superman not as heroes, but as man and woman.

Under the surface of super powers and arch-villains and heroic deeds, what Superman is really all about is the battle of the sexes. This is just what George Bernard Shaw was writing about in *Man and Superman*, and I think Jerry Siegel and Joe Shuster were well aware of the play. They titled an early comic on which they collaborated "Man or Superman."

The play has more in common with our Man of Steel than the name. In *Man and Superman*, Shaw makes his female protagonist the pursuer, the man the pursued. And he makes them universal: His Ann is meant to represent Woman, John is meant to be Man. (As we can view Superman and Lois—super man and super woman.)

Ann and John talk a lot about the "Life Force," a sort of existential kryptonite; love; or sex.

As baldly as Lois Lane, Ann makes a play for marriage.

"I will not marry you," John says in the last act.

"Oh, you will, you will," Ann replies.

After a few similar sallies back and forth, John persuades Ann he means what he says.

"Well. I made a mistake," she says sadly. "You do not love me."

"It is false," he says. "I love you. The Life Force enchants me: I have the whole world in my arms when I clasp you. But I am fighting for my freedom, for my honor, for my self, one and indivisible."

And Truth, Justice and the American Way? Does this not sound familiar? Just such notions prevent Superman from marrying Lois, the woman he loves.

Shaw's hero John refuses to marry because he believes marriage to be evil: "profanation of the sanctuary of my soul, violation of my manhood, sale of my birthright, shameful surrender, ignominious capitulation, acceptance of defeat."

This sounds familiar, too, so let us examine it.

First, notice how John mentions the "sanctuary of my soul"? Does that sound anything like a Fortress of Solitude?

Most men just call it a den.

Superman didn't always have a Fortress of Solitude. He got it in the 1950s, which fits, since most researchers place the invention of the den at about the time families moved from city apartments to suburban ranch houses, which occurred in the '50s. Superman's super-maleness makes his fortress a sort of super-den—no imitation maple panelling and remnant carpeting here, but walls of ice and rock, a den situated in the Arctic Circle and virtually inaccessible to mere mortals, especially women. (Arch-criminal Lex Luthor does find it in the '50s, and eventually Superman allows Lois a peek into it. Does it come as a surprise to you that every time Lois visits the fortress, near-disaster follows?)

The furnishings of these dens don't matter, though. Men don't even really need them, as Shaw, writing in 1902, was well aware. He called it a sanctuary of the soul, which women have known all along is the place into which men truly retreat. At their father's knee, girls learn that men's hearts are their fortresses.

Consider Superman. Since the '30s, his

110

personality has changed very little. As Clark Kent he went from newspaper reporter to television reporter. But other than that, things have changed around him while he stayed the same: honorable, strong, agile and single.

He loves Lois Lane, yet he has never told her the most basic facts about himself. He has never revealed himself to her. He has never, as far as I can see in the comics and movies, told her he loves her. (In the '50s newspaper strips he married Lois, but eventually that plot twist is revealed to have been just a dream. I wonder what Freud would say about these dreams.)

The "super" in Superman's name clearly refers not only to his superhuman powers, but to the fact that this guy is the exaggerated embodiment of what Tina Turner calls a typical male.

It's true. Look at his almost pathological fear of commitment. (Shaw's hero calls it "ignominious capitulation, shameful surrender.") He strings Lois along for 50 years, always holding out for her the hope that he will, finally, ask her to be Mrs. Superman. In story after story, she dreams of marriage. In some episodes, she even dreams she has a superbaby with him; she resorts to adoption in the story, "Marry Me, Superman!"

Poor Lois: If we are to believe *Newsweek* magazine and Phil Donahue, at this point in her life she has a greater chance of being killed by a terrorist than she has of being a bride. And Lois *has* been taken hostage by terrorists, countless times! This doesn't look good.

What prevents Superman from marrying Lois, besides honor? Superman *says* he's afraid that his wife would be instant prey to his enemies. She could be kidnapped, drugged, held for ransom, on and on. The fact that as his girlfriend Lois already has been drugged, kidnapped, held for ransom and on and on seems not to bother our Man of Steel.

The real reason he won't marry her, I've decided, is more or less the reason your typical Wall Street investment banker puts off his sweetie: his career. Superman is a workaholic. Work—fighting the never-ending battle for Truth, Justice and the American Way—takes precedence over everything else in his life. (This does not escape Lois' attention: In a 1975 story titled "Who was that Dog I Saw you with Last Night?" Superman and Lois are on a date when the Man of Tomorrow sees a fire. "Uh-oh," he says. "Looks like—" Lois chimes in, "Yes! I've heard it before…a job for Superman!" Later, the story continues, "as a stood-up, and slightly peeved, girl reporter dashes over," Lois somewhat sarcastically calls, "Superman! Remember me?")

And what about Superman's alter ego, Clark Kent, always eager to please Lois? Superman/Clark wants Lois to accept him for what he is deep down: a meek and bumbling, but good-hearted human. He wants her to love him not for his extraordinary powers, but to love him as an ordinary man, for himself, the way wealthy men are said to be searching for a woman who will love them for themselves, not for their money and success.

But Lois is blinded by Superman; she cannot see through the disguise to realize that the mild-mannered reporter she treats so callously is her true love.

The comics would lead you to believe that this is Lois' great flaw: She is unable to really see—and know—the man she loves. (Which many men argue is the problem with many women.) *She* is the only one who prevents her becoming Mrs. Superman.

But let's assume Lois did one day open her eyes to Clark Kent's solid qualities and fell in love with him. He still wouldn't be able to marry her, because if they were to marry, he would be unable to keep his secret very long. (Just taking her home—to the Fortress of Solitude—would give him away.) To Lois, that would be a scoop.

Which leads me to wonder whether Lois Lane doesn't have the same problem Superman has. Her own career proves an obstacle to their marriage. So perhaps we're looking not only at a duel of the sexes a la *Man and Superman*, but at a duel of the two-career couple, a la *Adam's Rib*, in which Katherine Hepburn and Spencer Tracy, as lawyers on opposing sides in a murder trial, find that the competition they feel in their careers makes their marriage rocky.

Of course, Lois lacks the sophistication of a Katherine Hepburn. Her desires are transparent: a scoop and marriage.

Sometimes the scoop wins out: In the 1970 story "The Man Who was Clark Kent's Double," Lois falls in love with a Clark Kent look-alike (the only difference is he's "manly," as she says). But she loses him when her curiosity overcomes her, and she discovers a secret he was trying to keep. After the dream-man angrily leaves her, Clark comes upon Lois in the *Daily Planet* newsroom. "Lois! What are you so unhappy about?" he asks. "I...I'm not (sniff) unhappy!" Lois answers. ' 'I'm (sob) overjoyed! Why shouldn't I be? I...I have a (sob) s-scoop!"

"Poor Lois," Clark says to himself. "Her curiosity got her a story...but lost what she wanted most. I wish I could help...but even Superman can't mend a broken love...or a broken heart!"

Lois also seems quite willing to sacrifice Superman's love to get the scoop of the century: Superman's secret identity.

With mere mortal men, Lois suffers no fools. Even in the early comics in the '30s,

when few women had such glamorous careers and fewer were willing to compete with men, Lois gets into unbridled scoop-races with male reporters, particularly Clark Kent. In the very first comic of 1938, Lois' first words are a cutting comment to Clark after he shyly asks her for a date: "I suppose I'll give you a break...for a change." When he proves to be a weakling on the date, she leaves him with "You're a spineless, unbearable coward!" Hardly an auspicious beginning, but it set the stage for her competitive attitude toward Clark.

Actually, the stage was set when they were kids: The first *Adventures of Superboy* comic shows "the historic moment...the first meeting of Lois and Clark" as adolescents, a meeting during which Lois thinks to herself, "Golly! He's so unexciting!" They meet when both are selected to work as cub reporters at the *Daily Planet*, and the editor (not yet Perry White) sets up a competition: The first one who brings in a front-page story gets a front-page byline.

This is Lois' immediate reaction: "I'll win...naturally! Any girl is superior to a boy...that is, any boy but Superboy...and you're no Superboy!"

While most girls drop such ideas as they become women—or at least they appeared to do so in the '30s—Lois kept it up, competing with Clark as an adult to get the coveted scoop even when it endangered her. After all, Superman was always there to save her.

A lot of women today would probably frown on Lois' constant need for rescue by Superman. She does sometimes bring to mind the women in horror movies who never remember to turn on the lights when they enter a dark house.

But Lois is different: She needs saving because she has a certain courage, a fool's courage sometimes, but nonetheless courage. And she has pride. What other woman

Visions of having superpowers come to me quite often. When I sat in Attica prison, representing the inmates who had taken over that institution's D-Yard for four days in 1971, I wished for the strength to tear down the walls and set the captives free. The same thought came to me when, as the chief negotiator for the Native Americans who had seized the hamlet of Wounded Knee in South Dakota two years later, I watched the encircling hordes of federal agents and longed for the wherewithal to push them back from their perimeter. Many times I have sat frustrated in one courtroom or another. If only I could find a convenient telephone booth, spin off my single-breasted suit and carry off my client far beyond the reach of leg irons, handcuffs and prison cells. Messrs. Shuster and Siegel, where are you when we need you most?

William M. Kunstler, attorney

of her time would have survived in such a tough profession (she's a news reporter, remember, not a writer on the society pages), going head-to-head with super criminals and, later, arch-villains?

Superman seems to be equally charmed and exasperated by this quality in Lois. He loves her spunk, but the spunk also leads to irritating scrapes. ("What a genius you are, Lois, for getting into trouble!" he says in a comic book from 1939, and, a few books later, "Here she goes again! What a mess! When'll I ever get time to do anything but rescue *her*?"

Still, at this point in their relationship, Superman seems delighted, overall, with

Lois Lane.

By the '60s, Lois had changed from a smart, tough girl reporter—in her first incarnation, she looked and sounded like a beautiful, sassy Claudette Colbert in the 1934 movie *It Happened One Night*—into a girl bent on marriage, a girl who looks like an ordinary sorority member and sounds like Miss Piggy. If Superman hardly changed, Lois Lane changed for the worse, making Superman lose his delight in her.

In the October 1961 issue of *Lois Lane* comics, Superman is transported to the year 2961, where he meets the Lois Lane of the future, the great-great-great-great-great granddaughter of Lois Lane. This Lois has

113

superpowers like Superman's and wears a futuristic costume, but her attitude is straight out of the past. When Superman insists on saving her, when she could save herself, she lets him, saying to herself, "But only because you're a man and even we 30th-century women find it smart to let men feel they're needed." Later, as they fly high into an atmosphere in which neither can talk, Lois finds herself unable to brake her super-speed. "If only he could tell me how to stop myself!" she thinks. "A girl *does* need a man after all!"

As the feminist movement took hold in the late '60s and early '70s, Superman not only lost his delight in Lois, he lost his patience with her—with the girl reporter who had been emancipated all those years!

In fact, Superman became downright hostile toward her. As did the *Superman* writers. Out of a random selection of comics from the early '70s, fully a third deal with Superman violently punishing Lois Lane in some way. In 1970, *Lois Lane* comics featured Superman prosecuting Lois for the murder of Lana Lang—for which Lois could get the death penalty. Later that year, the comic featured a cover with Superman holding Lois' body and saying, "Yes, Lana.. it's true! I killed Lois Lane!" In 1973 a cover featured Superman flying away from Lois, who is strapped to the front of a runaway truck. "You wanted to be with me to the end, Lois," he says. "This is it! So long!" Underneath a cover line reads, "Lois Lane never expected to be Superman's victim!"

During these troubled years, Superman alternately marvels and complains about Lois' status. "Lois is getting more liberated by the minute!" he says in 1972.

It's true. Losing her sorority-girl personality, Lois gradually becomes something of a human super-woman, fighting crime with only a little help from her friend. In the 1972 issue in which Superman remarks on her

liberation, for instance, Lois stows away aboard a space capsule and, alone in space, fights the evil henchmen of the secret criminal organization, the 100. When she finally attracts Superman's attention (by skywriting his "S" emblem with the capsule), she has already dispatched one man with a gun.

By this time, Lois has quit the *Daily Planet* and become a free-lance reporter. She lives with three roommates and actually does social things with them (though she still carries a torch for Superman, she doesn't mention marriage nearly as often). Even her competition with Clark Kent seems to be at bay.

Again demonstrating an ability to stay a quick step behind the trends of the day, by the '80s Lois Lane is offering Superman white wine and brie ("I never really acquired a taste for brie," Superman apologizes) and talking less of marriage and more of a ... relationship. Her career has become ever more important (she's won the Pulitzer Prize), which impresses that '80s kind of guy, Superman. "She's quite a woman, Lois Lane," he muses after their first interview, in the revisionist history of *Superman* begun by DC COMICS in 1986. "Quite a reporter, too!"

In the yuppie decade, Lois Lane finally decides to break up with Superman because, as a 1986 issue of *Lois Lane* comics puts it, "One day it didn't seem to be working anymore. They had gotten too close. It was too easy to get hurt. To misinterpret the moves. So they called it quits." In that issue, a two-parter on missing children, Superman doesn't even make an appearance. And the only relationship with which Lois deals is the one with her sister. Lois and Superman's duel of the sexes is the true never-ending battle.

But what of Freud's theory of flying? Remember the two interpretations—the erotic, and the one about flying reminding

114

the adult mind about the joy and freedom of childhood?

I think it comes down to this: Attractive as Superman is sexually — the possibilities must occur to most women — Lois Lane finds him attractive because he represents freedom. Freedom from a conventional life. Freedom from the roles women are expected to play. Freedom, in flying, from the gravity that pulls on humans.

Perhaps it's better that they never marry. The first thing Superman would probably do would be to settle Lois into the Fortress of Solitude, where she would finally discover that, super powers and all, Superman is a typical male.

POP GOES THE HERO

by DAVID GALLOWAY

My last encounter with Superman, in the summer of 1985, was on the high, sun-sloped plains near Avila. There, where Theresa nurtured her heavenly visions, the Man of Steel rippled his pectorals and leaped heavenward with a single bound. Oblivious to miracles and timetables, the bus swayed on toward Madrid. Whether the on-board video showed part one or two or three of the latest Superman film saga was never clear; entire segments vanished in bursts of sunshine or blasts of static. Still, the components were familiar enough to lifelong

acquaintances—including the damp adoration in Lois Lane's basset-eyed gaze and her murmured praise: "Bueno, bueno, bueno. Bueno, Superman." Senor Kent fumbled for his spectacles.

It is little wonder that I cannot date my first encounter with the Man of Steel, for I was scarcely more than a year old when he made his first printed appearance. He was, simply and obligingly, always there—as integral and essential to my childhood as Hershey's Kisses, roasted marshmallows, pin-on chameleons, earmuffs and scuffed knees. And just when I foolishly fancied I had put away such childish things, he reentered my life at a single bound—soaring across the improbable landscape of a show window at Bonwit Teller's. It was there, in April of 1961, that a young commercial artist named Andy Warhol hung his homage to Superman amid flowery spring fashions. With a mighty PUFF of his superbreath, the Man of Steel extinguished a forest fire, while clouds of smoke billowed around him.

Though Warhol had been painting seriously for several years, this was the first public exhibition of the results—a full year before the "scandalous" show of *Campbell's Soup Cans* at the Ferus Gallery in Los Angeles. It was, perhaps, an improbable site for launching an aesthetic revolution, but history has endowed the event (like so many Warhol events and non-events) with its own poetic logic. Despite its tentative British beginnings, Pop Art was the discovery (and celebration) of indigenous American motifs—not the local color of Benson or Wyeth, but the garish images of the mass media. Comic strips and consumer goods, film and television personalities, traffic signs and

neon and billboards became the sources of a vigorous, irreverent pictorial vocabulary. Above all, the artificial dichotomies of "high" and "popular" culture were shaken to their fusty foundations.

How appropriate, then, that one of the most popular and mass-produced of all American "folk heroes," the immigrant Superman, should have lent the movement such a mighty PUFF. For the record, however, it is not Andy Warhol but Roy Lichtenstein who is commonly credited with introducing comic-strip figures—Nancy, Donald Duck, Mickey Mouse—into painting. The first were intended to decorate his children's nursery, but in creating them Lichtenstein felt a tremendous relief at working without "the weight of art history" on his shoulders. A third-generation Abstract Expressionist, Lichtenstein began to introduce "hidden comic images" into his serious canvases as well. To stress the secondhand, printed sources of his oeuvre, he was soon rendering them in the "Ben Day dots" used for newspaper reproductions. Warhol saw those early works stacked in the Manhattan office of the Castelli Gallery in 1960, and they gave him the courage to ask Castelli's assistant, Ivan Karp, to have a look at his own diverse efforts.

Karp quickly sorted out the canvases based on "found" mass-media images as the best. Irving Blum, owner of the Ferus Gallery, did not agree: "Irving was one of the first people Ivan had brought to my studio," Warhol later recalled, "and when he saw my Superman, he'd laughed. But it was different the next year; after he saw that Castelli had taken on Lichtenstein, he came back and offered me a show." Lichtenstein's continuing exploration of comic-strip motifs discouraged Warhol from further experiments in that direction, but Superman had pointed the way. The significance of that painting cannot be measured in its "banal" source alone. The clear, strong, simplified drawing style suggested a new graphic technique to Warhol, himself one of the great draftsmen of the century, whose earlier "blotted" style had conspicuous baroque overtones. (*Superman* was painted in 1960, and the following year Warhol produced what remained his most distilled, elegantly reductionist drawings, as illustrations for *The Amy Vanderbilt Cookbook*.)

For Lichtenstein, too, the comics proved a powerful stylistic influence. Coincidentially, but once more with persuasive poetic logic, Lichtenstein had spent his apprentice years in Cleveland, like Superman illustrator Joe Shuster. After his studies at Ohio State University on the GI Bill of Rights, Lichtenstein set up an atelier in Cleveland, but worked there (when he was not painting houses for an income) in the then-fashionable abstract style. The graphic power of the comics was a discovery that followed his move to New York in 1957. For both Warhol and Lichtenstein, the adoption of mass-media imagery brought a new awareness of commercial (as opposed to "fine arts") techniques — the printer's dots in Lichtenstein's canvases, the photo-silkscreens used for most of Warhol's works after 1962. Its vulgar, representational subject matter alone is insufficient to define Popism; technique is even more crucial to the cool, distanced approach of its "hard-core" practitioners. It definitively separates the achievements of "Andy" and "Tom" (those comic book names) from those, say, of Robert Rauschenberg or Jasper Johns, with whom they sometimes share common populist sources. This is not a question of quality but of kind: Johns and Rauschenberg never abandoned

the elegant, eloquent painterly gesture. Warhol surpressed it almost entirely, while Lichtenstein studiously eliminated every trace of individual "signature."

In the Bonwit *Superman* Warhol had not yet achieved the calculated flatness of the *Campbell's Soup Cans*. There was still an echo of Abstract Expressionist antecedents in the thin paint that dribbled down the canvas. But where the prevailing school stressed composition at the expense of subject, Warhol had placed an instantly recognizable, heroically proportioned figure squarely in the foreground. And, like the timid Clark Kent metamorphosing into the Man of Steel, Warhol was about to emerge as *the* superstar of the transatlantic art scene. In the process, he set about reinventing his own past to account for his new, improbable role on the planet Earth. Biographers will long puzzle over the date (August 6, 1927 or August 8, 1931) and place (Pittsburgh or Philadelphia) of his birth, and whether his father — either a miner or a construction worker — was named Andrew or James. Perhaps, in giving such contradictory details, Warhol was attempting to disguise the fact that he was yet another rocket-launched figure from Krypton. His public-public life (as opposed to his private-public, public-private and private-private lives) often seemed to have the suspenseful but simplified contours of comic-strip narration. Even an assassination attempt would make its way into the scenario.

While Warhol seemed to grasp the hidden riches of popular culture intuitively, contemporaries like Claes Oldenburg, Tom Wesselmann, Jim Dine and Roy Lichtenstein were frequently more intellectual in their approach. Lichtenstein argued that the comics interested him primarily for their abstract, compositional properties, and not for their content. It is true that discussions of Pop Art are likely to lay undue stress on the

I am a fan of anybody who can make his living in his underwear.

David Mamet, playwright

movement's commonplace themes, too little on their rendering. Nonetheless, there is a dramatic contrast in the motifs chosen by Warhol and Lichtenstein: The former always showed a preference for cult figures, while the latter repeatedly selected images of teary, heartbroken females or valiant but anonymous soldiers. Warhol's *Superman* was the forerunner of a celebrity gallery that would eventually include Elvis Presley and Mick Jagger, Jackie Kennedy, Marilyn Monroe, Goethe, Mao, Uncle Sam and, at the end of his life, the reigning queens of the world. However explicit the source of such portraits, they are never so literal as they appear in the moment of viewer recognition. They are "transformed" through unconventional color, through the imperfect registration of silkscreens, through gestural amendments or merely through scale. Even the tongue-in-cheek literalness of *Black Bean Soup* is contradicted by the sheer monumentality of the image.

This aggrandizing of the original has much to do with the shock effect prompted by such early works as *Superman*. Even the most literal—*Before and After* or *Dance Diagram*—have something to say about the transfiguration inherent in the act (and choice and nature) of painting itself. The Bonwit Teller display of 1961 included five paintings, and four of them dealt with the theme of metamorphosis: a bodybuilding advertisement, before-and-after views of a woman's nose, Superman and Popeye. To

don a costume or down a can of spinach and assume new, superhuman powers; to achieve beauty through plastic surgery, a new hair style, bodybuilding or cosmetics: Such American Dream transformations were the recurrent subjects of Warhol's paintings in the early 1960s. The titles speak for themselves: *Wigs, Dr. Scholl's Corns, Strong Arms and Broads, Eight Points Program, Make Him Want You, Batman, Before and After, Saturday's Popeye, Do It Yourself*.

Their creator was well on the way to his own ultimate transformation into one of the most celebrated and photographed media personalities of the decade. He had long since evolved from the shy, pasty, pimply Andrew Warhola, son of a Czech immigrant, into the fey and fanciful commercial artist, Andy Warhol. With silver hair, black leather and wraparound sunglasses, he would soon become a symbol of the sexual-social revolution of the 1960s. If he never again chose Superman as his subject, Warhol created an entire galaxy of superstars (including transvestites like Candy Darling and Holly Woodlawn), whom he "immortalized" in impromptu films. I do not know Warhol's own youthful fantasies about the Man of Steel, but the muscular favorites of the Factory days on East 47th—Joe Dallesandro, Joe Spencer, Tom Hompertz—suggest they were not radically different from my own.

Despite his cultivated androgyne image and his repeated stress on the avoidable

119

inconvenience of love affairs, Warhol's "classic" work was charged with erotic energy. Portraits of Mick Jagger or Marilyn Monroe were studies of sex symbols; the Velvet Underground that Warhol promoted was an explosion of orgiastic sound; and his films made sex explicit even before Hollywood rediscovered the box-office appeal of the double bed. So it hardly seems farfetched to imagine that Warhol shared my own fleshly yearnings for Krypton's survivor. And he inadvertently brought about a reconciliation with my childhood hero. That achievement is but a small, intensely private part of the immense debt I owe to Warhol's visionary genius.

The subjective note, however, often carries its own objective lessons, and my romance with Superman—in essence, perhaps, no different from Warhol's—is inseparable from my art-historical view of the Pop revolution. But the romance itself began, of course, with the comics—even more tantalizing because they were forbidden. Then came the voice of radio's Bud Collyer plunging from tremulous tenor ("This is a job....") to baritone butch ("...FOR SUPERMAN!"). Weaned on tales of transformation—warty frog to handsome prince, pumpkin to coach-in-four, scruffy duckling to preening swan—I had no difficulty accepting the split-second metamorphosis. That the wan and weedy youth on the beach (the one who always had sand kicked in his face) would slowly swell to macho proportions and someday thrash the beach-bully: That seemed utterly, laughably preposterous. Billy Batson's "Shazam!" was far more credible than Charles Atlas's hollow promises.

As a certified bookworm, I, of course, identified with the sand-sprayed victim, but found my own subtle way to deal with Memphis bullies who lurked in ambush somewhere (anywhere, it seemed, and everywhere) between Messick School and Felix Avenue. Grasping the leather straps stoutly in my hands, I pummeled them with my roller skates. In the cavalier South, such weapons were considered unsporting, but this did not diminish their effectiveness. Is it any wonder, then, that the very wellsprings of empathy pumped and throbbed for Clark Kent? Like me, he was jeered as clumsy, sissified, weak-kneed, yellow-livered, absent-minded, and he wore GLASSES! How Miss Cole's pupils guffawed when I first entered the second-grade classroom with that dread accessory. Four-eyes sometimes forgot his lunch but never, ever his roller skates. We had our little secrets, Clark and I. (And when my parents divorced, I fancied that kindly old Jonathan and Martha Kent might adopt me.)

It was, in short, a complex, intimate relationship that early assumed an erotic dimension as well. In secret I sewed a fraying letter "S" onto an old jersey pajama suit, confiscated a red bathtowel and slipped away to the nearby woods. I pursued no dastardly villains but reveled in the half-naked feel of pajamas beneath the open sky, in broad daylight, and lying in the grass imagined Superman's pulsing thighs hovering over me. The forbidden world of comics thus acquired a fresh, engrossing dimension of taboo. Batman and Robin suggested nimble variations on the theme, but Superman remained my own tender, indigo-haired ravager. For his sake there were no limits to industry or ingenuity. With misshapen, hand-woven potholders sold door to door, funds were raised for a subscription to *Action Comics* and membership in the Superman Club, complete with certificate, button and decoder. (There might, at any time, be a message just for me.)

Together, my hero and I fought for Truth, Justice and the American Way. He sank Japanese destroyers, plucked Nazi bombers from the sky, brushed enemy tanks from their tracks. I dutifully hauled wagonloads

full of newspapers, stomped tin cans into glossy rectangles, peeled and balled the tinfoil linings from cigarette packages, hoed a victory garden, assembled Red Cross gift boxes, knitted woolen squares to be stitched into blankets for the troops and stirred saffron-colored powder into margarine until it blossomed into buttery peaks. And I dutifully saved my milk money for the stamp lady. Together, Superman and I won the war, but we lost the peace. As the first pink eruptions of adolescence crossed my brow and sunny woodland forays had turned to damp nightly frenzies, my hero perpetrated the ultimate, hitherto unthinkable betrayal: He married the meddlesome, moon-faced girl-reporter, Lois Lane. The year was 1949, and the connubial bliss was brief, for the following year the would-be Mrs. Superman awoke to discover (like Pam Ewing in her time) that it was all A DREAM.

For me it had been a nightmare—a trauma of separation and loss that not even television's Superman-impersonator George Reeves could fully mend. There were moments, to be sure, when a come-hither twinkle in his eye transformed the porthole-shaped screen of Zenith's futuristic TV, but this was not my future. In long shots, Reeves's tights could often be seen to BAG at the knees. No, the Superman of my childhood was beyond recall, and the string-bundled stacks of *Action Comics* and *Superman* comics were one day trundled away, without a tear, to a wastepaper drive. Little did I know that we would make a new beginning at Bonwit Teller's—one that helped to write a new chapter in American art as well. Whether I actually saw that historic window or only imagine it now, with the faded color

photographs before me, is irrelevant. I was often in New York in 1961, but jazzy Bonwit's displays were not my customary visual fare in those graduate-school days. My real infatuation with Warhol's work dates to the opening of Cleveland's New Gallery of Contemporary Art in 1968.

Long before Warhol's death, however, I had come to see *Superman* as an important clue to a personality repeatedly described as enigmatic, willful, mercurial. But the data is incomplete without the knowledge that in 1960 Warhol also painted a companion piece to *Superman*—a portrait of Clark Kent that remained in the artist's private collection until his death and, to my knowledge, has never been photographed or exhibited. One imagines it wedged beneath a mattress or stashed at the back of a closet for a quarter century, shrouded by faded '60s gear, rather like the hidden countenance of Dorian Grey. Clark Kent to Superman, Andrew Warhola to Andy Warhol: How that transformation progressed can be seen in the series of Byronic self-portraits the artist began in 1966 and exhibited for the last time in London's Gallery Offay in 1986. The metamorphoses continued: painter to filmmaker to rock impresario, publisher, novelist, businessman, historian, legend. But even before the end of the swinging decade, the rowdy, randy effervescence of the founding years had dimmed. Unlike the Man of Steel, Warhol could not stop bullets, and in the summer of 1968 two of them penetrated his stomach, liver, spleen, esophagus and both lungs. They were fired by Valerie Solanis, founder of the Society for Cutting Up Men: S.C.U.M. (Resemblances to villainous creations by Jerry Siegel and Joe Shuster were purely coincidental.)

In retrospect, that event, too, seems redolent with symbolism—a bizarre apostrophe to the violence inherent in the flower-powered 1960s. The decade began with Warhol at Bonwit's, John Fitzgerald Kennedy in the White House, but it would find its immolation in race riots, assassinations and the garish technicolor of napalm. Even Superman could not extinguish that blaze with a mighty PUFF. Yet the schizophrenic decade returned to me the heroes of my childhood. Overnight, it seemed, trash and trivia had become High Culture, the forbidden fruits were now Haute Cuisine, and the jeans for which I yearned as a boy were Haute Couture. We had come of age, America and I, and we shared a shock of recognition—above all, of self-recognition. While we were still dizzily appraising the territory, savvy European businessmen like Count Panza di Biumo, Peter Ludwig and Karl Stroher were already building premier collections of the new American art. And *Superman* was snapped up by ball-bearings playboy Gunther Sachs. He, of course, would never know the sweet intimacy of a boyhood friendship with the Man of Steel, "all in color for a dime," or the joys of a belated reconciliation with Pop's most powerful hero. I had a far other Superman than his, and with the mellowing of time I would even forgive Lois Lane her unscrupulous dream.

ST. CLARK OF KRYPTON

by EDWARD MEHOK

Seven centuries ago children, huddled around the fire in the huts of medieval Europe, were enthralled by marvelous stories of men and women gifted with extraordinary powers who waged a never-ending battle against the perpetrators of evil and injustice. Their eyes grew wide as they were told the story of a man who was taken captive by a cruel tyrant. Determined that his prisoner should not be rescued, the evil ruler had a deep pit dug within the stout walls of his keep. The prisoner was shackled and lowered into the pit. Over the mouth of the

123

pit, the tyrant ordered to be built a heavy wooden ark, into which he placed 1,000 armed soldiers.

Having completed these fortifications, the tyrant retired, confident and secure that he had outwitted any who would rescue the poor man. But the prisoner's abject cries were heard at a great distance by his hero, and suddenly he was there in the night. With superhuman strength he overturned the heavy ark in which the soldiers were sleeping, trapping the confused, scrambling army beneath it. Then, surrounded by a mysterious shining light, the one who had come descended into the dark pit, burst the prisoner's chains and bore the man away in his arms, returning him again to his home.

Thus ended another thrilling episode in the Amazing Adventures of…St. Leonard.

What's this, you say? There were superheroes running around Europe in the Middle Ages? Well, they weren't *called* superheroes, but their adventures would have made for some pretty exciting comic books.

There was Gregory the Wonderworker, who once dried up a lake that was the cause of dissension between two brothers, and, on another occasion, changed the course of a river. There was Sabas, a monk of Palestine, who crawled into an oven to retrieve a man's smouldering wet clothes and emerged unscathed, and, another time, having fallen asleep in the forest, survived being dragged into a lion's den without a scratch.

There was Hugh of Lincoln, said to have had "considerable power" over the squirrels and birds who populated his little enclosed garden, who was credited with once saving the English king, overtaken by a storm in the middle of the English Channel, by calming the winds. And St. Egwin, the Bishop of Worcester, who set out on a penitential pilgrimage to Rome to answer complaints against him, by first placing iron shackles

on his own legs and then tossing the key out to sea—only to find it in the belly of a fish he caught in Rome. There was Maurus, who walked across the water to save a drowning boy. And Gerard Majella, who could make himself invisible and even be in two places at once.

The children—and adults—of the Middle Ages were especially fascinated by the courage, patience and perseverence that mere human beings could demonstrate in the face of inhuman cruelty. "Unimaginable" tortures and sufferings were described in exquisite detail, elaborated and compounded. A classic example has been preserved by Chaucer in the *Second Nun's Tale*.

Cecilia, a woman of great beauty and intelligence, has dedicated her life to Christ. She converts her husband and his brother to Christianity and resists the efforts of the Roman prefect to force her to worship pagan idols. He orders her to be burned, but she is unharmed by the flames. He orders her to be beheaded, and, after three strokes of the blade, she is at last mortally wounded, but for three days she continues to teach the faith to people who are so impressed by her wisdom and courage that they, too, are converted.

Here was evidence that a faithful follower of Jesus could draw on amazing resources not only to withstand powerful political enemies but supernatural diabolical forces as well. When the devil changed himself into a handsome young man in order to seduce the virgin Justina, she realized who it really was. She made the sign of the cross over him and the devil melted away. The young and beautiful Barbara, locked in a tower by her overly protective father, became a Christian against his wishes. Informed of this, he tried to kill her, but the maid was miraculously transported to a mountain for refuge. There shepherds grazing their flocks

on the high slopes reported having seen a flying girl.

During the succeeding centuries such stories were told and retold with increasing elaboration and exaggeration. The genre of saints' legends in the medieval world was unrestrained by such considerations as historical fact or physical probability. It was an oral tradition characterized by great flexibility, even after written collections such as *The Golden Legends* of Jacobus de Voragine began to appear. It did not matter if it had really happened; what was important was that it *could* happen. The superpowers of the medieval saints were a way of expressing, in the external, visible world, a powerful internal reality that transcended the limitations of the flesh and of the physical world—and opened a realm of infinite possiblilties.

Nothing, the legends were saying, can prevail against such conviction. St. Felix was led to the temple of Serapis to be forced to offer a sacrifice. He blew into the face of a statue and it collapsed at once. Led to the statue of Mercury, he did the same; on to the image of Diana, the same. Then he was led to a sacred tree. He prayed and then blew on the tree, which was instantly uprooted and in its fall crushed an idol, along with its temple and its altar.

Similarly gifted, Martin set fire to a pagan temple but saw the wind was blowing the fire toward a house nearby. He went to the roof of the house, stood facing the fire that was advancing toward him and instantly the flames turned back against the force of the wind. A holy person concerned for the cause of justice relied on the power of God, and everything was possible with God. If faith could move mountains, then George could subdue and slay a dragon and Leo the Great could turn back Attila the Hun.

The marvelous attributes of Superman, indeed, would not have seemed all that outlandish to children brought up on the adventures of St. Kieran of Saighir or St. Finnian of Clonard. In fact, though none of these early super-people exhibited the full arsenal of awesome powers displayed by St. Clark of Krypton, practically every one of his wonderful abilities turned up in one or more of his medieval ancestors.

Can Superman burrow deep into the earth and release a stream of magma that will heat a lake to boiling? St. Finnian of Clonard is said to have caused a camp of Saxon marauders to be swallowed up by an earthquake. St. Gregory relocated a mountain. And we are told in the Venerable Bede's *Life of St. Cuthbert* that "even the sea" obeyed that remarkable man.

Can Superman withstand a rain of bullets, mortar shells and flame throwers? St. Elmo remained unhurt though beaten with whips and a lead-loaded club (this was before the days of machine guns) and rolled in pitch, which was then ignited. And good St. Vitus, when cast by the emperor Diocletian into a cauldron filled with (ouch!) molten lead, pitch and resin, emerged smiling (how like Superman!) "as from a refreshing bath."

Can Clark Kent, now a television news anchor, dash to the rescue of a sinking ship in the space of time it takes to air a commercial and be back in the studio to read the baseball scores? St. Kieran could say Mass for his brother monks at Saighir every Christmas night, show up moments later to give a homily at Ros-Bennchuir many miles away and be back in his cell at Saighir in time for matins.

Does Superman possess a wonderful costume that can survive a trip to the sun's fiery core? St. Kieran is said to have carried a glowing fireball in the lap of his tunic to his shivering guests so they might warm themselves on a cold winter's night. And a paralytic was cured, the story goes, simply by wearing St. Cuthbert's shoes.

Can Superman leap tall buildings in a single bound? St. Christina the Astonishing, believed dead of an epileptic fit at the tender age of 21, amazed her mourners by suddenly soaring to the rafters of the church where mass was being said for her. (Christina, a fastidious creature who could not tolerate the odor of human beings, is said to have done this on more than one occasion.)

Can Superman use his X-ray vision to see a tiny band of criminals tunneling beneath a bank? St. Kieran saw the bodies of the king of Munster's seven minstrels, who had been slain on their journey by the king's enemies, buried at the bottom of an Irish bog.

Even the more prosaic trademarks of the Man of Steel have their medieval counterparts. Is Clark Kent never seen without his glasses and the Man of Steel known far and wide by the large letter "S" emblazoned on his manly chest? St. Anthony's cloak invariably bears the symbol of a crutch in the form of a "T," and the followers of St. Bruno wore a blazon with seven stars.

Does Superman have a secret retreat in the far northern wastes to which he can repair when his spiritual batteries need recharging or when he is just plain tired of battling criminals? St. Martin of Tours (who escaped certain death miraculously at the last moment, on several occasions, by defying the laws of gravity) had a fortress of solitude in the hills outside of town. The only trouble was he was so beloved that 80 men eventually followed him there and turned the poor man's getaway into a monastery.

What was the powerful attraction of the saints to these medieval Europeans? Why did they never tire of hearing about them and their fabulous deeds? And are there any parallels between the facination these holy men and women held for medieval Christians and the appeal of Superman for 20th-century Americans? Are there, indeed, some ways in which our times, our needs and even our aspirations are similar?

Life in the Middle Ages was difficult and devoid of creature comforts, and, given the state of medicine and science, existence itself was uncertain. Women died in childbirth, and children often did not survive to adulthood. Those that did were faced with eking out a living on someone else's land, in the words of one historian, "sharing the same pot, fire and loaf,' working the same piece of earth for generations."

In the small towns that were springing up around marketplaces in Europe, unskilled workers were miserably paid, owned no equipment and had as yet no guilds to protect their interests; they were at the mercy of marauding bands of Brabancons, or unemployed soldiers, who roamed the countryside taking what they needed. There were periodic famines and plagues, the most terrible of which, the Black Death, is believed to have killed one quarter of the population of Europe; and there was, finally, a seemingly endless succession of wars (over things like the control of the wool trade or some royal snub) and crusades for which the peasantry was continually being rounded up and pressed into service.

Is it any wonder that the people hungered not only for food for their bellies, but for stories of escape and hope? For some reassurance that good will finally triumph and the downtrodden be delivered from their enemies? It was a time of heretics and witches

Of *course*, Superman is a Clevelander. How else would the Cuyahoga River have stopped burning?

James Naughton, journalist

burned at the stake, and, periodically, of the hunting down of Jews. Did ever 20th-century superhero battle more sinister foes? In a world so often dismal and menacing, the legends of the saints eventually collected in such "best-selling" anthologies as *Acta Sanctorum* and *The Golden Legends* offered hope, as did the comic-book tales of Superman for those Americans swept into a profound uncertainty and helplessness by the Depression, then menaced by the looming spectre of Facism.

When Martin the Pope went to the emperor for help, he was locked out of the palace. After being twice repulsed by the emperor, the holy man went home and prayed and fasted for a week. Returning to the palace, he made his way to the emperor, hindered by no one. The emperor was so angry that Martin had been admitted he refused to arise to meet him until suddenly his throne was engulfed by flames, a conflagration which ended by wounding more than his pride. Medieval audiences loved such stories. When evil powers threaten and are challenged by simple goodness, there is excitement and, even in the little triumphs, much pleasure.

The worldly wise may regard some of these revered figures as naive and innocent in the ways of the real world, but underneath the meek and often puny exterior of the saint, medieval audiences knew, was a

dazzling figure with super-sensitive sight and sure-footed strength ready to step suddenly forth and do amazing things. The transformation occurred not in a telephone booth, but in the believer's space of communication with God: the church, a private oratory, wherever prayer could strip away the ordinary and lift the heart and mind to awareness of the divine presence and power. (Joseph of Cupertino levitated so often during prayer that the monks insisted he pray in a low-ceiling room because he was doing so much damage to the ceiling of the church.)

Like Superman, these heroes derived their extraordinary powers from their roots in "another world." Because they are in touch with the spiritual dimension, the saints are able to transcend that nagging obsession with the physical that keeps most of us earthbound; because they anticipate a greater reward, they can disregard the material values of this world; because they respond to a higher love, they are able to pour forth a universal compassion.

It is in this context that virginity and celibacy take on a special importance, leading someone like Cecilia, who loved God above all, to commit her life entirely to God's service. By embracing celibacy, instead of each other, St. Francis and St. Clare acquired the time for continual prayer and for the giving of themselves to all who were in need. If the hero or heroine is truly dedicated to this more extensive love, it necessitates the sacrifice of any personal desire for an intimacy that would restrict such love. Indeed, Superman's pre-Hollywood relationship with Lois Lane was characterized by this kind of altruism. In the earlier comics, he belongs to the world and is dedicated to caring for all of humanity: a full-time occupation and a most demanding relationship.

The gods of ancient Greece were irrevocably diminished by just such preoccupations with personal fulfillment. Indeed, their dalliances with human partners in turn resulted in a race of superhumans who were capable of performing extraordinary feats such as cleaning out the Augean stables or carrying the world on their shoulders, but proved even more vulnerable to the heartache and the thousand natural shocks that the flesh is heir to. These superheroes triumph magnificently or fail miserably depending on the whims of the gods and their own personal rivalries.

The Hebrews eliminated such rivalries in their belief in one God, all-powerful and just and fearsome, but also loving. This was a deity who blessed his people as long as they were faithful, and on those specially chosen and favored he conferred extraordinary powers. The results were: a leader who could part the waters, a king who could experience persecution and continue to love those who stood against him, a prophet who could call down fire from heaven, even a spoiled and bullish strongman who wasn't always sure if he was on God's side.

Then the ultimate hero appears on the world stage: Jesus of Nazareth. Sent to Earth, like that hero of contemporary fable, to be a superman among us, he is found, not in a tiny rocketship come to rest in a cornfield, but in a manger, surrounded by farm animals and simple shepherds. Raised by a humble couple who are aware of his uniqueness and assume their role in his

human development with dutiful humility, he is to be the fulfillment of Israel's messianic hopes, while the city people will always see him as only a boy from the country. As he moves through Palestine, only a few will come to know his secret, but many will benefit from his superhuman powers.

Endowed with more than X-ray vision, he can see through the facades of people and read their minds and hearts. He knows that Nathaniel has been resting under a fig tree in the next town, that the Samaritan woman has had multiple husbands and lovers, that Judas is going to betray him. He will walk on water and command the elements with a word, have power over sickness and do battle against the forces of evil. Even as he is crushed by these forces, he will rise to a new life with a body that can pass through walls and be in two places at once. Now there is no longer any remnant of his human nature to render him helpless, no leaden material that can impede his vision. The shroud of his humanity has been destroyed, and he is transfigured to reveal a divinity that is immortal and indestructible.

The parallels with the story of Superman are obvious. Both Christ and Superman represent the fulfillment — one religious and the other secular — of basic human hopes for a messiah. Both are savior figures that people of all ages and religions have dreamed about and longed for. Both stories are great poetry expressing humanity's highest aspirations and providing much-needed encouragement and inspiration.

Not that the legends of the saints lacked the occasional glint of humor that softens the harshness of daily existence. A group of monks were refused permission by their prior to sing a new office dedicated to Saint Nicholas because the new canticle sounded too much like minstrels' songs. When the saint's feast day arrived, the brothers performed the traditional vigils with a certain

sadness and then went to bed. That night, Saint Nicholas appeared to the prior, dragged him from his bed by the hair and threw him on the floor. Then the nocturnal visitor intoned the antiphon and proceeded to sing the new canticle carefully to the end, beating out the meter on the prostrate prior's back. The prior soon awakened the house with his cries. And when the monks entered the room, he quickly granted permission for the new music.

There was a playfulness about the descriptions both of grand accomplishments and of human foibles that more serious minds could find ludicrous. A young man, filled with desire for the virgin Justina, was transformed into a sparrow by the devil and flew to her bedroom window. But as soon as she looked upon him, he was suddenly a man again, now finding he could neither fly away nor jump. The considerate and resourceful Justina, fearing lest he fall and dash himself on the ground, had him taken down by a ladder and warned him to give up his foolish pursuit.

When Clark Kent finds himself in similarly foolish circumstances, we are not only invited to laugh, we are given an opportunity to identify with the human side of Superman — his path blocked by a lumbering freight train or his pursuit of some heroic cause frustrated by a crying baby handed him to watch. But these little human moments end, as they did in the saints' lives of medieval times, by making the adventures of Superman all the more satisfying and his sudden transcendence of the physical laws of nature all the more exhilarating. Today, as in the Middle Ages, we continue to crave such images of the wonderful and the transcendent. No matter that Superman is not an overtly religious figure and that St. Clark of Krypton preaches a secular gospel (though one shaped in its idealism by the long Judeo-Christian tradition of intense belief in the dignity of the individual human being). The fact is that humanity still yearns for a deliverer. Even the most cynical of us discover a sudden rush of delight in the fantasy — indulged ever so briefly in a movie theater's cool darkness — of a Super-man.

THE ART AND SCIENCE OF LEAPING TALL BUILDINGS

by JOHN D. McGERVEY

Mary Poppins can fly. So can Superman. The difference between the two is the difference between fantasy and science fiction. Fantasy does not attempt to explain why the known laws of nature are being violated, but science fiction often includes some scientific rationale for the action, which may add to the appeal of the yarn.

A popular explanation of superstrength, for example, is that the hero (or villain) has somehow acquired the "proportionate strength" of an insect or a spider. Horror movies get great effects by showing giant-

sized bugs, which somehow are more terrifying than, say, giant pandas. But many giant creatures have walked the Earth, and none of them resembled bugs. Why not?

Suppose you take a bug and multiply each of its dimensions by 100. Its weight would go up in proportion to its volume, so the weight would be multiplied by a factor of 100 for each dimension. The cube of 100 is one million; a one-gram bug would become a one-ton monster. But your superbug wouldn't be able to stand up! The strength of its spindly legs is not proportional to their *volume*, but to their cross-sectional *area*, which would be multiplied by the square of 100, or a mere 10,000. If its original legs could support five times its weight—say five grams—its new legs could only support 50 kilograms, or 1/20th of its new weight. An elephant doesn't have those heavy legs for nothing.

In the early *Superman* comics, on the other hand, the writers seemed to sense a danger in making their hero a purely magical or fantasy figure; they invented many explanations, some of them plausible, for his feats. Let us examine some of his superpowers (and his one weakness) to see how we can "dream things that never were, and ask 'Why not?' "

Superman's superstrength was explained by his origin on the planet Krypton, where gravity was so strong that the inhabitants needed superstrength just to stand up. Thus it seems reasonable that someone who could jump to ordinary heights on Krypton (say about one meter) could "leap tall buildings in a single bound" on Earth. There is a germ of real physics in that concept; you need only accept the premise that human-like

creatures could develop on a planet whose gravity is several hundred times the gravity of Earth.

One early leap by Superman was described as covering an eighth of a mile. If this was a single leap (following a ballistic trajectory, like a cannonball), a simple physics calculation shows that Superman had to leave the ground with a speed of more than 100 miles per hour. That is indeed "faster than a streamline train," to quote an early Superman description.

But as Superman matured, the descriptions blossomed. Soon he became "faster than a speeding bullet" (about 1,000 miles per hour). That speed corresponds to an energy of about ten million joules, for a man of normal weight. Superstrength doesn't exempt you from the law of conservation of energy, and to gain that energy from food requires more than 2,000 food calories—just to reach that speed once. The conclusion: Clark Kent must eat like a pig.

Besides the energy requirement, there are also force and acceleration to consider. How much force must Superman's legs exert to reach 1,000 miles per hour—and thus leap a tall building in "a single bound?" If he is pushing off against the ground, as people do when they leap, he has to get up to this speed before his feet leave the ground. A high-school physics student can compute the acceleration that takes you from zero to 1,000 miles per hour in a distance of, say, two feet; it is 20,000 times the acceleration of gravity. This means that Superman's legs have to exert a force that is 20,000 times Superman's weight, or about 2,000 tons (coincidentally, just about enough to stop a speeding locomotive in a fraction of a second).

But as his greater speed was introduced and Superman's leaps became higher and higher, it became clear that they were not "leaps" at all. We could see Superman changing direction in mid-air or even circling the Earth like a satellite. At this point all traces of science had disappeared; the feat had entered the realm of pure magic or fantasy. Nevertheless, it's fun to try to apply the basic laws of physics to these flights.

With a speed of 1,000 m.p.h. at "liftoff," and no air resistance, Superman could reach an altitude of three miles and cover 12 miles in one leap. But even Superman can't turn off air resistance. Any object thrown through the air at great speed will be slowed down by air resistance and eventually fall earthward at a constant speed, called the terminal speed. For a body of human size, shape and weight, the terminal speed is about 120 miles per hour. So even if you could survive a blast that started you off at 1,000 miles per hour, you would quickly slow down, and you would complete your flight by falling toward Earth at a mere 120 miles per hour.

Some skiers do a little better than that; they achieve a speed of 150 miles per hour by streamlining themselves with skintight suits and special headgear. Superman needs none of that. Defying the laws of physics, he even trails a cape behind him on his supersonic flights!

To reconcile Superman's flights with the laws of physics, several possibilities come to mind. For example:

1. His superstrength might permit him to propel himself as he flies, as an airplane does. Superman's early flights sometimes displayed a vigorous thrashing of his legs, as if he were swimming through the air. This calls to mind the problem of pushing on the end of a rope. No matter how strong you are, you cannot push off against something unless that thing pushes back. Action must equal reaction, and your souped-up car goes nowhere if its wheels have no traction. Pushing hard enough on thin air to sustain these flights would create super-hurricane winds. People near Superman's launch point would be knocked flat, or worse.

2. Perhaps Superman has some means of jet or rocket propulsion. If that is the case, no evidence of it ever appears. In the comics he often moves as if he were simply running on the air; the running motion would be superfluous if he were rocket propelled.

3. He might weigh a lot more than the ordinary mortal. Then his initial speed would not be reduced so quickly by air resistance, for the same reason that you can throw a golf ball farther than you can throw a ping-pong ball. This view is consistent with an early episode in which an enemy found Superman impossible to lift, and another one in which Superman cracked the sidewalk when he landed. (Notice that Superman is a bit of a showoff—he lands on one foot, not even bending a knee to minimize the shock! In the later stories, Superman apparently has the magical ability to slow down and make a soft landing—no more cracked sidewalks.)

What about flying through outer space, as Superman has done almost from the beginning? One of Superman's more mind-boggling feats of flying occurred when he was a boy; he carried his earthling father to the moon. He took care to outfit the father with a space helmet, but not a spacesuit. You can imagine what problems that could pose for an ordinary mortal. Even if the father's clothing didn't burn up from air friction during the liftoff, it would not provide any pressurization to keep poor dad's blood from boiling in the vacuum of outer space. (Superman often carries people through the air or catches them as they are falling. In real life, poor Lois Lane would go "splat" all over the Man of Steel after a typical catch;

132

Superman and I have a lot in common. He has the strength of ten men, and I have the weight of ten men. Superman and I are a lot alike—we both like to wear full-body blue tights under our regular clothes. I like Superman because he uses his power for good—to help people. That's something I *never* would have thought of.

William M. Gaines, publisher, *MAD* magazine

the impact on his "steely" body would be just like an impact on the concrete below.)

Although Superman himself has no worries about air pressure (or breathing, in space or underwater), flying in outer space has to create problems for him. In space there is nothing, not even air, to push against. No matter how strong he is, Superman cannot violate the law of conservation of momentum; he cannot increase his momentum in one direction unless he gives an opposite momentum to something else. In empty space, this means he must use rocket propulsion any time he wants to speed up, slow down or change direction. Thus, when Superman is circling the globe like a satellite, he will be there for a very long time unless he can eject something in the forward direction to slow himself down.

One possible source for his rocket braking would be his superbreath. He might blow his superbreath out in front of him and thereby be pushed backward, just as a rifle recoils when it ejects a bullet. If he is already moving forward, this recoil would slow him down and let him come down from orbit.

Another way for Superman to slow down would be by using his X-ray vision. It is well known that X-rays, like all forms of radiation,

carry momentum; thus Superman would recoil backward as the rays went forward, and you can imagine his slowing down sufficiently to descend into the atmosphere, where atmospheric drag could bring him down. (Of course, those X-rays would have to be superstrong.)

Superman's orbital flights pose yet another physics problem when superspeed is involved. When Superman is circling the globe seven times per second, his speed approaches the speed of light. Even if he had such prodigious energy, how could he avoid flying off into interstellar space? There has to be a force keeping him in orbit. Gravitational force keeps a body in a low earth orbit only if the orbital period is about 90 minutes.

Could Superman send out superbreath or X-rays to keep himself in orbit? If he did, how much force would these rays have to exert? And how does that force compare with the force needed to stop a locomotive in, say, one tenth of a second, from a speed of 60 miles per hour?

The force needed to keep Superman in this superspeed orbit is close to a billion tons, even if Superman's body only has the mass of a human. This clearly means that Superman is far "more powerful than a locomo-

133

tive"; the force needed to stop the loco-motive is a few thousand tons—about 30 times the locomotive's weight, according to a high-school physics calculation. (If his breath is that powerful, Superman could stop the locomotive just by blowing on it—carefully, of course, so he doesn't launch it into outer space.)

The whole concept of motion in outer space is an interesting one. Superboy was once shown disposing of a dangerous object by throwing it directly toward the sun, saying "There it goes, right into the sun." But because of the Earth's motion around the sun, the object still has the angular momentum that it had before he threw it, and it will be in an orbit that whips around the sun like a comet. To hit the sun in an orbit like that, he would have had to throw the object at a speed of about ten million miles per hour. This object appeared to have a mass of at least 100 tons. That would make the required energy more than three quintillion joules—ten times the energy of the largest H-bomb ever made.

A much easier way to hit the sun would have been to throw the object in a way that just cancels out its motion with the Earth around the sun. That is, throw it toward the east at midday (in the direction that the sun appears to move past the distant stars). Then if its speed leaving Earth is equal to the speed of the Earth's orbital motion (a mere 60,000 miles per hour), the object will be momentarily at rest relative to the sun, and it will then fall straight into the sun. If Super-boy had thrown the object that way, only 100 trillion joules (equal to a 25-kiloton bomb) would have been required.

Actions involving the Earth's curvature as well as its motion are sometimes presented in Superman's adventures without regard to the physics involved. A good illustration appears in an episode in which Superman became a substitute teacher. To show how

exciting a classroom could be, Superman ground a plate-glass window (with his hands) to make it into a "super-telescopic lens." Through this lens students could see a tropical jungle! But a lens can only help you to see the light that strikes the lens. The light rays from that jungle would have to pass through many miles of earth to reach the lens. If teachers other than Superman wanted to show their classes a tropical jungle, they'd have to fly them there.

Superman often displays an astounding ability to manipulate materials. A favorite trick is to make huge diamonds from coal. This feat depends on the fact that diamonds are a form of carbon that is produced when sufficiently high pressure is applied. Super-man is shown pressing on the coal with one flat palm on each side. A human doing that to a real lump of coal with a strong vise would have to watch out for flying fragments when the coal shattered, long before it could be turned into a diamond.

The numbers quoted here make it obvious that Superman can't get his prodigious energy from food. His ability to generate X-rays suggests that he might use nuclear energy—he might be a walking nuclear power plant! But that seems unlikely; if he were, the people of Metropolis would have been fried a long time ago. This, and the fact that his head has a fairly normal shape, makes us wonder how he produces those X-rays. Or are they really X-rays?

Superman's X-rays have only one char-acteristic in common with the real rays; they are stopped by lead. Real X-rays are stopped, with varying degrees of effective-ness, by many different materials; that is the only reason why you can use them to see anything. If the rays went through every-thing in their path, then they would be useless for vision; they have to be reflected or absorbed in order to show us anything. Real X-rays are even stopped by air; at sea

Although a comic-book figure, there has never been anything "comic" about Superman. For five decades, Superman has shown generations of kids what being a hero really means.

John Glenn, U.S. senator and former astronaut

level they can't penetrate from one end of a football field to the other. We now know that some X-rays come from outer space, but to detect them we have to fly a detector above 99 percent of the atmosphere (on a satellite or a balloon).

Superman's X-rays, on the other hand, are magical. They are reflected in a convenient fashion; they will go through the wall of a building, then bounce off a newspaper so Superman can read it! They are also absorbed, but only when Superman wants to use their energy for some special purpose, such as starting a fire or melting something. At other times Superman can see for an enormous distance with the rays. When he wishes to do so, he can even send the rays through miles of earth, as when he said, "I'll send an X-ray beam to my Fortress of Solitude hidden in the Arctic."

Giving Superman powers that are more than superhuman — that are not even limited by the laws of nature — created the potential for something really dull. Where is the suspense in the adventures of a creature who has no limitations? As a student once wrote, "Achilles was dipped in the River Stynx [sic], and he became intolerable." To make Superman tolerable, the authors had to give him a weakness, so they invented kryptonite, the

celestial debris left over from the explosion of his natal planet, Krypton, which occasionally falls to Earth in meteorites — and, invariably, into the hands of evil persons.

The original kryptonite simply made Superman weak, without affecting anybody else in the slightest. There is a vaguely "scientific" basis for this effect. Just as a tuning fork resonates at one frequency and no other, the alien molecules in Superman's body could resonate to (and be damaged by) the radiation from kryptonite, while our molecules are unaffected. But the weakness theme could only be worked so many times before it became tiresome, so other forms of kryptonite were conjured up.

The spookiest of these is "red kryptonite," whose effects add spice to the proceedings by being "unpredictable." One consequence of this is to threaten the exposure of Superman's secret identity, by producing physical changes that show up in Superman and Clark Kent at the same time. For example, Superman suddenly grew a beard and ridiculously long fingernails after one encounter with this material. How, you ask, could that be a problem? Answer: He couldn't cut them; they were superstrong. The nails were even too strong to cut with his X-ray vision. How did the writers get Superman out of this jam? When all else fails, try luck. By an amazing stroke of it, the nails yielded to the combined X-ray vision of Superman, Superdog and Supergirl!

So we see that a little imagination lets us relate some of Superman's feats to the laws of nature. Many of them, though, remain in the realm of magic or fantasy.

SUPERMAN AND THE DREAMS OF CHILDHOOD

by JANE W. KESSLER

To understand something of Superman's appeal to the young, you must imagine yourself as an infant. Though a newborn's parents are very conscious of the infant's helplessness and dependence, the infant does not perceive himself or herself as helpless. Far from it. The competent infant quickly masters the art of calling for its "slaves," who then struggle mightily to divine what would restore happiness and contentment.

With the acquisition of language, the toddler acquires new powers and for a while enjoys the illusion of omnipotence. It appears that if one can only utter the right sound, all kinds of things materialize like magic. But the illusion does not last. Somewhere in the early years, the fledgling magician finds that words do not always control people's actions or events in the real world, and the child is catapulted into a feeling of total helplessness. Observations indicate that something or someone else is in control. The small child feels very small indeed, but derives some comfort from the presence of the big people who can do all the things that he or she cannot do. There is someone who knows what is going on and can take care of everything. For a while, the child attributes the parents with the omnipotence he or she has lost, but gradually the fact that even the parents have some limitations of power becomes all too apparent.

It is hard to relinquish the faith that one has control over events, at least by proxy of one's parents. Although in reality growing children become more independent and capable, they also become more aware of their vulnerabilities and limitations. You can't cross the street alone until you are five years old; you can't read the words until you go to school; you can't stay up late until you are much older; you can't go in the water alone until you can swim; you can't drive until you are 16 years old. There is always something you can't do until you are older and bigger.

It is no wonder that children who have given up so much in the way of magical beliefs and have to wait so long for new powers turn to fantasy for comfort. For satisfying this need, Superman is absolutely perfect. He sees everything and can conquer all kinds of danger. When you add to this his moral certitude and determination to fight evil, he is a hero in every sense of the word. The fact that he has some vulnerability only provides a necessary touch of suspense, but

not enough to be really worrisome. What a comfort compared to the perils and uncertainties of everyday life.

But there is more to Superman than his ability to conquer all odds. The plot line of the Superman story is tailor-made to fit the fantasies that persist in most of us from our childhood days. First, there is the secret of his birth and the origin of his special powers: The nice, but very ordinary, parents who raised him were not his real parents at all. Many children around ten or 12 years of age have entertained the idea that there is something mysterious about their birth and that their parents are not the real ones. A girl is likely to create a new mother and a son another father who is far superior to the real thing. These real parents are more noble, famous, rich or beautiful than the humdrum man and woman who are claiming parentage. This is also the time when the young child may become interested in ancestors, patiently searching for something remarkable to counteract the ordinariness of the parents. But the conviction that one has been adopted flies in the face of all evidence to the contrary, and the child half knows that it is only a dream.

Freud described these "family romance" fantasies as part of the child's effort to come to terms with the growing awareness of the limitations of the real parents. The child has come to realize that these people are not always right. They make mistakes. They don't know everything and their powers are limited, perhaps even inferior to some other parents with whom the child has a passing acquaintance. The idea that one is going to grow up to be like these imperfect people is not at all appealing, so one looks for substitutes, if only in fantasy. Lest parents feel merely rejected, one should keep in mind that the replacement of the real father by a more distinguished one harkens back to an earlier time when the child was much

I have always been very ambitious and Superman fit my idea, on a very grand scale, of how one should live one's life.

Ed McMahon, television personality

younger. The effort to replace the real father by a more distinguished one is merely the expression of the child's longing for the vanished happy time, when his father still appeared to be the strongest and greatest man, so the fantasy reflects a kind of memory.

Furthermore, the child often feels slighted and unappreciated by these same imperfect beings, giving further support to the notion that somewhere there must be some parents who would be all-loving as well as perfect. All of this disillusionment and disappointment is the natural beginning of the emancipation of adolescence. But it is still hard for young children to think of total independence—instead they conjure up an improvement on the familiar themes of the child-parent relationship.

Otto Rank, who at the age of only 20, was already a highly respected colleague of Freud, analyzed the role of the family romance in the mythological stories of the birth of the hero and his subsequent heroic deeds. He suggested a parallel between the "secret" parentage of legendary heroes and the family-romance fantasies of childhood. Superman's expulsion from the planet Krypton fits all the necessary conditions, with the substitution of outer space for Valhalla or Mount Olympus in accordance with our times. But the heroes of mythology were somehow transported out of our world or

met some unhappy fate, whereas Superman lives happily ever after as part of Metropolis. This makes him an ordinary person with whom anyone can identify.

This brings us to the second secret that adds to Superman's irresistibility, namely, his double identity. Clark Kent is a pleasant but unremarkable young man who even has a visual problem that requires that he wear glasses. With the instant magic of a change of clothes, he reappears with all his extraordinary powers to command the awe and gratitude of practically the whole world. Everyone can respond to this fantasy transformation, which appears in such classic fairy tales as the Frog Prince and such romantic classics as *The Scarlet Pimpernel*. The reversal-of-roles fantasy is particularly satisfying because of the surprise element. The weak one or the small one who is usually the butt of ridicule beats out everyone and rises to fame. Undoubtedly our pleasure in such a surprise twist has its roots in the memories of feeling small, weak and helpless compared to older siblings and parents.

There are other details in the Superman story that are psychologically "right." The wonderful costume that goes with the magic was made from the blankets in which Superman's mother wrapped him for protection on his journey from Krypton. Martha Kent, the adoptive mother, unravelled the blanket and reknitted it into his costume—a true "security blanket." The blanket is almost the only indication we have that Superman had a biological mother; it was his two fathers who made the big decisions and guided him towards a missionary role in life. This plot line is in keeping with the fact that school-age boys admit to no interest or need for mothers, but the baby-blanket motif hints at some recognition that, once upon a time, the mother had special protective powers.

What about Superman's relationship with Lois Lane? Lois loves Superman but is only fond of Clark Kent in a sisterly kind of way. She sees him as helpless, weak and frightened, even perhaps needing protection. Although Superman is the embodiment of manly strength, he is not required to make sexual advances to Lois Lane—an appealing situation for a boy between six and 12 who wants to love and be loved...but from a safe distance. In this so-called latency period, physical sex does not figure into the fantasies of the child.

It is possible to analyze the Superman/ Lois Lane/Clark Kent triangle in terms of an Oedipal theme. A child's first love relationship outside the family is colored by his relationships with his parents. For the sake of argument, let's assume that Clark Kent loved his adoptive mother, who is long gone, and Lois has stepped into her place. Lois, fulfilling the role of the mother figure, loves a fantasized father figure of great power and authority—Superman—and there is no room for the "small boy" represented by Clark Kent. Clark loves Lois in hopeless frustration, and Superman cannot return Lois' love because to do so would be to reveal that he is in reality Clark, whose love relationship with Lois is, in Oedipal terms, forbidden. It is a classic triangle where all is fantasy and nothing is real.

It is also right that Superman should be more brawn than brain. It is his superior physical powers that enable him to over-come his enemies, not his cleverness. He does not have to read about things because he knows everything with his X-ray vision. His school career seems to have been very brief and unimportant. In this respect, he contrasts with Batman, who has no super-powers but relies on a variety of modern technological devices and his mental powers of deduction. In his analysis of the comic book as contemporary mythology, Widzer, a child psychiatrist, related particular attributes of different superheroes to specific developmental levels of childhood and suggested, for instance, that Batman appeals more to the older child. With the gradual giving up of magical thinking, there is more appreciation of the rewards attained by hard work and a more realistic assessment of the world. Most children aged ten to 12 perceive power as the result of diligence and personal effort rather than magical endowment. The heroes for this age rely on training, physical condition and their intelligence to conquer the world.

Younger children enjoy the simpler magic in Superman. Superman's ability to fly is a good example of pure magic as the "easy way out." The idea of flying has an irresistible appeal, and every child tries on wings and envies the birds. James Barrie's Peter Pan flies from home when he is seven days old—still young enough to remember how to fly. Children are birds first, in Barrie's fantasy, and it takes about two years for them to become completely human. Perhaps it does take years to relinquish completely the hope.

The fact that Superman, story and person, embodies so many childhood fantasies helps to explain his awesome popularity, but some might question if it is good for children to indulge in such fantasies. It is certainly possible for children to be confused about the difference between reality and make-believe. The double identity of Superman, however, seems to make this difference very clear as the "pretend" Superman defies all rules of reality. If something is presented clearly as a "story," confusion between real and unreal is highly unlikely. Another possibly harmful effect is that children will become so absorbed by fantasy that they lose interest in reality. This, too, is possible, but only for the unhappy child whose reality is filled with hideous disappointments. Again, the problem is with the reality, not the fantasy.

But it does not necessarily follow that make-believe is "good" even if it does not harm. Plato suggested that the education of children should begin by telling them stories which, though not wholly destitute of truth, were in the main fictitious. He recommended a censorship of writers of fiction and wanted mothers and nurses to tell their children only authorized stories that were to be highly moral, idealized versions of how one should behave. Good and evil should be clearly distinguished and good should always win, hands down. Superman clearly passes Plato's test. With the bad people obviously and clearly doomed from the start, there is no ambiguity in the Superman stories. Young children think in terms of clearly drawn opposites and are uncomfortable with mixed portrayals in which you cannot tell the good folks from the bad.

In more recent times, psychologist Bruno Bettelheim, after years of experience in the treatment of emotionally disturbed children, wrote a book on the importance of fairy tales and "the uses of enchantment" in the young child's life. In contrast to Plato, he advises parents not to choose stories simply for the enhancement of virtues they illustrate, but to present the full array of traditional and unadulterated fairy tales. In Bettelheim's view, the common themes of fairy tales symbolically represent common inner conflicts that children cannot express on their

own. The stories open "glorious vistas" that permit children to overcome momentary feelings of utter hopelessness. He emphasizes the importance of telling the stories many times so that children become completely familiar with them and can make them their own. What is scary on first exposure becomes reassuring with repetition.

Superman is something like a fairy-tale hero in that he can perform miraculous deeds. Bettelheim wrote that the young boy listening to a fairytale fantasizes that he, too, can climb into the sky, defeat giants, change his appearance, become the most powerful or most beautiful person—in short, have his body be and do all one could wish for. He goes on to say that after the child's most grandiose desires have thus been satisfied in fantasy, he can be more at peace with his body as it is in reality. But there is an important difference between Superman and fairy-tale heroes, who become ordinary mortals at the story's end. Superman is no ordinary mortal, so his is an epic tale rather than a fairy tale.

We started with the statement that Superman is perfect, but is he timeless? Does he have less appeal now than he did in the 1930s and '40s when the world was faced with a simpler version of good and bad? Certainly there have been changes in the nature of childhood, sometimes described as the "erosion of innocence." Partly because of the medium of television, children of all ages are exposed alike to programs designed for older children or adults. Toy manufacturers have discovered that preschool children demand the Barbie dolls and action figures that are marketed for older children. Of more serious consequence, young children are exposed through television to the dilemmas of adult life: questions of sexual behavior, complications of morality and the misdeeds of real "folk" heroes in sports and politics. Children learn too soon to devalue adult omniscience and omnipotence. They have very little time to enjoy the illusions of simple "good" and "bad." What was a perfect hero for the ten-year-old boy of yesteryear may be better suited for the contemporary six-year-old.

In his book, *The Hurried Child*, David Elkind, a distinguished child psychologist, discusses other kinds of pressures on children today, such as the push for early academic achievement. Parents are exhorted to provide formal academic instruction at early ages so that life becomes a real and serious business. It is his contention that rushing children through childhood is stressful and contributes to the depression which is now frequently seen in school-age children. He also cites the increase in teenage suicide, teenage pregnancy, drug use and school dropout rates as further evidence of stress.

The accelerated pace of childhood does not mean that childhood fantasies have changed, but that there is less time for reflection and working through them with the help of play and make-believe. Superman is a simple morality tale with lots of magic. There is a time for simple things. It would be a pity for Superman to lose out altogether to *Miami Vice*.

THE GOOD, THE BAD AND THE OEDIPAL

by LESTER ROEBUCK

You can learn a lot about a man by knowing who his enemies are.

Unlike real people, comic-book heroes can't always pick their foes. They are obliged to fight evil in whatever form it occurs.

Sometimes, though, certain enemies become more important than others. Long-standing relationships form — not unlike marriages — in which heroes and villains become partners of sorts, each shedding light on some facet of the other's character or offering an opportunity to explore hidden parts of a complex psyche.

143

In the early years of the comic book, Superman fought a lot of villains who weren't *his* enemies so much as society's. There were thugs and gangsters robbing banks and pushing people around, corrupt officials, arms merchants during World War II and, later, corporate tycoons who placed profit above the common good. Superman fought and defeated them all.

But there have also been the super-bad guys with powers beyond those of ordinary men, villains with a malignant craftiness capable of challenging Superman on nearly equal terms. These guys are the real enemies of the Man of Steel who together reveal the nature of evil at work in the *Superman* mythos.

In the September 1943 issue of *Action Comics*, Superman battled a bespectacled old man with shoulder-length grey hair and a wide-eyed, smiling countenance. The Toyman, as this villain was known, came to be one of the most fiendish of Superman's foes in the first decade's of our hero's saga.

Toyman's grandfatherly appearance disguises the true nature of his evil genius. Described in the comics as a superbrain, he is a cunning, vain and publicity-mad inventor who has a secret workshop hidden well beneath the streets of Metropolis. There he devises ingenious toys with which he can execute bizarre crimes throughout the city.

For example, in one episode Toyman uses an army of radio-controlled miniature toy soldiers equipped with tiny guns that fire knockout gas to rob an armored truck. In another, he invents an elaborate computer toy that translates the sound of his voice into electrical impulses to operate a plastic extrusion molding machine. All Toyman has to do is describe a crime he wants to commit and the machine creates an array of miniature automatons which act out the crime ahead of the fact. In this way Toyman can conduct a projection study of all the elements of his scheme and minimize the possibility of error.

Toyman always gets caught, of course, but even in prison he uses his grandfatherly charm to win over wardens who let him set up shop and eventually effect an escape. Toyman has a wide range of escape devices, including a flying pogo stick and, in one bizarre episode, a bronze statue of Superman himself, erected on the roof of a prison, whose arm is really a catapult that Toyman can use to fling himself to freedom.

The key to Toyman's evil—the kink in his character, if you will—is less his vanity or greed than his egocentric fixation on the trappings of childhood. By 1947, stories in which he appeared were describing Toyman as a "genius who never graduated from kindergarten."

No episode illustrates this failing more clearly, nor underscores the meaning of Toy-man's evil in the *Superman* mythos, than "The Wind-Up Toys of Peril" (*Superman* # 63, March/April 1950). In an effort to make Superman look ridiculous, Toyman invents a vending machine called the Superman Toy-O-Mat that dispenses, among other toys, Superman dolls capable of leaping over a replica of the *Daily Planet* building or knocking down the wall of a miniature version of the Strongbuilt Construction Company. When the executives of these businesses see the dolls, they are so charmed that they buy the toys to display in their offices. Toyman's scheme is that the dolls, once inside, will activate themselves and perpetrate robberies.

Both Toyman and the toys he creates are charming and dangerous. They betray people who are enchanted by seeing themselves reflected in the miniaturized world of childhood. If there is a lesson in the Toyman episodes, it is the danger of holding onto the external trappings of our youth, a lesson likely to appeal to people anxious about the transition to adulthood.

Toyman isn't the only childish villain Superman has had to face. In August of 1942 a gat-toothed man in his mid-thirties with a Franklin Pangborn moustache and the wardrobe of a carnival barker showed up in Metropolis and began a crime spree that lasted for almost two decades. It was the Prankster (a.k.a. the clown king of the underworld, the chuckling charlatan, the mirthful miscreant, the rollicking rogue, the comedy crook, Ajax Wilde, Mr. Van Prank, Colonel P.R. Ankster, Mr. Frank Ster and Professor Smythe).

Whereas the Toyman's evil genius expresses itself in a remarkable mechanical ingenuity, the Prankster is a gifted amateur psychologist whose understanding of human frailty makes him one of the most daring and effective confidence men in American literature.

A typical Prankster scheme is illustrated by an episode from 1943 in which he borrows $100,000 from a racketeer on the basis of a promised 1,000 percent return on the investment. The Prankster immediately donates the capital to the Society for the Prevention of Cruelty to Ostriches, thereby earning lavish approval from Metropolis' wealthiest and most well-connected matrons with whom he establishes saccharine mutual admiration societies. Soon he is invited into all their homes and a series of spectacular burglaries ensues. Ultimately the racketeer receives his $1,000,000 payoff, just as the Prankster promised, but then himself falls victim when the Prankster robs *him*, proving beyond a doubt the Prankster's fiendish cleverness is so extreme that he is a threat to decent citizen and criminal alike.

Probably the Prankster's most inventive scheme of all is chronicled in "The Great ABC Panic" in the May/June 1943 issue of *Superman*. The Prankster places a confederate in the U.S. Copyright Office and proceeds to copyright the alphabet. Immediately the nation is thrown into a panic as everyone has to pay the Prankster exorbitant royalties whenever they wish to write something. The *Daily Planet* is faced with the prospect of going broke; skywriters are suddenly out of work, not to mention typists, librarians, novelists; school children become delirious with joy when it is discovered that teachers can no longer assign written homework. Civilization teeters on the verge of total collapse because—as even Superman is forced to admit—the Prankster's racket seems totally legit. Not until the Prankster breaks the law by trying to kill Clark and Lois can Superman intervene.

Immensely egotistical, the Prankster schemes as often for publicity as for profit, and the need to humiliate the Man of Steel is an ever-present theme. The Prankster is content to pretend to rob a bank simply so that when Superman arrives on the scene to free a bank employee locked in the vault the Man of Steel will be surprised by a mechanical device planted by the Prankster that throws a custard pie in Superman's face.

The Prankster also holds the distinction of being the first supervillain to best Superman in a fist fight, if only momentarily. Toward the end of "Crime's Comedy King" (*Action Comics*, February 1943), Superman gets set to stop the Prankster with a super-haymaker to the jaw when the fiendish felon squirts him in the face with a watergun and ducks, causing the Man of Steel to miss badly and—unbelievably—knock himself out cold.

There is a degree of malevolence in the Prankster's behavior, a persistent delight in committing mayhem, which makes him more pernicious than many of Superman's other foes. The Prankster carries a real gun, for example, and he almost always tries to eliminate his cohorts, usually by violent means. This aspect of his character is all the more chilling in light of his habit of involving children in so many of his schemes.

Once, when the student/inmates of the Manley Academy for Problem Children vote the Prankster as the man they most admire, he is inspired to pattern a series of crimes on pranks typically played by children. In another episode, the Prankster renders Superman ineffective by convincing Perry White to have the *Daily Planet* sponsor a contest in which a prize will be given to the child who writes the best essay containing an eyewitness account of Superman's exploits. As a result, the Man of Steel is so mobbed by kids that he cannot act to stop the Prankster's plotted crimes for fear of hurting the children.

In the most bizarre of all the Prankster's many schemes, he accidentally discovers the location of the fountain of youth and brings its magic water back to Metropolis to assist him in his crimes. Lois Lane soon falls victim. She is turned into an infant, and the Prankster threatens to withhold the antidote unless Superman stays out of the villain's way. Even the criminals themselves employ this magic path back to infancy. The Prankster transforms one of his henchman into a baby so that he can enter a bank through an air duct to perform a robbery. Eventually Superman discovers that only sugar can bring people back to normal, making him the first comic-book hero to acknowledge, if only tacitly, that candy is the surest antidote to childhood.

Both the Toyman and the Prankster are perilous bridges to childhood. Each character seems quaintly out of place—the Toyman with his long hair and 19th-century style

of dress, the Pranskter with his rich lingo peppered by such Elizabethan curiosities as "aye" and "verily." It is as though each has grown up clinging to some vestige of an outmoded time, or, like Peter Pan, having refused to abandon his childhood.

In the *Superman* mythos, such characters can be appealing, but they are dangerous as well. Their playfulness is a disguise for malicious trickery and their innocence is sham. In short, they are children with adult powers, or adults with childish passions—in either case, not to be trusted.

Superman also clings to a vestige of his childhood: his costume, woven by Martha Kent from the raveled baby blanket that swaddled him on his journey to Earth. He, though, sacrifices many of the rewards of maturity—children of his own, for example—to remain innocent and pure, carrying into adulthood the best qualities of youth. No wonder he goes out of his way to pursue villains who preserve only the worst side of childhood, its egotism and anarchy.

Of all the childish troublemakers Superman has ever had to face, the most childish of all—bar none—is the infamous Mr. Mxyzptlk. Fans of the Man of Steel who know only the TV series and the movies may never have heard of Mxyzptlk, but those familiar with the early comic books will remember him as the bulb-headed, two-foot-tall, derby-wearing doofus from the fifth dimension whose amazing extradimensional powers make him an unbeatable foe.

There was some confusion in the early years as to the exact spelling of this imp's name. At one time known by the tongue-tying monicker Mr. Mxyztplk, he eventually began appearing in episodes of *Action Comics* and *Superman* with the more easily pronounced name Mr. Mxyzptlk (Mix-yez-pitel-ick, according to Michael Fleisher in *The Great Superman Book*, published by Warner Books in 1978).

If not for Superman, there might have been no Spider-Man, which is far too horrendous a possibility to contemplate. Therefore, not only has the entire reading public been enriched by the fabulous creation of Jerry Siegel and Joe Shuster, but your friendly neighborhood web-slinger and I consider ourselves personally and irrevocably in their debt.

Stan Lee, writer, editor and publisher, Marvel Comics

In what was perhaps a covert dig at Mickey Mouse's role in the Sorcerer's Apprentice episode of the phenomenally popular 1940 animation feature *Fantasia*, Mr. Mxyzptlk entered the *Superman* mythos in 1944 as a humble court jester in his native land of Zrfff, who, while playing in the research library of a brilliant scientist, bumbles onto the discovery of a magic word—qrdmlzf. Saying it transports him to our world of three dimensions. Here he is immune to the laws of physics and wreaks havoc by playing super-tricks on Superman.

Like Superman, Mxyzptlk can fly. He also has the ability to effect profound physical transformations in the world that defy any thing Superman can do with his super-powers. For example, in the first episode in which he appears (*Superman* # 30, 1944) Mr. Mxyzptlk survives a head-on collision with a truck, drives an ambulance up the side of a building and hurtles it into space where it explodes, makes a river flow uphill, single-handedly builds a bridge across one of the Great Lakes (the much longed for Lake Erie causeway to Canada, no doubt), brings a statue to life, uses his superbreath to litter an entire city and even survives, through the marvelous elasticity of his body, a direct roundhouse punch from the Man of Steel that would knock any three-dimensional villain to kingdom come.

In subsequent episodes, this elfin foe exhibits even more amazing powers. In one he uses a super-sneezing powder to make Superman unleash a sneeze so powerful that it destroys an entire solar system. In another he infantilizes the entire city of Metropolis with a magical "second childhood gas." He is even capable of casting a spell over the entire Earth, causing all of humankind to forget that Superman ever existed.

Luckily for Superman, the magic which brings Mr. Mxyzptlk to our world can also carry him back. All Superman needs to do is trick the imp into spelling or saying his name backwards—Kltpzyxm (Kel-tipz-yex-im)—and he is transported instantly back to his own dimension for an indefinite period of time. In the course of their many confrontations, Superman employs numerous ruses to catch Mxyzptlk, including tricking him into submitting to an ophthalmological exam in which the magical reverse spelling is hidden in the letters of the eye chart. So successful is this scheme that Superman actually uses it twice.

Mr. Mxyzptlk is unique among Superman's many antagonists in that he is the only one not really associated with evil in any way. He is not motivated by greed, like the Toyman. Nor is there a vein of cruelty, like the Prankster's, underlying his irrepressible playfulness. What there is in him, at heart, is a pure spirit of infantile egoism, unrestrained by social conscience, that turns the entire universe into a playpen.

Mr. Mxyzptlk, moreover, is the one villain most like Superman in that he too is an alien creature. Against his extradimensional magic, Superman's superpowers are useless. He cannot prevent the chaos Mxyzptlk causes. The best the Man of Steel can do is rush around, like the vexed parent of a hyperkinetic three-year-old, and clean up the messes. Every single time they meet — and there have been many, since Mxyzptlk appeared regularly in the comic book until well into the '60s — Superman's only available resource is his ability to outfox the little dickens with supersubtle guile.

Perhaps the weirdest of all of Superman's super-foes is Bizarro Superman No. 1, introduced into the comic book in 1959. Designated No. 1 to distinguish him from the hundreds of other Bizarro Supermen living on the cube-shaped planet Htrae, this Frankensteinian version of the Man of Steel is created by a dangerous duplicator ray that can produce flawed imitations of any person or thing it is trained on.

Bizarro is Superman *sans* the Apollonian beauty. He is so ugly, in fact, that his mere presence scares the bejeebers out of the Abominable Snowman. He has chalky white skin, unkempt hair, a grotesquely faceted face, a dimwitted mentality and a penchant for misusing pronouns ("Me unhappy," he would say, or "Lois! You had baby while me was gone! Oh, me happy father now!").

Apart from these few imperfections, he is the exact duplicate of Superman, right down to the herculean physique and full complement of superpowers.

Like Mr. Mxyzptlk, Bizarro is less an evil threat than a phenomenal nuisance. He is well intended, even sentimental, but because of his superpowers and his superclumsiness, he tends to be a menace. Lost in a reverie, he may fly too close to a smokestack and knock it to the ground.

This capacity for havoc is enhanced by the fact that his value system is skewed. Whereas Superman remains aloof from Lois Lane, Bizarro pursues her like a moonstruck suitor, even to the point where Superman is forced to save her by using the duplicator ray to produce a Bizarro Lois capable of returning Bizarro Superman's love.

Together this Bizarro couple take up residence on Htrae (which is you know what spelled backwards), populated by further duplicates of themselves, where they live a bizarre parody of an American middle-class life style with their son, the Bizarro Baby Buster. On Htrae, ugliness is beauty, corners are never square, flags fly upside down, street cleaners throw dirt in the gutters, alarm clocks announce when it's time to go to sleep and fathers reward bratty children by taking them to cowboy movies with titles like "The Slowest Gun in the West."

Bizarro is an unusual enemy for Superman in that there is little direct conflict between them. In one episode Bizarro threatens Earth with an army of Bizarros when he thinks that Superman has kidnapped Bizarro Baby Buster, but direct warfare is avoided. In fact, Superman and Bizarro never really fight each other. What would be the use, since their superpowers are perfectly matched?

Superman's profound decency and his godlike abilities are what most people think of when they try to explain what this world-class hero means to his millions of youthful believers. But Bizarro shows us that decency and ability, however important, are simply not enough. These qualities he has in abundance, and he's still a freak.

Even more than the Toyman and the Prankster, Bizarro is a radical distortion of Superman's character. He adds to Superman's decency and power a bland middle-American normalcy of thought, as though in him Superman and Clark Kent have been grotesquely integrated. The preposterous life of suburban housekeeping and backyard barbecues led by Bizarro Superman and Bizarro Lois on Htrae is a reminder of how freakish it would be if Superman's aloof treatment of Lois were to be replaced by Clark Kent's mundane yearnings. Bizarro's role, then, in the *Superman* mythos is to remind us that the Man of Steel's heroic stature depends on his ability to keep the Clark Kent portion of his psyche carefully segregated.

Central to Superman's heroic stature, of course, is his profound sense of humanity, and it is this quality which another of the supervillains of the mythos—the monstrously evil Brainiac—totally lacks.

Brainiac is a humanoid computer invented by a race of computers who revolted against their own creators on the distant planet Colu. Listed in the DC *Who's Who* vol. III as a professional "would-be world conqueror," Brainiac stalks through the universe in his spacecraft accompanied only by his monkey-like alien pet Koko. His original mission, programmed by his creators, was to repopulate their world by collecting specimen cities from all the inhabited planets of the universe. This Brainiac does by shrinking the cities and all their inhabitants with a powerful ray and sealing them in bottles aboard his spacecraft. His never-ending grudge against Superman begins when he arrives on Earth and shrinks Paris, London, Rome and finally Metropolis.

As villains go, Brainiac is a fairly standard version of the contemporary myth of dehumanized, machine intelligence run amok. His importance in the *Superman* mythos, however, stems from the single fact that before arriving on Earth he had stolen the Kryptonian city of Kandor prior to that planet's cataclysmic end. Superman is able to retrieve Kandor but cannot restore the city to its original size. He therefore preserves it bottled in his Fortress of Solitude, where he can, by occasionally shrinking himself to the size of a fly, make periodic visits to this last remaining fragment of his home land.

Kandor and its inhabitants represent all that was good about Kryptonian culture, but not all of Superman's contacts with his past are benign, certainly not those involving villains from the Phantom Zone.

Zod, Ursa and the massively repugnant Non—who made their spectacularly villainous film debut in *Superman II*—are certainly the most notorious denizens of the Phantom Zone, but there have been others since fans first learned of the zone in 1962, including Professor Vakox, Dr. Xadu, Ral-En, Jax-Ur and Ras-Krom.

The Phantom Zone is a non-material dimension—a purely spiritual state of existence, in effect—first discovered by Superman's Kryptonian father Jor-El. Thanks to the Phantom Zone Projector, an ingenious instrument invented by Jor-El, the forces of law and order on Krypton are able to punish hardened criminals by banishing them to the Phantom Zone. There they serve their sentences in a form of telepathic imprisonment, fully capable of observing the goings-on of the universe but totally unable to participate. Because of its non-material existence, the Phantom Zone is not destroyed with the cataclysmic end of Krypton. Thus the planet's most inveterate evildoers are left in an indefinitely suspended state with no thought beyond the desire to avenge themselves on the sole surviving son of the man they hold responsible for their predicament—Jor-El.

Over the years there have been occasions—during nuclear weapons tests, for example—when small holes in the Phantom Zone are created, and one or more of these villains squeeze through. At such moments the *Superman* mythos reveals glimpses of its potential tragic side: The dark consequences of the father's accomplishments are visited on the son.

Many of the great myths of human culture have an Oedipal dimension in which sons and fathers are pitted against each other. Oedipus' unwitting murder of King Laius is only the most straightforward example of this tragic human tendency. Zeus battled his father Kronos for the throne of heaven. Often the conflict is symbolic, as when an African tribesman must kill a lion to succeed in his rite of passage. Tragic heroes in literature regularly struggle against father figures—Hamlet against Claudius, MacBeth against Duncan—and the world of fairy tales and legends is filled with stories of princes who plot against kings and youths who must slay ogres in order to become men.

Superman is blessed—and cursed—in mythic terms. When Jor-El dies that his infant son might live, he eliminates himself as Superman's fated opponent. Thus Superman is saved from Oedipus' fate. But because fortune casts him in the role of hero, the logic of myths would force him to create, even if unknowingly, a symbolic or surrogate father who becomes the Oedipal antagonist. In the *Superman* mythos, young Kal-El creates his own worst enemy—the mad scientist Lex Luthor.

Luthor—the most important of all the supervillains and Superman's sworn archenemy—first appeared in *Action Comics* # 23 (April 1940). He has remained an integral part of the mythos to this very day.

In the early years there was no explanation for Luthor's origins. He merely appeared in a cleverly levitated city in the clouds and began a reign of terror that has lasted for nearly 50 years. Not until the 1960s did fans learn that Superman and Luthor were boyhood friends in Smallville. In a laboratory accident that he mistakenly blamed on Superboy, Luthor suffered a humiliating total baldness. So began a resentment that festered into a maniacal hatred of the Man of Steel.

In symbolic terms, Jor-El and Luthor create the perfect good father/bad father dichotomy. Jor-El was a responsible citizen of Krypton, and he used his scientific genius to serve humankind. Luthor, on the other hand, is a monstrosity.

Nothing conveys his character more clearly than the endless stream of grotesque technology *his* scientific genius spews forth. Among his more horrendous inventions are the wormcar, which allows him to tunnel through the Earth, the underwater city Pacifico, whose construction causes world-threatening tidal waves, and the infamous duplicator ray with which he creates the horrific Bizarro Superman.

That these unrivalled scientific geniuses from different worlds—Jor-El and Luthor—are mysteriously bound together in the mythos is underscored by a 1952 episode in which Luthor extracts from outer space a large vault inscribed with the words "I, Jor-El, have gathered in this vault my greatest scientific powers, that they may survive to benefit other men even though our own world must die." Luthor opens the vault to discover such marvels as a lightning projector, levitation bombs that reverse the

effect of gravity, an invisibility spray and a secret weapon labelled for use only by those who desire power over all humanity. The secret weapon is a ruse, however, cleverly designed by Jor-El to disarm anyone who attempts to use it, since an individual who desires power over all of humankind can only be evil. Thus does the good father prove his dominion.

Luthor is not only an evil version of Superman's father, he bears a perverse similarity to the Man of Steel himself. There is even a distant world — Lexor — where Luthor does good deeds and is considered a hero. On Lexor, Superman, true to his earthly moral code, pursues Luthor and earns a reputation as a villain among the Lexorian people.

In a very real sense these evenly matched combatants are spiritually wedded to each other. Luthor is every bit as much Superman's alter ego as is Clark Kent. Perhaps this explains the intensity of their conflict.

Of all the supervillains in the *Superman* mythos, Luthor is the only one who repeatedly, obsessively plots the annihilation of the Man of Steel. Others may be vexed and resent the persistence with which Superman foils their schemes. But for Luthor the death of Superman *at Luthor's hands* becomes the sole reason for being. This is why Luthor becomes the one villain to identify himself with the consistent use of kryptonite. He even counts among his more notable accomplishments the invention of luthorite, a synthetic form of kryptonite every bit as lethal — for Superman — as the genuine article.

Among the countless tales spun out of the struggle between these two characters, one theme in particular emerges that casts light on their relationship. Luthor envies Superman's phenomenal powers and schemes repeatedly for ways to redistribute their relative strengths. He may attach himself to electric dynamos, for example, to boost his own strength, or he may fabricate an odd metal capable of absorbing Superman's energy, then fashion it into bullets that his henchmen fire at the Man of Steel, gradually sapping his superpowers so they can be tranferred to Luthor. So obsessive is Luthor's jealousy of Superman's invulnerability that it becomes virtually indistinguishable from a lust for immortality. Superman's very existence marks the limits of Luthor's being, just as the existence of the son is the indisputable evidence of the father's mortality.

In what may be the most profound episode in the 50-year history of Superman, Luthor uses his scientific genius to travel through time back to Krypton before Jor-El's marriage to Superman's mother, Lara (*Superman # 70, July 1964*). His plan is to woo her away from Jor-El, marry her and thus insure that he can gain control of the universe by eliminating before the fact the very existence of Superman.

The Oedipal resonance of this episode is overwhelming. Not only does it underscore the role Luthor plays as the symbolic evil father, it introduces the other half of the Oedipal myth as well. Luthor — the evil alter ego with whom Superman is inextricably bound — dares to enter into a sexual relationship with the Super Mother.

The battle with Luthor will last for as long as Superman lives. Theirs is a fundamental and irreconcilable conflict. They are bound together as inseparably as an object and its inverse reflection in a mirror. Luthor is the yin to Superman's yang, the NO that makes YES possible. Against this most implacable foe, Superman is stretched to the very limits of his being. No exercise of his wits can win against Luthor. Such tactics are best saved for the Toymen and Pranksters of the world. More than with any other villain in the mythos, Superman must fight Luthor with strength and courage alone.

In this never-ending battle Superman becomes humankind at its noblest — fighting the ultimately unconquerable foe, who is within himself and therefore within all of us. Against Luthor, Superman takes a stand to oppose the evil that we can become and against which our only defense is an abiding faith in the importance of the struggle.

NECESSARY HEROES

by LEE K. ABBOTT

In December of 1979, the start of a winter otherwise remarkable for its mildness, we bought our first house, a three-floor Colonial typical of the innermost ring of Cleveland's oldest suburbs. We took possession of it, I say, eagerly and happily and hopefully, the same way — but without the money and the paperwork — that we hoped to take possession, metaphorically speaking, of our neighbors. They were not to be folks from Charles Addams' neighborhood, we hoped, nor those from the imagination of Peter DeVries or Gahan Wilson or John

153

Cheever or even the smug minds which had given the world the Beaver clan. They were to be, my wife and I had convinced ourselves, neighbors like those we'd grown up with in southern New Mexico: inoffensive as white bread, the sober sort who appreciated what Frost had to say about good fences, the gray-flannel kind who might come and go quietly; what the middle class in every Metropolis ought to be about.

On the east, as it turned out, living behind barricades of newspapers, were Bill and Mildred, veterans of doughboy America—old, gray as bad coffee, roly-poly, survivors of a time before ambiguity and self-doubt situational ethics. On the west, however, flashing like a thundercloud from modernity itself, were . . . well, I never did get their names (and maybe this is the speeding bullet of truth even Himself is not faster than). These people, instead, were states of mind: Dad was an *In the Heat of the Night* police sergeant, animated as a tree stump, pastyfaced, a man who met the world belly first; Mom was a harridan, unstable as blasting powder, pear-shaped, loud and impossible to look at directly, her inner life as collapsed as botched souffle; and Billy, their son of six, was sullen and tortured and crazy, whose first words to me, where our sidewalk met his, were, "I could kill you instantly."

He was sitting in a Big Wheels, eyes narrowed with contempt, head shaved like a samurai.

"How?" I wondered.

He was small and harmless, I was big and not; and wasn't this, after all, just joshing in the neighborhood?

"With this," he snarled, and up snapped a grimy and well-dinged fist.

He could kill me, I learned, because he was Superman. He could kill me, I was given to know, because he could, like the legend he aimed to be the image of, fly and bend steel and go fast and see through. He could

kill me because he knew what was right, what wrong, and who was responsible for both. He could kill me, with fingers or X-ray eyes or sharp wits, because I, his next-door nemesis, was obviously a lowdown, scheming, underhanded, garden-variety Lex Luthor; and he, in his shorts and cape, was the sworn defender of Truth, Justice and the American Way.

So, vigilant as a Gurkha, I watched.

That winter, in galoshes and parka and soiled ski cap and tattered mittens, Billy battled all the caped wonder's enemies. Early and late, in good weather and bad, he rampaged outdoors, leaping and flailing and zapping cats and dogs, cars and passing clouds. He nailed the paperboy, the metermen, the trash folks, the joggers—all those, to his dark mind, who stood between him and his better self. Regularly, and in a routine that favors Freud's view of relations, he vaporized his father. In the evening, the old man would roll his cruiser into their drive and hoist himself out, his 200-plus pounds as fallen as some crests we know of. And there would be Billy—ooopps, Superman—in the shadows, up a tree, skulking behind an evergreen, hidden in the lilacs, ready to vault one tall building or another.

"I got you!" he'd holler. "I really got you!"

But it was his mother who was really got. Often, I heard her screaming and bellowing, making those threats it is a mother's cheerless duty to make. "Billy, you wait till your Dad gets home!" "Billy, I'm gonna tell your father!" "Billy, you put down that right now or I'm gonna blister your butt!" Mayhem and Old Night and frightful row—all of it I heard that winter. Yet what I also heard, besides the loud ("Billy, you slob, you ungrateful SOB, put down that bat, that golf club, that A-bomb, stop looking at me that way, get off that table, come down from there....") was, translated into the other language that is love, this: Billy, *please behave so that life*

Imagine if Superman had played for the Cleveland Browns in the '50s. I would have been gathering splinters on the bench.

Otto Graham, pro football hall-of-famer

will be easy and we can all live in peace and be successes.

And then, in the spring, she exploded outdoors and I came to the understanding I am half here to tell about.

She was the Curse Queen of East Scarborough Road that early May afternoon, holding forth against all the vile forces. She cursed the weeds she snatched out of her meager garden, as well as the birds and the bees, the sun in the morning and the moon at night. Like a fetchingly mad Hyde Park orator, she issued her opinions on the subjects most desperately close to her heart: food, shelter, child-rearing, our craven government, the wretched beings we sometimes are. Wielding a hoe, brandishing a rake, she scuttled hither and yon in her yard. She was Hurricane Mom—digging, scratching, whacking, flinging, pounding. "God Damn!" she howled. "Jesus H. Christ!" A bush was yanked up, a maple branch lopped off. "What in hell is this!" Pruning shears went tumbling, a Weed-Eater roared.

Then it was quiet. As is said, and meant, in the hokey mysteries we read: tooooo quiet. I glanced up from the rusted bumper of the Nova I was washing. Across the way, bent like a coolie Ethel Mertz, was Billy's mom, mouth open, teeth wet. Ravaged. Wracked. Ruined inside and out.

Her head turned slowly, suspiciously.

My sponge went plop in the bucket.

Maybe the world lurched a bit.

Maybe a cold wind went through us. Maybe not.

But, as we caught each other's eye, we had the same thought: "Where, oh where, has that Billy-boy gone?"

Moments before, he had been here—and here and here and here. Moments before, clad in his superhero's get-up of blue T-shirt shirt and red underpants and Sears towel cape, he'd charged up my drive and toward the street. Vanquishing this scourge or that, he'd swooped across the tree lawn, plunged into her flower beds, made a racket in the garage. And now?

I looked left. And right. I looked high. And low. And then, in an instant too perfect for fiction, I spotted him.

"What're you doing there?" she had hollered. "Get off that right now, mister!"

She was yammering and pointing, and yonder he stood, inside the house, apparently on the back of their sofa, his pug's nose smack against their picture window. He was Superman, all right. Like his TV god—certainly he was too young for the comics themselves—he stood feet apart, fists on his hips, chest puffed out, chin strong. His was the expression of the dauntless everywhere: "I am six and fearless and big as any adventure you have for me. Hail, wholesomeness! Hail, virtue!" He had, as any art is supposed to, taken dominion of his everywhere.

He'd also locked, and bolted, the doors.

Parts of me—the parts, at least, that have made me a story writer—want to report that I had a good chuckle that spring of 1980; but I did not. While she pounded and he posed, while she ranted and he waved, I was creeping to my own door. I wanted to slip inside, to sit quietly for a minute. As we know, there is watching and there is seeing, as there is listening and hearing, and I report to you now that suddenly, as unexpected and sometimes terrible as is lightning on a clear day, I was seeing. An alarm had clattered off in me, something I had been carrying inside for nearly 25 years and, in ways as dramatic as Billy's mom's antics, it was warning me to wake up. What I had seen, I tell you, was not Billy.

What I'd seen, defiant and proud, was myself.

Years ago, growing up in the baked badlands of New Mexico, I, like Billy, had flung myself into the comforting clutch of fantasy. Like Billy, I was Incorrigible—sulky, smartmouthed, a daytime manic, a huggermugger of anger and pride; for, like Billy, I had parents who had cosmically failed the ideal sold to me by Dick and Jane and by the TV wonderland I often got to ogle. Specifically, my mother, otherwise tenderhearted and sharpminded, was a drunk who would vanish into an institution when I was 12. My father, Ivy-educated and reared in New England boarding schools, was too old and stern to be the daddy I yearned for. A career military officer, he took as his mission in life to play golf and canasta at the country club and to bend the world to his impossible code of Honor, righteousness and fine manners. And me? As my third-grade psychologist once said, I, uh, internalized.

Because my parents' despair had become, in the juicy crenulations of my psyche, my own, I self-destructed: I ran away from school every day; one afternoon I went hysterically blind; I got in fist fights; I lied, pitched tempest-sized tantrums, choked my brother; yet, I even locked my mother out of the house for seven hours; and then, when I was eight, fate and circumstance, the poles of my extraordinary world, combined to bring me my Superman: Francisco "Pancho" Villa, Mexico's cutthroat bandito.

You can get booze cheap in Mexico; so every Sunday our family outing became a trip to Juarez, through one of its three ports of entry, or further west and south to Las Palomas, across the border from Columbus, New Mexico, the hardscrabble garrison town General Villa invaded one starry morning in March 1916. I remember clearly (as I now hope Billy remembers his first encounter with the thing that set him free) my moment of self-discovery: Riding in our black-over-yellow '57 Ford Fairlane, the desert flat and hostile but for this tumbledown town of clapboard and crumbling adobe, my father said that there—and there and there!—were the honest-to-goodness no-kidding-buster actual bullet holes made by Pancho that night. I was hooked. Wearing cap guns and holsters (you see how fortune works?), I understood, in ways not so mysterious to my now-older heart, that Pancho Villa—a mouth-breathing, mule-thieving, virtually illiterate genius of a guerillo—was my Superhero.

Like Superman, Pancho Villa was bigger than the meanness I lived in. Though only flesh, he was, to the Billy in me, that stronger, faster, cagier creature who could put right both public and private times. In an age before the trivialization of Superness itself, he rose above neighborhood and town and country to take up residence, as Superman has, at the crossroads of metaphor and symbol. Like all heroes, the worship of whom we are partly obliged to forsake for the contrary credentials of adulthood, Pancho Villa held me in the same thrall Billy thrived in. Billy and I were not unalike, I saw that sun-splashed afternoon in my driveway; rather, we were, one grown and one not, two people who had, once upon a time and as all who want to be saved must, given themselves over, at the expense of what was banal and thus horrifying, to dream and to vision and to hallowedness.

Lordy, we wanted to ''fly,'' and, shown how and why by our made-up heroes, we could.

How tidy it would be to report, now eight winters down the line, that Billy and I became pals. Hardly. He was the before, I the after; there would be no going back for me and only a sad going forward for him. Anyway: They moved, packed up and vamoosed in two days. To the country, we heard. To the outlands. To a better life. The father had put in his 20 years; the mother was out of breath.

Billy would be 14 now—quieter, probably, and riled by new but not different things. There are times, especially when I lay me down to sleep, when I think of him. Not a kid anymore, he's facing other rites whose passage we are supposedly better for. From my own teenager, I know the kinds Billy could be: a hood, a burn-out, a jock, a nerd, a dweeze. Whatever. Somehow, though it's only sentimental and silly to presume so, I hope he still believes in Superman. Yes, I hope he's still out there—stoner or dipstick or dork or dimwit—still attending, as we all should, to the figure, or figures, who spring from the imagination to show us a certain shining way to go.

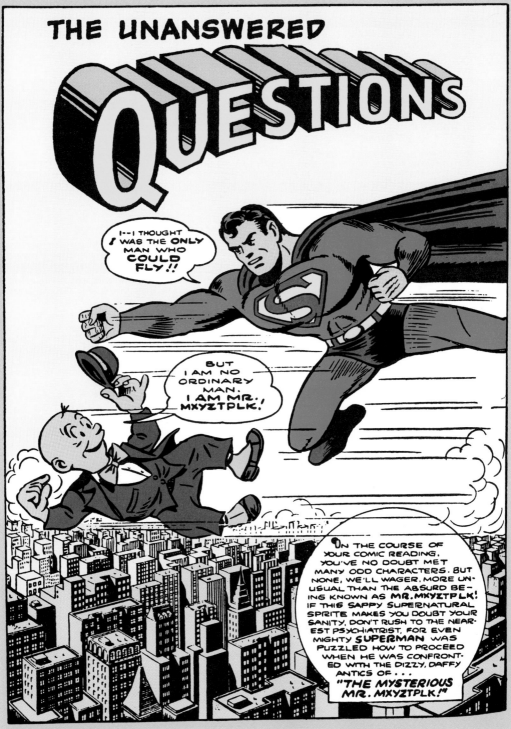

IS SUPERMAN THE ONLY HUMAN BEING WHO CAN FLY?

One of the earliest accounts of humans who could fly involves Zetes and Calais, twin brothers and members of the argonauts, that stalwart band who accompanied Jason in search of the golden fleece. Zetes and Calais are remembered for saving their brother-in-law, the blind king Phineus, from the harpies. Mythological creatures with women's heads on vultures' bodies, the harpies nagged poor Phineus whenever he tried to eat, until Zetes and his brother (to quote Rex Warner's translation of Ovid's *Metamorphosis*) "drew their swords and sprang into the air, since they were winged. The Harpies fled away…and the chase went on over land and sea till…Iris, the goddess of the rainbow appeared and said, 'Cease your pursuit, Calais and Zetes!'….The brothers obeyed her and, lightly turning in the air, flew back to the palace of Phineus where, for the first time in years, the king was able to enjoy an unmolested meal."

The question, of course, is whether Zetes and his brother were human beings, since they were the offspring of a liaison between Oreithyia, daughter of Erechtheus, and Boreas the North Wind. According to Rhodius Apollonius' account in the *Argo-nautica* Book I (Seaton trans.), Zetes and Calais were conceived when "…Boreas snatched [Oreithyia] from Cecropia as she was whirling in the dance, hard by Ilissus' stream. And, carrying her far off…he wrapped her in dark clouds and forced her to his will. There they were making their dusky wings quiver upon their ankles on both sides as they rose, a great wonder to behold…." This raises the possibility that Oreithyia may have preceded her twin offspring as the first flying human.

Humans who can fly might, of course, be found among the literally hundreds of Catholic saints, Indian fakirs and occult mediums whose documented levitations can be found in hagiographies and proceedings of societies devoted to the study of parapsychological phenomena. Likely candidates would be those holding the records for the longest and highest levitations.

The longest levitation, in terms of time, is attributed to Joseph "The Gaper" Desa (1603-1663), a Franciscan ecstatic canonized as St. Joseph of Cupertino. Most of his 70 documented levitations lasted for only a few seconds, minutes at most. But on one occasion he is said to have risen in the open air to the level of the surrounding trees and remained suspended for over two hours.

The record for the highest levitation is held by an unnamed Indian fakir. According to the *Proceedings of the Society for Psychical Research* (vol. 38, p. 276) a witness named Perovsky-Petrovo Solovovo estimated the fakir's elevation at over 100 feet, the height of a ten-story building.

Whether levitation constitutes real flying is debatable, though, since it is unclear that levitation is ever voluntary. St. Joseph, for example, couldn't turn *his* power on and off. He needed a cue, or trigger, most often a statue of the Virgin Mary, sight of which could send him into a rapture that lifted him heavenward. Once, it is recorded, he levitated after looking at a sheep.

The famous English healer, Valentine Greatrakes, while visiting the castle of one Lady Conway in 1665, claimed to have seen Lady Conway's butler levitate with such irresistible force that Greatrakes, even with the help of another male guest, could not pull the floating servant back to the ground. This suggests that levitation isn't like flying so much as it is like being stuck to the air with Super Glue.

For voluntarily leaping tall buildings with a single bound, the most likely precursor to Superman was the celebrated "Jumping Man" of Queen Victoria's day. According to accounts in London newspapers of the period, the Jumping Man was first spotted in 1837 by a Londoner named Jane Alsop, who described him as taller than average with furious white eyes capable of emitting a fiery blue ray. He wore, according to Alsop, a white jump suit with metallic claws for hands and a clear, bubble-like helmet. When frightened, the Jumping Man would leap to safety with a bounding gait of unhuman proportions. Within days of Alsop's sighting, the Jumping Man was frightened by a butcher and escaped by leaping over a 14-foot brick wall.

In the 1840s, similar sightings were recorded in other districts of London. To the incredible leaping ability was added the detail that the Jumping Man had a habit of shrieking whenever he left the ground.

Similar accounts were recorded in the 1860s and '70s, when repeated stories of a hedge-hopping stranger were told in several rural English counties. The most reliable documentation of the Jumping Man's existence occurred in 1877. Two sentries at an army post near Aldershot reportedly fired on a stranger wearing a white jump suit with a globe-like helmet and belching blue fire from what would have been his mouth. According to the transcript of the sentries'

subsequent court-martial, the stranger escaped by performing superhuman leaps that carried him an estimated 30 feet at a time.

The last reported sighting of the Jumping Man occurred in Liverpool in September of 1904. Crowds of people watched awestruck for more than ten minutes while a curious stranger in a white suit performed antic leaps over houses. None of the witnesses to the event could believe the leaper was human, which leaves the possibility that for 67 years England was a sanitarium for a very nervous creature from outer space, who posed no threat to Superman's claim to be the only *human being* who can fly.

Claims of voluntary flying are also made for the Lung-gom-pa, an order of Tibetan mystics who practice a secret breathing ritual that so reduces their body weight that they can, according to the *Encyclopedia of Occultism and Parapsychology*, "...sit on an ear of barley without breaking its stalk...." Some among the Lung-gom-pa claim to be so prone to liftoff that they wear heavy chains of iron wrapped around their bodies to prevent themselves from floating away. Witnesses able to confirm having seen Lung-gom-pa walking with extraordinarily springy steps are far more common than witnesses to actual flight. Most common of all are witnesses to the wearing of chains. The Tibetan challenge to Superman's power of flight, therefore, remains open to question.

Breathing exercises also serve to explain the remarkable leaping ability of many male dancers, the greatest of whom are sometimes credited with flying. For example, so spectacular were the jetes of Vaslav Nijinsky, the premier dancer of the 20th century, that he could, according to Diaghilev, cross a stage diagonally in two leaps, regularly achieving elevations in the range of three feet.

An even more likely candidate for King of the Terpsichorean Aeronauts was the great

162

Marie-Jean-Augustin Vestris (1760-1842), regarded by many as the greatest dancer of all time. The fact that he was the star of the Paris Opera ballet for 44 years is amazing enough, but his leaping ability was such that his father, Gaetano Vestris (himself a dancer of some repute capable of a wicked *pas de cheval*), once boasted that Vestris junior only returned to earth during his leaps in order not to humiliate other dancers on stage. This is an extraordinary claim, weakened somewhat by the fact that proud fathers aren't known for their objectivity.

A more persuasive case could be made for Jesse Owens. In 1935 he set the world record for the broad jump at 26 feet 8 $1/4$ inches, a mark which stood until August 12, 1960, when Ralph Boston shocked the sports world by ending Owens' quarter-century hold on the record with a leap of 26 feet 11 $1/4$ inches. Boston upped the mark again that same year to 27 feet 2 inches, then in 1965 to 27 feet 4 $3/4$ inches, which stood until the 1968 Olympics when the phenomenal Bob Beamon "flew" 29 feet 2 $1/4$ inches, a mark that has stood to this day.

There's a strong argument for not counting these men as challengers to Superman's claim. First, broad jumping really isn't flying. An athlete runs fast, jumps as hard as possible and falls into a pit of sand, invariably in an ungainly sprawl. Such shenanigans lack the grace and swooping changes of direction of true flight. Moreover, if three men can jump close to 30 feet in a single life span, it seems unlikely that any one of them is really flying. Humans who can fly simply can't be all that common.

If there is to be a real challenger to Superman's status as the only human being who can fly, it has to be someone who leaves the Earth at will and comes down when he wants to, not when gravity demands; someone who, once airborne, can change direction faster than the eye can follow, and who, reacting like an eagle, can tip his wing to swoop ever higher, stretching the limits of his world every bit as certainly as he stretches the credulity of those who watch him; someone who is genuinely one of a kind. Someone like Michael Jordan.

As rare and gifted as Michael Jordan is, though, he is no *real* threat to the Man of Steel. Anyone who has ever witnessed one of his star-spangled, acrobatic, two-steps-and-we're-airborne, sky-walking high slamma-jammas knows that, unlike Superman, Michael "the flying Bull" Jordan cannot possibly be for real.

—Buster Jackson

Buster Jackson lived in Kansas before moving to Cleveland. At the age of nine he jumped off the roof of his father's garage and sustained no visible injuries.

WHO WOULD
SUPERMAN HAVE
VOTED FOR
FOR PRESIDENT?

Superman maintains a scrupulously nonpartisan stance, of course, befitting his role as a good newspaperman and pop culture hero for the entire family. In fact, he has never had an impure (read controversial) thought. But it is equally obvious that such a model citizen must dutifully cast his vote for President. The tantalizing question, then: For whom would Superman have voted over the years?

It is known that he had graduated from Smallville High and was already working at the *Daily Planet* under an assumed name as early as 1934 (see "The Man of Tomorrow and the Boys of Yesterday"), although word of his exploits was not widely bruited until 1938, when his adventures began to appear in comic books. We can deduce, then, that he would have been at least 21 and eligible, as a naturalized citizen, to vote in the 1936 election.

A longtime janitor at the *Planet* has confided that a search of Clark Kent's wastebasket on the day after election day invariably turns up odd scraps of paper containing box-score-like tables which use a complex point system to rank the candidates, though the columns have been cryptically labelled

"A" and "B" so as not to reveal his choice.

It is believed that Superman/Kent makes up his mind based on the candidate who most closely resembles himself. This is the same system used by many yuppies, Marine veterans and prison guards.

Reconstructing the races since 1936, one is able, with a little ingenuity, to match the candidates with the categories, yielding the following: candidates who wore a cape—Roosevelt (1 point); candidates who take their clothes off in public places—Johnson (1 point) and Kennedy (1/2 point); candidates with honesty and integrity—1 point for everyone except Johnson and Nixon (deduct 1 point); candidates certified to fly solo—Goldwater (1 point); candidates with absolutely no political sense at all—Willkie (1 point), McGovern and Mondale (1/2 point each); candidates who played without a helmet—Ford (1 point); candidates who have not had sex since World War II—Nixon (1 point); candidates from another planet—McGovern (1 point). In addition, beginning in 1960, 1 bonus point seems to have been awarded to every candidate who was not Richard M. Nixon.

Several races, however, yield no clear winner by this system. The theory has been advanced that, for a tie breaker, Superman gave the nod to the candidate he believed would win an arm wrestling match between the two contenders. This system is widely used today in South Carolina, Alabama and Texas.

The envelope, please!

In 1936 and 1940, it's Roosevelt over Landon and Willkie, respectively (it was widely believed that even Landon and Willkie's mothers voted for Roosevelt). Dewey takes it in 1944 with the tiebreaker; but in 1948 Truman gets Supe's vote (it is thought he scored better than Dewey on the sex-since-World-War-II question). In 1952 and 1956, Stevenson wins the nod over

Eisenhower (who loses points for having Nixon on the ticket). In 1960, Kennedy takes it (Superman likes Robert Frost). In 1964, Goldwater edges out LBJ (Flyboy beats Slyboy). In 1968, Humphrey wins over Nixon, the only candidate who actually scores negative points.

It's McGovern in 1972 (see previous answer). In 1976, Ford trounces Carter (Superman's X-ray vision had detected lust in Jimmy's heart long before the *Playboy* interview). In 1980, it's Reagan over Carter (Reagan and Superman are both members of Actor's Equity). And in 1984, it's Ronnie again (this time for stopping a speeding bullet).

—John J. Boyle

John J. Boyle, who served as mayor of Cleveland Heights (1974-75), was Ohio Governor Richard F. Celeste's 1986 campaign manager.

WHAT BREED OF DOG IS KRYPTO?

The American Kennel Club currently recognizes seven groups of pure-bred dogs: Sporting Dogs, Working Dogs, Terriers, Toys, Non-Sporting Dogs, Herding Dogs and Hounds. Since neither Superdog nor his parents were ever registered with the AKC, a systematic process of elimination of the recognized groups appears to be the simplest means of determining what breed Krypto is.

Group 1—Sporting Dogs. This category is easily eliminated from the list. Quite simply, Krypto was not bred for the specific purpose of hunting feathered game. He does have the hanging ear of such Sporting Dog breeds as the English Setter and the Brittany Spaniel and consequently may, like them, be subject to ear infections if he is allowed to ride in a car with his head out of the window. There is, however, little evidence to suggest that Krypto, though able to fly, would ever use his extraordinary abilities for the sole purpose of retrieving birds, which is the definitive characteristic of the 24 distinct breeds in the Sporting group.

Group 2—Working Dogs. Though Krypto is dedicated to the service of humankind, which is the philosophy uniting the 18 breeds in this class, he is forced to spend the majority of his time on a meteor in outer space, relaxing in his Doghouse of Solitude, and therefore may not qualify as a Working Dog. Alsatian, Boxer, Bouvier des Ardennes, Great Pyrenees, Komondor, St. Bernard—Krypto looks like none of these breeds, nor any of the others in the group. If by chance he *is* a Working Dog, he is so far off the standard that he would never qualify for show points.

Group 3—Terriers. The 23 recognized breeds of the Terrier group were all bred for going to the ground. Krypto was bred for taking to the air. In no way could he be a Terrier.

Group 4—Toy Dogs. From the Bichon Frise to the Pomeranian, the breeds of this group are distinguished by their small size and by their extraordinary service as companions to humans. The companionship Krypto provides Superboy makes him deserving of inclusion in this group. But there is the inevitable problem of size, since Krypto stands, by some accounts, as much as 20 inches at the shoulder. Moreover, as lap dogs with many idle moments in their days, Toys often become the objects of elaborate grooming rituals. Realistically, a superdog could not effectively fight criminals adorned with a Shih Tzu's hair ribbons or a Pekingese's bows. What criminal would ever take a dog so decorated seriously?

Group 5—Non-Sporting Dogs. As the AKC classified and reclassified breeds over the years, the shuffling resulted in the need for a category that now contains 12 breeds ranging from the Bulldog to the Poodle. Everyone knows, though, that Krypto is, if anything, a good sport and thus cannot be considered for the Non-Sporting class.

Group 6—Herding Dogs. This is the most recently formed of the AKC's seven groups. The 14 breeds in the group are the good right hands of farmers and shepherds every-where. Gentle and intelligent, Herding Dogs are often referred to as the "lions that lie down with the lambs." Though Krypto has this temperament, he does not fit the physical standards of the herding breeds, most of which have lengthy fur, with the exception of the spotted Canaan and the solid-black Kelpie, neither of which could be mistaken for the snow-white Krypto.

Group 7—Hounds. This group holds the greatest potential in an investigation of Krypto's lineage. His exceptionally keen sense of smell makes him a likely member of this group. The Bloodhound's scenting ability is well-known and utilized by law enforcement worldwide. "Sniffing to fight crime" is a talent this superdog has repeatedly demonstrated.

Of the 20 hound breeds recognized by the AKC, Krypto most closely resembles the Greyhound and the Whippet. What other breeds, for example, have the speed necessary for keeping up with Superboy? Krypto, moreover, has a deep chest, a feature of these breeds. In size, he comes closer to the 65 to 70 pounds of the Greyhound than to the much leaner Whippet. Contrary to the Greyhound standard, however, Krypto does not have the requisite semi-pricked ears. Nor is he well cut up in the flanks, though he does have an admirable depth of muscle in the loins.

Krypto, then, is perhaps part Greyhound, with the ears of a Setter and the coloring of a Bichon Frise. In a phrase, he is an All-American mixed breed, or mutt, and thus the perfect companion to an All-American hero.

—Melissa Spirek

Melissa Spirek, a master's candidate in communication at Cleveland State University, is a member of the Cleveland All-Breeds Training Club.

IS SUPERMAN JEWISH?

The year is 1931. Instead of Jonathan and Martha Kent of Smallville, Julius and Gussie Kleinman of Cleveland, Ohio, discover the infant Superman — Kal-El — thrown from his rocket ship in the alley next to Julius' tailor shop on Gooding Avenue. As the Kents would have, the Kleinmans turn the child over to the authorities, but the baby haunts them until they appear at the orphanage to request adoption.

Of course the boy will have to be a Jew, so Julius arranges a bris and engages the mohel Pertz to do the honors.

Pertz arrives and asks Julius to state that the mohel is acting as the father's agent in the rite of circumcision. The Kleinmans and their friends make the ceremonial vow of wholehearted involvement in the act. Pertz draws his double-edged knife across the baby's stretched foreskin and cuts.

And cuts, and cuts, and cuts.

Is Superman Jewish?

To be honest, no. The man has all the ethnicity of Formica. Some immigrant: Mr. Krypton, Mr. Blue Eyes, Mr. Square Jaw.

Had Kal-El come to Earth for real in Cleveland's Glenville neighborhood, we'd all be speaking Yiddish today.

Jerome Siegel, Superman's creator, grew up in a place and time that seem legendary to many Cleveland Jews. Not only was the city then a major — you'll pardon the expression — metropolis, but Glenville itself was a neighborhood of nearly 40,000: a small gathering of *landsleit* who would have had the Man of Steel wrapped in a *tallis* faster than a speeding bullet.

Along 105th Street from Euclid Avenue almost to Lake Erie lived half of Cleveland's Jewry. The flavor was intellectual, political, committed and, above all, Jewish. Parents sent their children to Hebrew schools at a rate double that of the Jewish communities in New York and Chicago. At Glenville High School, more than 75 percent of the students were Jewish. In block after block could be found *shul* after *shul*, bakery on top of bakery with the smell of pumpernickel heavy in the air.

There were Jewish supermen around, to be sure. Older boxing fans still rank Benny Leonard with the greatest lightweights in history; lesser known are the other two dozen or so Jewish prizefighters who held world championships. Cleveland had its own "Jewish Angel," Glenville welterweight Jackie Davis, who fought 125 professional bouts from 1930 to 1935 and wore a Star of David on his trunks. And Jonah Goldman, the Cleveland Indians' first Jewish ballplayer, was a hero to thousands of boys in Glenville.

Superman might be "Jewish" in the sense that he will always be of Krypton, subject to laws, in his case physical, that are foreign to his countrymen; no matter how assimilated Superman seems, he is both strengthened and haunted by a past he relives over and over.

Superman fights two basic battles: He fights for Truth, Justice and the American Way; and he fights to maintain his identity. Jews and the fight for social justice are, after all, old friends; so too are Jews and the struggle to assimilate, but not too much.

Both Superman and Siegel have small homelands, Siegel's Eretz Yisroel and Superman's Kandor, irreversibly miniaturized by the evil Brainiac and stored safely in a bottle at Superman's Fortress of Solitude amidst the Arctic waste. Cast into a comic-book Diaspora, Superman fits so perfectly into American myth that he has recast the myth with his own hands.

Yet however American the myth, our man, be he Super or Jewish, looks within to find strength to live—to a heritage, an elsewhere, he knows in his bones.
—Scott Raab

Scott Raab, who attended Hebrew School in Cleveland Heights, is a graduate of the Iowa Writers' Workshop.

WHY DIDN'T LOIS LANE WRITE TO ANN LANDERS?

I couldn't help but feel sorry for Lois Lane, played by Margot Kidder in the first *Superman* movie, as she tried to manoeuver into an appropriate stance vis-a-vis the title hunk. There she was, with the most desirable man in American life and literature ready to fall at her feet, and she dithered like a ditsy 13-year-old.

Lois went at things all wrong. She needed specialized advice, but information on dating superhumans is scarce. Even underground, subcultural stuff dealing with extra-species relations tends to harp on how to avoid them: Do not drive pickups down lonely desert roads known to be extraterrestrial landing strips, avoid strange men whose names begin with Z (Zeus, Zontar), etc.

Poor Lois needed the assistance of a good advice column, along the lines of those "Twenty Ways to Keep Your Man on Tenterhooks" sagas in the women's magazines, of which I, at a certain age, read an uncountable number. Since, while watching the movie (consumed with envy and scorn), I became convinced that I could do better than our hapless heroine, I here undertake to provide such advice, thereby proving that Superman should have shown up on my balcony, instead.

First: clothes. Lois scored low in the what-to-wear department. In the movie, she was continually off the mark, wavering between an appeal-to-seriousness wardrobe of uninspired separates and the most sentimentalized feminine-statement garments — the baby-blue, dripping chiffon dress she wore on their first date being the primary example (whose appearance also marks the point in the movie when I began to be seriously annoyed with her). What psycho- or sociological motives are revealed by these couture choices, I hesitate to explore — to say nothing of the fact that she acted like she'd never seen a man, never mind a superhero, before.

Let us be practical. What are the right clothes to wear for flying? (She *knew* if Superman came over, they'd go flying: It was as inevitable as ending up in the back seat at the drive-in on high school dates.) The proper attire is obviously dependent on the weather; whether it's a night or day flight; a public or private flight. But the chiffon dress is wrong in every case: too clingy, too unserious, too dangerous (possible interference with line of sight), too altogether dippy. The best all-around flight outfit would be simple, functional, fitted, no-iron: Those shiny exercise leggings plus a leotard would be my pick — sexy, flexible, offering a lot of body contact. Color-coordinating with Superman: Is it necessary? Probably a mistake — it will look calculated. Can you wear a cape, too? *Vogue* says, "Why not?"

Other tips:

While out with Superman, do not wear jewelry with attractive but unfamiliar gemstones bought from street vendors, even (especially) if they emit an alluring green radiance.

One's hairdo is very important, as is a salon that caters to consorts of superheroes.

A sort of Dorothy Hamill cut that falls instantly into place would be ideal. Too-long hair is out — what if it gets in his eyes when you're landing? Also too-short hair — hair less than three inches long on women in comic books indicates an evil or power-mad nature; you can buck this if you want to go counter-symbol.

Give some thought to how to wave while flying in a parade — a large, hammy wave is a must in order to be visible to the huddled masses below.

The underwear question. Of course, Superman, being perfect in every way, would never use his X-ray vision to look at your panties: The movie is clearly in error on this point. BUT, just in case — for instance, if his mind were on saving the world from attack by gamma-ray-spewing kryptonite dragons — wear something really nice. What if, God forbid, you were in a helicopter accident? If a superhero showed up to save you, would you want him to see you in underwear that should be a dustrag?

Where should you go on your first date? This one is easy. Go to a movie or a play so you'll have something to talk about besides how he can pick up a bus. The real problem arises when you're past the initial stages. Whom could you double with? Does it have to be another mixed (superhero/human female) couple? And whom can you invite to dinner with a superhero? Can you seat them superhero/ordinary slob/superhero, or can you be casual and mix it up?

How about conversation? What sort of subjects/questions ought you to avoid?

"Gee, I wonder if your parents would have liked me."

"So, who is this Lana I keep hearing about?"

Don't complain if he spends evenings at the Hall of Justice without you. Superheroes need some time to take off their capes and network away from mortals.

Don't show a feigned interest in his work: Superman will know if you're not *really* fascinated by saving lives and defending the universe, and he will lose respect for you as an independent woman with your own life and interests.

But why bother with all this, you (and Lois) may ask? There are lots of perfectly okay men around *sans* special needs, even some with impressive builds. They don't have blue hair, of course, but this can be faked. So what is it about Superman, son of Jor-El?

First, the mystery: a man with no last name, only a title, a man with no past, no family (read: no in-laws) — all this is practically irresistible. It offers a lifetime of finding out secrets, cross-referencing motives, puzzling out behavior patterns.

Then, he is a man who does tricks: He flies, he balances automobiles on his palm, holds up bridges, sees through walls. What a wealth of boasting opportunities! No one will be able to top your spousal anecdotes.

And finally, best yet, if you're in on his secret identity, he offers a sensitive, shy side: He is Clark Gable crossed with Leslie Howard, Sylvester Stallone with Alan Alda, John Wayne in *The Quiet Man*. Who could resist?

— Mary Grimm

Mary Grimm is a native Clevelander whose fiction has appeared in *The New Yorker*.

IS THERE ANYTHING SUPERMAN CANNOT DO?

Some wags think that committing suicide is the only thing Superman cannot do. What do they know? Actually, having superpowers isn't all it's cracked up to be. Any number of disadvantages tend to accrue.

For example, Superman cannot have a vasectomy. Not that he wants one. Probably he *could* have children, but he *wouldn't* out of wedlock. And since he can't get a blood test, he can't get a marriage license and therefore would never need a vasectomy.

Superman cannot get a tattoo. This raises doubts about whether he'd ever fit in as a Marine.

Superman cannot get a vaccination. This places restrictions on the number of countries in this world where he can travel.

Superman cannot buy clothes off the rack, given his super-physique. It is doubtful that he could ever win a limbo contest, either.

A tan? Forget it. Beach time is wasted time for the Man of Steel.

Superman cannot ride a pogo stick. Probably.

If you've taken a close look at his leotard, you'll no doubt agree that Superman cannot carry loose change. This eliminates a number of options open to the normal citizen: vending machines, subways, parking meters. The super-guy is virtually closed out of public transportation. No wonder he flies.

Superman *can* go to the dentist, but not much can happen when he gets there. This raises the interesting question of what Superman uses to floss.

Because of his X-ray vision and super-hearing, it's impossible for anyone to sneak up on the Man of Steel. This means he'll never get to play "Guess Who!" or experience the joy of a surprise birthday party.

Superman will never win a Billy Barty look-alike contest.

Finally, as much as he might wish otherwise, Superman will never be drafted. Even the notoriously heartless Selective Service System would be moved to exclude from conscription the last surviving son of a planet that exploded.

—Arvydas Berkopec

Arvydas Berkopec, an iridologist practicing in Cleveland Heights, Ohio, is proud of the fact that he can do any number of things that Superman can't.

WHY IS SUPERMAN STILL A VIRGIN?

American popular culture has often treated virginity as being primitive or foreign. Witness *The Last American Virgin*, the 1982 film whose title implies that virginity is out of style in America, that there is only one virgin left, like the last unicorn.

Recent teen films, such as *Risky Business*, *About Last Night* and *Porky's*, send the same message: Anyone who has not "gotten laid," especially if he is a young man, had better do so quickly, usually by means of hiring a prostitute or picking up a "hot number" at a singles bar. All-time American film heroes—Burt Reynolds, Warren Beatty, Errol Flynn, Clark Gable, Tyrone Power—have certainly not been known for their monogamy—on screen or off. Divorce and infidelity are often the main attractions in publications such as *The National Enquirer* and *The Star*. The popularity of such films and sex heroes reinforces the notion that one should lose one's virginity at a young age and promotes infidelity in love relationships as THE American Way.

In once popular TV cop shows such as *Starsky and Hutch* and *Baretta*, in which the main characters are supposed to represent law and order, one-night stands are the norm. In one episode Hutch spends a night with a psychotic, who then fancies Hutch her fiance. He responds by treating her as if she were a casual acquaintance. That Hutch should never have entered into the liaison is not an issue. Baretta is another cop who sleeps with a different woman every week, often a woman he is protecting from harm.

Moving away from "realistic" shows into science fiction, we find Star Trek's Captain James T. Kirk, whose prime directive of noninterference with other civilizations seems to exclude his seduction of female aliens, who often end up beaming off the ship in tears when Kirk announces his "complete" dedication to one woman, the starship Enterprise. In one episode Kirk, when asked by a former lover how long it will be before she will see him again, witlessly replies, "That's up to the stars."

The law enforcers, the starship captains, the model "good guys" are all sexually indiscreet. Not so Superman. He, at least, retains values of chastity which seem lost in America.

When Miss Teschmacher wonders in Mario Puzo's Superman why she "can't get it on with the good guys," her wistful smile tells us she feels that some inadequacy as a woman must make her off limits to the Man of Steel. Superman's response to Miss Teschmacher's inquiry—a reassuring caress delivered safely under her chin and a "Step back now!" before blasting through the roof in pursuit of Lex Luthor's missiles—redirects his attention, as well as the viewer's, to the original purpose for which Superman was created: to protect America, a role which it seems can be played out to its fullest only if his virginity remains intact.

Superman's young creators seemed to understand this intuitively. In the early comic strips, Superman is somewhat of a ruffian with female criminals, sometimes threatening them with physical violence if they try

to charm him into releasing them. Quite shocking to those of us whose image of Superman has primarily been shaped by Christopher Reeve's portrayal of him as a super-gentleman. But not so out of the ordinary if we think about how young boys of our culture traditionally, or perhaps stereotypically, treat little girls: They pull their pigtails and put frogs in their desks.

Superman specifically appeals to boys not yet interested in girls because he is concerned with physical action, freedom, never being tied down to one place. Superman's only responsibility is to perform heroic deeds on behalf of the whole world rather than a single individual. This chivalrous way of life would be lost, or at least diminished in importance, if Superman were to tie himself to a single woman (or keep a little black book).

It is only when the story is adapted to the movies for consumption by adults that Superman is conceived of as a sexual being. "How big are you?" Lois asks in Superman I, then quickly correcting herself, asks, "How tall are you?" But not fast enough for us to have missed the allusion to the super-sex she imagines he can give her. Lois' language becomes even more euphemistic in this memorable scene. "I assume then that the rest of your bodily functions are normal?... Well, putting it delicately. Do you.... Do you.... Eat?" What tasty morsels she must have in mind!

Yet Superman cannot be a super-American if he cannot transcend the human weaknesses, the vices typically associated with Americans. To be a hero to Americans, Superman must value and himself exemplify that which in America is sacrificed too easily. The love triangle of Clark-Lois-Superman protects not only Superman's identity but also his virginity; Lois' crush on Superman distracts her from a potential relationship with Clark, and Superman's love for the

172

country keeps him forever distant from Lois. Both identities, Kent and Superman, must remain chaste so that the triangle is not broken.

Until *Superman II*, that is, when Lois discovers that Clark is Superman. One may very well argue that Superman loses his virginity in this movie; however, Lois does not make love with Superman. She must settle for the ordinary human male he becomes after relinquishing his powers in a strategem to outwit his enemies. In the end, even *Superman II* reinforces the idea that Superman must remain a virgin. At the movie's end Superman converts back to the superhero he is, and Lois' memory of their love relationship is erased.

Superman's virginity is a large part of what makes him so godlike, not in the classical sense but in the Judeo-Christian sense. Unlike the Roman and Greek gods, who have human vices, Superman more closely resembles the Judeo-Christian God, whose super-goodness stands as an example for humans to imitate (as boys imitate Superman) as closely as possible, even though they can never attain that perfection. The superior being has to be sexless; furthermore, it must be thought a taboo or a desecration even to look upon him/her as a sex object, just as Christ and the Virgin Mary are not thought of in a sexual sense. Loss of virginity is weak and human, while the state of virginity is nearly divine.

—Rosa Maria DelVecchio

Rosa Maria DelVecchio, a doctoral candidate at Case Western Reserve University, is writing a dissertation on horror as an analogue for sexuality in Edgar Allan Poe's tales.

WHAT SIGN IS SUPERMAN?

It's a pretty straightforward process, given the exact time and date of birth, to ascertain the influence of the stars. That he was born in another solar system and failed to record the exact moment he came under the influence of our solar system makes the work a little difficult. You have to go by his character.

A Gemini, right? Too obvious.

Superman is a Leo. You're not surprised, are you? Of course a Leo, and a classic Leo to boot. Little things and big things point only to the most majestic of fire signs. Plumage is one; the Man of Steel is easily and immediately identified throughout the world because of his, shall we say, unusual combination of blue, skin-sucking leotard, bright red cape and the "S" across his chest. For many Leos, a simple, 18-karat signet ring would suffice; this Leo is, make no mistake, not bound by earthly considerations of taste and decorum.

There is more, of course, and it all points to the inescapable conclusion that Superman's sun sign was Leo, the most favored of all astrological signs. Leos walk straight, head up, shoulders back, a certain and unshakable confidence behind the measured gait. In emergencies, no sign responds better than Leo, known for assuming responsibility quickly and fearlessly on broad shoulders. Equally telling is Leo's sympathy for the defenseless.

Leo is a fiercely loyal friend; he is a powerful enemy. Leo has not a single malicious bone in his body. Malice is not part of his makeup, and he has great difficulty coping with cruelty. When romance is in the air, Leo is a chivalrous and gallant suitor. You may recall that Lois Lane, when in the Man of Steel's arms, never once appeared immodest.

Superman's sun sign, then, is Leo.

More difficult to guess is his rising sign. A Leo with Cancer rising is a sensitive, versatile and shy man who is easily influenced by kindness or sympathy. Does this begin to sound familiar? Cancer rising also tends to retreat into a shell or womblike shelter, some place where he can restore his confidence. The Fortress of Solitude comes to mind almost immediately, doesn't it?

But Virgo rising also makes sense, indicating an energy level so high that it almost seems charged with electricity. And Libra rising could be Superman, too; he is ruled by Neptune, the planet of dreams, idealism and vision. Even closer to describing Superman is Aquarius rising, an air sign that is ruled by the moon, the fastest moving body in the heavens.

Each is close, but none as perfect a fit as Leo with Leo rising, a man whose thought processes are impenetrable and who often assumes a faraway look. His profile is one of nobility and he prefers quality to quantity. More telling, he has few intimates and seldom settles down in a relationship.

We can guess that Uranus was in retrograde when Superman first came under the influence of our solar system. Uranus is the planet of sudden change and ruled his fourth house, which concerns the home and mother. Furthermore, the fourth house directly opposes the tenth house, of father and profession. Mercury, the planet of communication, was in Superman's third house, so he became a journalist. No doubt his moon was in Scorpio, which enhances his fearlessness and his desire to make things fair and right.

Skeptical? Not under the influence of the stars, you say? Then answer this one: How do you explain his going to work for the *Daily Planet*?

—John H. Tidyman

According to his past lives' regression, John Tidyman was a Mongol soldier in the 11th century. He currently works in the public relations department of a public utility company in Cleveland.

WHY IS SUPERMAN SUCH A SQUARE?

We encounter Superman for the first time in 1938. He is new to Cleveland, as Metropolis was called then, an ambitious young man trying to land his first reporter's job. He undertakes an inaugural good deed (punching out a lynch mob at the county jail) because he sees it as "my big chance to impress the editor."

It seems reasonable to say that Superman is probably in his early twenties at this point. If we count back from 1938, we can hypothesize that he must have arrived on Earth as an infant just after the First World War. He grew up in Smallville during the Roaring Twenties and matured to superman-hood under the sobering influence of the Great Depression. Understanding that several of Superman's formative years came during the administration of Calvin Coolidge helps explain a troubling aspect of our hero's behavior: his tendency to act like an over-grown Boy Scout.

Superman is a square, a straight arrow, a Man of Steel in the polymer age. For close to five decades he has been leaping and bounding through urban America without ever learning how to swing. Perhaps he simply *can't* swing. As a product of the '20s,

he may still have entertainers like Whispering Jack Smith crooning "Me and My Shadow" inside his head.

Today we tend to regard the Roaring Twenties as a long party, the decade in which Flaming Youth rebelled under the influence of writers like Sinclair Lewis. Dashing Rudolph Valentino thrilled audiences at palatial theaters; Jack Dempsey demolished all comers in the ring.

But in a burg like Smallville the party never got started. There soil conditions were better suited for the seeds of Prohibition, Revivalism and the record growth of a secret society known as the Ku Klux Klan. The screen at the Smallville theater (if there was one) was filled with the image not of Rudolph Valentino but of Roscoe "Fatty" Arbuckle, and Dempsey's Smallville fans were probably outnumbered by followers of Alvin "Shipwreck" Kelly, who earned his fame by doing nothing more than sitting on a flagpole for 23 days and seven hours. In Smallville Boy Scouting (imported from England in 1910) was booming, teaching Clark Kent and his fellow American youths to be trustworthy, loyal, helpful, friendly, courteous, kind, obedient, cheerful, thrifty, brave, clean and reverent, 12 virtues that would distinguish Superman in adult life as certainly as the familiar blue body stocking.

Historians verify that Superman's small-town '20s were extraordinarily dull. Arthur Schlesinger, Jr., finds the decade so gray with conservatism that he suggests Americans might have created the New Deal, even without the stimulus of the Great Depression, out of sheer boredom. And the well-known Rabbi Abba Hillel Silver dismissed "Flaming Youth" in 1931 when he noted in his book, *Religion in a Changing World*, that most of the raccoon-coated collegiate disciples of Sinclair Lewis were "as orthodox, as unimaginative and as submissive as the most hidebound Babbitts of their day."

The '20s did move America toward modernism in many respects, introducing problems and changes that affected Superman permanently. After World War I the nation cultivated a strong distrust of foreigners that forced him to conceal his superpowers behind the disguise of fainthearted Clark Kent. Women won the vote and began acquiring a new assertiveness that troubles him to the present hour.

When Superman came of age, he participated in another phenomenon characteristic of the era: mass migration to the cities. What lasting challenge could he find in Smallville? The tallest structure to leap over was probably the spire of some fundamentalist church. Every evening the radio brought word of burgeoning skyscrapers and human turbulence in the big towns. The fast pace of metropolitan life disoriented newcomers, encouraging a crime wave that must have tempted young Superman, a warehouse of hidden strength whose foster parents had told him, "When the proper time comes, you must use it to help humanity." So it is no surprise that he appeared, in 1938, flying around Cleveland/Metropolis looking for work.

He got the newspaper job, of course. Over the years it has provided ideal cover from which to help humanity. His days have been filled with heroism, adventure and achievement. As a professional crime fighter he has grown with the times, adapting to the schemes of the Toyman, the Prankster, Mr. Mxyzptlk and the resourceful Lex Luthor.

But socially Superman continues to dwell in the past. One can't imagine how he spends a weekend.

Superman still approaches the woman he loves in his clumsy Kent disguise, apparently confusing Lois Lane with the shrill Helen Morgan who warbled these words from her 1928 hit, "Bill":

His form and taste

His manly grace
Are not the kind that you
Would find in a statue.

Will Superman ever be able to stop being such a square? Probably not on his own. He has been conservative for too long. But the situation is not hopeless.

DC COMICS has already implemented a number of modifications to help Superman shed his lonely-guy image. But will they go far enough? Will they make him really hip? A public relations counselor might be called for. Manipulating a few of his obvious assets might do wonders.

For example, one of the best things he has going for him is the logo. But not that slap-in-the-face version emblazoned on his chest. Let's scrap that yellow shield and relocate the high-impact "S" on a back pocket to subtly capitalize on the full power of the Superman buns. And he's simply got to quit flying. Those windy, Cape-Canaveral takeoffs don't impress people anymore. Today's Superman belongs on a set of sporty American-made wheels. When he's out of the car, he should cover downtown sidewalks with a springy stride that says, "I jog."

A hip Superman is a man of the '80s. Perhaps he spends time at the university casually working toward an advanced degree in communication. Or he paints (not seriously), experiments with an investment portfolio and collects jazz LPs. The metal in *this* Man of Steel would be strictly custom alloy and his character, like his muscles, well rounded.

—Stuart Kollar

Stuart Kollar, director of publications for Cleveland State University, is a free-lance writer and card-carrying baby boomer.

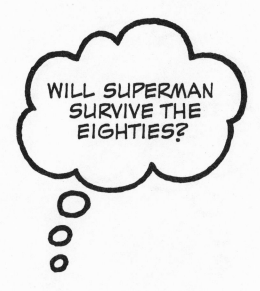

WILL SUPERMAN SURVIVE THE EIGHTIES?

Modesty has kept me from saying anything about this until now, but Superman and I—Dick Feagler—have a lot in common.

We are the same age. Both of us were born in Cleveland. Both of us started out in the newspaper racket. Both of us moved from that into television.

Like Superman, I find that when I walk about the streets of Cleveland, people point at me and shout things.

"Look! Over there!" they say. "Is it the guy on *Bowling for Dollars*? Is it your cousin Louie? No! It's Whassisname. The guy on the news! The Loudmouth!..."

Naturally, I ignore this. Like Superman, I let such things bounce off me.

Until now, I have refrained from mentioning the uncanny similarities between myself and Superman. I am not particularly mild-mannered, though I fight a never-ending battle to be well-mannered. I have avoided cashing in on Superman's notoriety, and— as far as I know—he has never tried to cash in on mine. In fact, we have never met.

I only speak out now because I am worried about what's happening to Superman. According to what I read in the newspapers, he is undergoing a lifestyle change.

"We're trying to revitalize him," says Paul Levitz, executive vice president of DC COMICS.

According to Levitz, Superman is trying to slim down his physique so he looks a little less muscular and a little more like Jim Palmer in an underwear ad. He is trying, and I quote, "to become less of a nerd and more of a yuppie."

We all know what this will mean. He will find television unfulfilling. Knowing there's no money in the newspaper game, he'll turn to writing books.

The only thing about himself he doesn't plan to change is his super-suit. His every-day, Clark Kent clothes, however, will presumably become less nerd-like and more like the duds you see on MTV. We'll see a lot less of his business suit and a lot more in the way of pleated slacks and an unstructured linen jacket. If he can figure out a way to keep his X-ray vision from boiling the water in the Bausch and Lomb soft contacts, he may even dump his trademark horn rim glasses.

Clark Kent will probably start hanging out in fern bars, drinking the house chablis and making leering approaches to women who are too young and too liberated for him.

"How'd you like to fly me?" he will say.

"Bounce off," they will tell him. It will get so bad that when he walks into a joint, people will point at him and whisper:

"Look. Over there. It's a bird—it's a plane—it's a boor."

If Superman is reading this, I hope he'll listen to me like a brother. Some may call it a lifestyle change, but what Superman is up to has all the earmarks of a midlife crisis.

A man gets to a certain place in his life and all of a sudden he doesn't feel so super anymore. Especially a man born in 1938— pre-baby boom.

If Superman isn't careful, he will drown in the sea of baby boomers who were born after him. If a man isn't careful, he will change his ideas of Truth, Justice and the American Way to conform with the lifestyle polls in *USA Today* and *People* magazine.

Trying to do that is worse than a dose of kryptonite. It makes you silly. I've tried it and I know.

—Dick Feagler

Dick Feagler delivers opinions on the news for WKYC-TV in Cleveland.

I'm a fan. A TRUE fan.

There are essays in this book that deal with Superman as immigrant, sex object and icon. They discuss his choice of friends, his clothes, his powers. I offer no such learned critique. All I have to offer is the loads of trivia about Superman and the industry that has grown up around him, gleaned from 25 years of wishing I could fly like the guy on TV.

Having, at age 32, given up almost all hope that I could accomplish this, I've compensated by absorbing as much of the lore surrounding The Man of Steel as anyone possibly can. My friends and family will be pleased that I've found some other outlet for displaying my mastery of such arcana as: "Did you know that kryptonite was invented on the old Superman radio show so Bud Collyer could have two weeks off?" (This allowed another actor to moan and groan his way through the part without anyone noticing Collyer's absence.) I thank you on their behalf.

Those who wish to lay claim to the distinction of being a TRUE fan should likewise be able to reel off all manner of minutiae without pausing for breath.

178

Such as: By now even my aunt Sadie knows that Superman was created in Cleveland, but only a TRUE fan can pinpoint the location of Siegel and Shuster's Cleveland studio, where the newspaper strip was first produced. (East 105th Street and Euclid Avenue)

And name the year the strip was launched. (1939)

And when it was finally cancelled. (1984)

Surely only the TRUE fan knows that when the Max Fleischer cartoons premiered at the State Theatre in Cleveland one weekend in October 1941, Siegel and Shuster signed autographs in the lobby.

Or that *Superman II*, estimated to have cost more than $53 million, has been rated by Guinness as the most expensive film ever produced.

And that Guinness claims that Marlon Brando received the highest salary ever given an actor for his work as Jor-El in *Superman, the Movie*.

A TRUE fan especially relishes George Reeves trivia. Like where he was born. (Ashland, Kentucky)

And the year of his birth. (1914)

And the names of two other notables born the same year. (Siegel and Shuster)

Even his final resting place. (Forest Lawn)

But perhaps only the truest of the TRUE fans knows how Noel Neill, who played Lois to Reeves' Kent/Superman on the TV show, touchingly refers to the actor to this very day. (As "My Superman")

As you can see, I'm a pretty true-blue fan.

I am not, however, a collector.

I wish I had a dime for everyone who's ever said to me: "I/my brother/my kid had a box/closet/semi full of Superman comic books, but *my mother threw them out*. Collectors have the mothers of America to thank, because if everybody had saved their Superman stuff it wouldn't be worth diddly.

Thanks, Mom.

As I said, I'm not a collector—although many TRUE fans are—so my information on Superman collectibles comes from friends. Here's a brief look at what's hot and what's not.

Action Comics # 1. If you don't have it, you're not a super-collector. Period. The price most widely quoted for one in mint condition these days is $38,000. This is not the most expensive comic extant, however. That distinction belongs to *Marvel* # 1, valued at $42,000. *Action Comics* # 2 is extremely rare, but, for some reason, not that highly prized. Subsequent issues are valuable for specific content (first team-up with Batman, for example, or first appearance of Supergirl).

A George Reeves costume. Three complete sets of the red and blue costume are known still to exist, but none of the earlier brown and gray ones. Jim Hambrick of Fountain Valley, California, has refused $40,000 for his red and blue. (Hambrick's collection, by the way, is stupefying, encompassing every Superman comic, most of the Superman toys made since 1939, the director's scripts from the TV show, complete with blocking notes ("George: wink at Noel," "crash through window," etc.), every Fleischer cartoon, a Christopher Reeve costume and hundreds of other precious items.)

An animation cel from a Fleischer cartoon. Based on the Joe Shuster model sheets (Superman, Clark Kent and Lois, drawn from every conceivable angle), these are highly coveted and very rare.

Siegel and Shuster's Science Fiction. This high-school fanzine was a five-issue series produced in 1932-33. In issue # 3, Jerry and Joe postulated a bald villain called "the Superman," the first time they used the name, making these mineographed sheets an historical treasure. Noted sci-fi collector

Forrest J. Ackerman is a character in Issue # 3's "Reign of the Superman" story and has the only known complete collection of this fanzine.

George Reeves' signature. He just didn't sign for much. Seriously, a signature on any Reeves photo is worth $1,000; on a photo of George as Superman, $2,000 to $2,500. His autograph is more valuable than those of Clark Gable or Errol Flynn.

The best of the rest.

A Christopher Reeve costume.

A secret-compartment decoder ring sold through the Superman of America Club. For ten cents you got the ring, a certificate and a button.

A Krypto-Ray Gun movie projector circa 1939-40 used to show Superman filmstrips on the wall.

Superman # 1 published in 1939, now worth about $5,000.

A copy of George Lowther's 1942 novel, which, among other innovations, gave us the names of Superman's parents. A copy with a dust jacket is very hard to find.

The Holy Grail of Superman collectibles is the first drawing Joe Shuster ever did of Superman in 1933, when Jerry Siegel ran to Joe's apartment to describe his idea about a "visitor from another planet." Joe had been sketching a girl at the time and drew Superman in the corner of the paper. The sketch is owned today by Joe Shuster's friend, Gary Coddington of Pasadena, California. Coddington also owns some of the original art from *Action Comics* # 1. All of these items would have to be considered priceless.

Listen up! Clear off your desks. Get out a clean sheet of paper. Put your name in the upper right-hand corner. We're going to have a pop quiz.

If you can answer 50 percent of these questions correctly, consider yourself a TRUE fan. If you can't, give the test to someone you know and lie about how well you did. The answers are at the end of this book.

Ready?

1. Who was the first to utter the immortal words, "Faster than a speeding bullet, more powerful than a locomotive, able to leap tall buildings in a single bound....?"
2. Who was the announcer on the TV show, *The Adventures of Superman*?
3. Who was Kirk Alyn's stunt double in the serials?
4. Tommy Bond played Jimmy Olsen in the serials. What cast member of the Christopher Reeve films shares a common history with Mr. Bond?
5. Who did George Reeves portray in *Gone With the Wind* (the character's first *and* last name)?
6. Why did George Reeves first wear a brown and gray Superman suit?
7. In Michael Fleisher's encyclopedic *The Great Superman Book*, how many times are Jerry Siegel and Joe Shuster mentioned?
8. What advertiser sponsored the radio and TV show?
9. What performer holds the distinction of appearing in all three live-action film versions of Superman (serials, TV show, 1978 movie)?
10. In which of the following films and plays are references to Superman made?
    a) *The Man Who Came to Dinner*
    b) *White Christmas*
    c) *West Side Story*
    d) *Beverly Hills Cop*
    e) *Jacques Brel Is Alive and Well and Living in Paris*
11. Who directed the final episode of the TV series?
12. What's wrong with question No. 3?
13. Name three songs that mention Super-

man ("The Theme From Superman" doesn't count).

14. What special-effects pioneer, later renowned for his work on *The Six-Million Dollar Man*, devised the breakaway walls, liftable cars and simulated natural disasters of the Superman TV series?

15. Who has spent the most time as Superman (on-air and screen time)?

16. What TV sitcom character is without a doubt a TRUE Superman fan?

17. What other Cleveland legend has his own DC comic book?

18. Who played Lois Lane in the ABC TV production of the Broadway musical *It's a Bird...It's a Plane...It's Superman*?

19. What other '50s icons costarred with George Reeves in *Westward Ho the Wagons*?

20. What, besides a secret-compartment decoder ring, did ten cents buy you as a member of the Supermen of America Club?

21. What three attributes marked every member of the Supermen of America Club?

22. Who was the producers' first choice to play Superman in the 1978 film?

23. Who was the producers' first choice to play Clark Kent's mother?

24. What real-life public official was entrusted with the knowledge of Superman's secret identity and once pretended to be Clark Kent in order to preserve the secret?

25. Who has the better claim as the location for a Superman museum: Cleveland, Ohio, or Metropolis, Illinois?

BONUS

Essay question, 25 words or less: On TV's *The Adventures of Superman*, the Man of Steel was shot at in almost every episode, calmly letting the bullets bounce off his chest. When the crooks were out of ammo and threw their guns in desperation, how come Superman always ducked?
—Tim Gorman

Tim Gorman, a native Clevelander, is president and chairman of the board of Neverending Battle, Inc., a non-profit organization planning a variety of activities to honor Jerry Siegel and Joe Shuster during Cleveland's celebration of Superman's 50th birthday.

Answers to the quiz beginning on page 178:

1. Jackson Beck, announcer for the Super-man radio show on the Mutual Network.
2. Bill Kennedy, who would later host an afternoon movie for a Detroit television station.
3. Paul Stader.
4. Jackie Cooper, who played Perry White. Both were members of the *Our Gang* comedies. Cooper was Jackie, Bond was Butch.
5. Brent Tarleton.
6. On black-and-white TV, it looked better than a red-and-blue costume.
7. In a 512-page book *they are not mentioned once*.
8. Kellogg's.
9. Noel Neill. Look for her on the train that young Clark Kent runs past in *Superman, the Movie*.
10. All of them.
11. George Reeves.
12. Stader's footage was never used. He didn't move as well as Kirk, so Alyn had to do his own stunts.
13. A partial list:
    "Superman" by Barbra Streisand
    "Sunshine Superman" by Donovan
    "I'm Your Superman" by Rick Springfield
    "(I Wanna Fly Like) Superman" by the Kinks
    "You Don't Mess Around With Jim" by Jim Croce
    "Land of Confusion" by Genesis
14. Thol Simonson.
15. It isn't even close. Bud Collyer. Forty-five minutes a week for ten years, plus the first six Fleischer cartoons, plus the Saturday-morning TV cartoons.
16. Hawkeye Pierce on *M*A*S*H*. He refers to Superman in at least 12 episodes and spends one entire episode in a Super-man costume.
17. Bob Hope.
18. Loretta Swit.
19. Mouseketeers Cubby, Doreen, Tommy and Karen.
20. A membership certificate and a button.
21. Strength, Courage, Justice.
22. Robert Redford.
23. Joan Crawford.
24. President John F. Kennedy in *Action Comics* # 309, which appeared on newsstands in November of 1963.
25. Cleveland, of course. As early as *Action Comics* # 2 and *Superman* # 1 Clark Kent worked for the Cleveland *Daily News*. *Action* # 11 clearly identifies Cleveland as Superman's home town. Metropolis isn't mentioned until *Action* # 16.

BONUS. Why do you think? The prop gun was made of metal. He could have been hurt. Geez!

CONTRIBUTORS NOTES

Lee K. Abbott, an army brat raised in the deserts and country clubs of southern New Mexico, has published three collections of short stories, the most recent of which is *Strangers in Paradise* (Putnam). His honors include two National Endowment for the Arts fellowships (1979 and 1985), the St. Lawrence Award for Fiction (1981), the Cleveland Arts Prize (1982), the O. Henry Award (1984), the Editor's Choice Award (1986) and the Pushcart Prize (1986). He is currently professor of English at Cleveland's Case Western Reserve University.

Joanna Connors grew up in Miami, Florida, and Chicago, Illinois, observing the girl and boy reporters who worked with her father. She resisted entering the family business (her grandfather worked for the *Knickerbocker News* in Albany, New York), choosing instead to study theater at the University of Minnesota. The tug was too strong, however, and after a hurtful career as a free-lance writer she went into the newspaper biz—first at the *Minneapolis Star*, where she was feature writer and then film critic, and then at the *Plain Dealer* in Cleveland, where she was theater critic and is now arts and entertainment editor.

Dennis Dooley has driven a bread truck, worked in an envelope factory, served as a member of a team conducting research in a state mental hospital and taught medieval literature at Case Western Reserve University. In 1980 he helped to found *Northern Ohio LIVE*, a monthly magazine of the arts and entertainment. Currently on the staff of The Cleveland Foundation, he is the author of an award-winning book, *Dashiell Hammett*, a critical analysis of that writer's work.

Patrick L. Eagan chairs the department of political science at John Carroll University in University Heights, Ohio. As a specialist in science and technology policy, he has written reports for the U.S. Department of Commerce on policy regarding the exportation of technology and has published in *Policy Perspectives Journal* and *Policy Studies Journal*. He received his Ph.D. from the University of California Riverside and has been a John Hay fellow at Columbia University, a NASPPA fellow at the Bureau of Standards in Washington, D.C. and an NEH fellow at Vanderbilt University. In 1988 he will be a resident Grauel fellow at the University of Madrid, studying the relationship between the Spanish government and the scientific and technological community.

Gary Engle, who earned a Ph.D. from the University of Chicago, is a member of the English department at Cleveland State University. He has authored more than 100 articles on American popular culture and edited a collection of minstrel plays for Louisiana State University Press. He is a regular columnist for *Northern Ohio LIVE*.

A journalist and novelist, **David Galloway** holds the Chair of American Studies at West Germany's Ruhr University. He has been a gallerist, art consultant and chief curator of the Tehran Museum of Contemporary Art. From 1968 to 1972 he was associate professor of modern literature at Case Western Reserve University. His art criticism appears regularly in *Art in America* and the *International Herald Tribune*.

David B. Guralnik is the editor in chief emeritus of *Webster's New World Dictionary*. He recently retired from his position as vice president and dictionary editor in chief of Simon and Schuster, current publisher of that Cleveland-based line, to whom he still serves as consultant. He holds a B.A. and M.A. from Western Reserve University and a Litt. D., *honoris causa*, from the Cleveland College of Jewish Studies. He is the author of *The Making of a New Dictionary* and of articles for various journals and anthologies.

Timothy Joyce chairs the English department of Nauset Regional High School in Cape Cod, Massachusetts. He was born on Cleveland's West Side, attended St. Edward's High School and received degrees from Cleveland State University and University College, Dublin. Before moving to Massachusetts, he spent six years as associate administrator of the Classification and Rating Administration of the Motion Picture Association of America. A collection of Joyce's poems, *Those Lucky Days* (Burning Press), was published in 1986.

Jane W. Kessler, a former Lt. (jg) WAVES (hospital corps) USNR, holds degrees from the University of Michigan, Columbia University and Western Reserve University. She is presently Lucy Adams Leffingwell Distinguished Professor of Psychology at Case Western Reserve University. Author of *Psychopathology of Childhood* (Prentice Hall), she is a member of the American Psychological Association and American Orthopsychiatric Association. She also serves on the Child Development Advisory Board of Mattel, Inc.

John D. McGervey is a professor of physics at Case Western Reserve University. He earned his B.S. from the University of Pittsburgh and an M.S. and Ph.D. from the Carnegie Institute of Technology (now Carnegie-Mellon University). He is author of *Introduction to Modern Physics* (a textbook published by Academic Press), *Probabilities in Everyday Life* (published by Nelson-Hall, Chicago, 1986) and numerous articles on physics, teaching physics, general science

and contract bridge (he became a Life Master in bridge at the age of 22).

Edward Mehok, a native of Akron, Ohio, has been a priest of the diocese of Cleveland since 1957. He received a Ph.D. from Case Western Reserve University, specializing in medieval and Renaissance studies, and is currently vice president and dean of students at Borromeo College of Ohio.

Dennis O'Neil's first published work was a feature piece in a Junior Achievement newspaper. His most recent is a comic-book adaptation of the old Doc Savage pulp adventures. In the 31 intervening years, he has sold hundreds of magazine articles, reviews, short stories and comic scripts, five books and two teleplays. He also has extensive experience as a reporter and editor, has lectured at dozens of colleges and universities in the United States and Canada and is a frequent guest at comic-book conventions and on radio talk shows. He lives alone in lower Manhattan, reads voluminously, travels often and enjoys listening to music, taking courses and wandering through the city.

Lester Roebuck grew up in Lawton, Oklahoma, and lived in Lincoln, Massachusetts, Paris, Rome, Hydra, Greece, Chicago and Jemez Springs, New Mexico, before retiring in Cleveland. A former sanitation worker and free-lance writer with a bachelor's degree in anthropology from Northwestern University, he is currently working as a part-time landscaping consultant in Cleveland Heights, Ohio.

Philip Skerry is professor of English and film at Lakeland (Ohio) Community College, where he has taught since 1973. He received his B.A. from the University of Massachusetts, his M.A. from Case Western Reserve

University and his Ph.D. from Indiana University of Pennsylvania. He has published numerous articles in scholarly journals and is currently at work on a book on Lord Byron. Dr. Skerry was assisted with the research for his contribution to this book by Chris Lambert, who has written for *Scene* magazine, a Cleveland entertainment tabloid, *The Golden Age of Comics* and *Trouser Press* magazine.

Frederik N. Smith is presently chair of the department of English, University of North Carolina at Charlotte. He has previously taught at Case Western Reserve University and the University of Akron. He is author of *Language and Reality in Swift's "A Tale of a Tub"* (Ohio State University Press), editor of a forthcoming collection of essays entitled *The Genres of "Gulliver's Travels"* (University of Delaware Press) and has published articles on Swift, Samuel Beckett, William Faulkner, John Fowles and William Styron. Dr. Smith was theater critic for *Cleveland Magazine* during the first two years of its existence.

Curt Swan is, after Joe Shuster, widely regarded as the preeminent illustrator of Superman.

187

Superman at Fifty: The Persistence of a Legend was set in Univers 55, a typeface that was chosen for its simplicity and resemblance to traditional comic-book lettering. The boldface accent type is Univers 65. Chapter headings, balloons and initial caps were hand-drawn by book designer Eugene Pawlowski. Pawlowski is a member of the faculty of the Cleveland Institute of Art, where he teaches graphic design. Among his many credits are the institute's annual student catalogue and *Cleveland Institute of Art: The First Hundred Years*, a history.

BOOKS OF INTEREST FROM OCTAVIA PRESS

Photocopy this coupon to order additional copies of *Superman at Fifty: The Persistence of a Legend* — or any of these other popular titles.

YES! Please send me:

Quantity

_____ *Superman at Fifty: The Persistence of a Legend*, edited by Dennis Dooley and Gary Engle, $16.95 hardback

192 pages, four 4-color plates

_____ *The Ultimate Benefit Book: How to Raise $50,000-Plus for Your Organization*, by Marilyn E. Brentlinger and Judith M. Weiss, $22.95 hardback

224 pages, including a variety of adaptable forms and planning aids

_____ *Halle's: Memoirs of a Family Department Store (1891-1982)*, by James M. Wood, Geranium Press, $29.95 hardback

224 pages, duotone photography and graphics

_____ *America's Soapbox: 75 Years of Free Speaking at Cleveland's City Club Forum*, by Mark Gottlieb and Diana Tittle, Citizens Press, $17.95 hardback

256 pages, illustrated; foreword by David S. Broder

Please add $1.50 postage and handling for one book, 50 cents for each additional book. Ohio residents add 6.5% sales tax. Deduct 10% on orders totalling $50 minimum before shipping and applicable sales tax.

_____ Payment enclosed _____ Please charge my: _____ MasterCard

_____ VISA   _____ American Express

Account no. _____ Exp. date _____

Signature _____

Name _____

Street address _____
(no P.O. Box numbers, please; we ship UPS)

City _____ State _____ Zip _____

Send form to: Octavia Press
3546 Edison Road
Cleveland, Ohio 44121